Management of Event Operations

Books in the series

Management of Event Operations
Julia Tum, Philippa Norton and J. Nevan Wright

Innovative Marketing Communications: Strategies for the Events Industry
Guy Masterman and Emma Wood

Events Management 2e
Glenn A J Bowdin, Johnny Allen, William O'Toole,
Rob Harris and Ian McDonnell

Events Design and Experience
Graham Berridge

Event Feasibility
William O'Toole

Marketing and Selling Destinations and Venues:
A Convention and Events Perspective
Tony Rogers and Rob Davidson

Management of Event Operations

Julia Tum, MBA MHCIMA
Philippa Norton, BA (Hons)
J. Nevan Wright, PhD

ELSEVIER
BUTTERWORTH
HEINEMANN

AMSTERDAM • BOSTON • HEIDELBERG • LONDON • NEW YORK • OXFORD • PARIS
SAN DIEGO • SAN FRANCISCO • SINGAPORE • SYDNEY • TOKYO

Butterworth-Heinemann is an imprint of Elsevier
The Boulevard, Langford Lane, Kidlington, Oxford, OX5 1GB
30 Corporate Drive, Suite 400, Burlington, MA 01803, USA

First edition 2006
Reprinted 2006, 2007, 2009

Notice
No responsibility is assumed by the publisher for any injury and/or damage to persons
or property as a matter of products liability, negligence or otherwise, or from any use
or operation of any methods, products, instructions or ideas contained in the material
herein. Because of rapid advances in the medical sciences, in particular, independent
verification of diagnoses and drug dosages should be made

British Library Cataloguing in Publication Data
A catalogue record for this book is available from the British Library

Library of Congress Cataloging-in-Publication Data
A catalog record for this book is available from the Library of Congress

ISBN: 978-0-7506-6362-5

For information on all Butterworth-Heinemann publications
visit our website at www.elsevierdirect.com

Transferred to Digital Printing in 2009

Working together to grow
libraries in developing countries

www.elsevier.com | www.bookaid.org | www.sabre.org

ELSEVIER   BOOK AID International   Sabre Foundation

Julia dedicates this book to Les Trois J
Nevan dedicates this book to Joy and their 25 years
Philippa dedicates this book to Simon, Samuel and Jake

Contents

Figures

Tables

Case studies

Series editors

Glenn A J Bowdin is Principal Lecturer in Events Planning at the UK Centre for Events Management, Leeds Metropolitan University where he has responsibility for managing events-related research. He is co-author of *Events Management*. His research interests include the area of service quality management, specifically focusing on the area of quality costing, and issues relating to the planning, management and evaluation of events. He is a member of the Editorial Boards for *Event Management* (an international journal) and *Journal of Convention & Event Tourism*, Chair of AEME (Association for Events Management Education), Charter Member of the International EMBOK (Event Management Body of Knowledge) Executive and a member of Meeting Professionals International (MPI).

Don Getz is a Professor in the Tourism and Hospitality Management Program, Haskayne School of Business, the University of Calgary. His ongoing research involves event-related issues (e.g. management, event tourism, events and culture) and special-interest tourism (e.g. wine). Recent books include *Event Management and Event Tourism* and *Explore Wine Tourism: Management, Development, Destinations*. He co-founded and is a member of the Editorial Board for *Event Management* (an international journal).

Professor Conrad Lashley is Professor in Leisure Retailing and Director of the Centre for Leisure Retailing at Nottingham Business School, Nottingham Trent University. He is also series editor for the Elsevier Butterworth-Heinemann series on Hospitality Leisure and Tourism. His research interests have largely been concerned with service quality management, and specifically employee empowerment in service delivery. He also has research interest and publications relating to hospitality management education. Recent books include *Organisation Behaviour for Leisure Services*, *12 Steps to Study Success*, *Hospitality Retail Management*, and *Empowerment: HR Strategies for Service Excellence*. He has co-edited *Franchising Hospitality Services* and *In Search of Hospitality: theoretical perspectives and debates*. He is the past Chair of the Council for Hospitality Management Education. He is a Chair of the British Institute of Innkeeping's panel judges for the NITA Training awards, and is advisor to England's East Midlands Tourism network.

The authors

Julia Tum is a Senior Lecturer in the UK Centre for Events Management at Leeds Metropolitan University. Her main areas of professional interest are in the field of operations management and strategic management. These are topics taught to under-graduates and MSc students and also from part of her outside work when contracted to external organizations. She led the development team for the Honours Degree in Event Management in 1996 and was Course Leader from 1996 until 2000. Prior to that, amongst her other commitments, she was the Course Leader for the MSc in Hospitality Management.

Philippa Norton works freelance within the events industry involved in operations management and marketing and is currently working on a project for Bradford Industrial Museum and the Imperial War Museum in connection with the 60th Anniversary of the ending of World War II. She has a first class honours degree in Events Management and has lectured part time at Leeds Metropolitan University. Philippa has a project administration background and has lived and worked in Namibia, Somalia and Pakistan. Throughout her life she always has been and still is involved in organizing local events on a voluntary basis.

Dr Nevan Wright is a Professor of Management at Auckland University of Technology in New Zealand, and is an Associate Member of Faculty at Henley Management College UK, where he lectures for several months each year. Prior to joining academia Nevan was a Director/General Manager for a group of multinational companies oper-ating in New Zealand. He is a Justice of the Peace for New Zealand and an Associate Fellow of The New Zealand Institute of Management. Nevan is the author of several management books.

Series preface

The events industry, including festivals, meetings, conferences, exhibitions, incentives, sports and a range of other events, is rapidly developing and makes a significant contribution to business and leisure related tourism. With increased regulation and the growth of government and corporate involvement in events, the environment has become much more complex. Event managers are now required to identify and service a wide range of stakeholders and to balance their needs and objectives. Though mainly operating at national levels, there has been significant growth of academic provision to meet the needs of events and related industries and the organizations that comprise them. The English speaking nations, together with key Northern European countries, have developed programmes of study leading to the award of diploma, undergraduate and post-graduate awards. These courses focus on providing education and training for future event professionals, and cover areas such as event planning and management, marketing, finance, human resource management and operations. Modules in events management are also included in many tourism, leisure, recreation and hospitality qualifications in universities and colleges.

The rapid growth of such courses has meant that there is a vast gap in the available literature on this topic for lecturers, students and professionals alike. To this end, the *Events Management Series* has been created to meet these needs to create a planned and targeted set of publications in this area.

Aimed at academic and management development in events management and related studies, the *Events Management Series*:

- provides a portfolio of titles which match management development needs through various stages;
- prioritizes publication of texts where there are current gaps in the market, or where current provision is unsatisfactory;
- develops a portfolio of both practical and stimulating texts;
- provides a basis for theoretical and research underpinning for programmes of study;
- is recognized as being of consistent high quality;
- will quickly become the series of first choice for both authors and users.

Preface

The structure of this book is built around a proposed event operations management model, which has its origins in Wright (2001) and has been augmented for the events industry. The model provides a way of approaching how to plan and organize each event that is staged . . . from planning a series of recruitment interviews between two or more people to planning the Olympic Games. The approach is essentially the same. The authors believe that each event is in fact a project, and that the wealth of literature that is available on both operations and project management can be used to assist an event manager in the complex management of an event.

The aim of the book is to present a theoretical model which can be used by an event manager. The chapters in the book lead the reader gently through this management process, and enable reflection to take place as the different concepts become linked together.

There are four sections within the book, and each examines in depth the elements within the four stages of the event operations management model. At the start of each new section readers are reminded of the structure of the book, and where they are within the model. The start of each section therefore reintroduces the model, explains the importance of what has already been covered and how it leads onto the next section.

It is the growing importance of the event industry that has necessitated the writing of this book. The book brings together in one publication the intricacies and complexities of event management, and shows by using an event operations management model that the approach can become more structured. Bowdin *et al.* (2001) identify how the event industry dates back thousands of years. The Romans were masters at staging events. Many examples can be found throughout history – Greek and Roman gladiatorial games, the ancient Olympic Games (first held in 776 BC), events held in the Middle Ages which celebrated harvests, and events that celebrated Royal ceremonies and military feats. Getz (1997) identifies the world of event management covers a myriad of cultural, sport, political and business occasions.

Events have long played an important part in daily life. Shone and Parry (2004) offer the thought that in most societies the slightest excuse could be found for a good celebration and that routine daily activities were often interspersed with festivals and carnivals.

In more modern times, in the last century The Daily Mail Ideal Home Show was launched in 1908 and the first British Industries Fair was held at the Royal Agricultural Hall (now the Business Design Centre) in London in 1915 (Bowdin *et al.*, 2001). Each one of these events was a project, managed by teams of people working towards common objectives.

Following the World Wars, celebrations became a thriving sector and existed alongside events celebrating cultures of new communities in the UK from the West Indies and South Asia. McKay (2000) highlights the emergence of festival culture with its origins in the 1950s.

The 1970s and 1980s saw a range of multi-purpose venues being built, funded by local authorities (Bowdin *et al.*, 2001). Wood (1982) believes that governments used community festivals and festivities to provide a focus for society, and to enable social and economic regeneration.

Sporting events have risen in their prominence alongside corporate hospitality and entertainment. The 1984 Olympic Games in Los Angeles began a trend of blending sports, events and creative expression, bringing together production and marketing, media and an awareness of economic benefit (Bowdin *et al.*, 2001). In every detail these events are projects, and they need an event manager to be following an event operations management model to ensure successfully coordinated management.

The trend for professionally staged events continues into the twenty-first century, with increased funding from sponsors, local authorities, industry, government and private individuals. These all demand a return on their investment, and need to be assured that the event is well managed and realizing its objectives, and will be delivered both on time and within budget. It is this growth of events that has led to the emergence of an events industry, with its associated industry associations, training and education.

The companies within the event industry, like those in most other industries, are facing strong pressures on cost, whilst the market is demanding increased quality and service (Lee-Kelley, 2002). As Lee-Kelley (2002) cites, information and technology is now offering advanced communication possibilities. Improved communication also increases the expectations of our customers, and similarly our expectations of suppliers.

Journals, newspapers and advertisements can be scanned to see a myriad of different event companies offering a complete event service – from managing a wedding or planning an international conference, to the development of major sporting or charity events. On further investigation it can be seen that many of these companies do not directly employ the relevant specialists, skills and resources, but manage the event by the use of outsourced or subcontracted specialists. For example, catering, sound and lighting provision, security, stage and seating and possibly the venue itself may be hired by the event company for the duration of an event.

Thus it can be deduced that many event companies bring together and manage a variety of companies and services to produce the final event. These are complex projects, and the industry deserves an event operations management model that it can follow methodically to be assured that it is using well-researched best practices and concepts.

As rapidly as the event industry has emerged, so also has the need to be efficient in the many ways that money and time can be spent upon securing the right resources and delivering a successful event. O'Toole and Mikolaitis (2002) identify that, as growth in the demand for events has occurred and the events themselves have become increasingly complex, the event companies which are emerging have become increasingly professional. It is imperative that these companies are able to work methodically, be organized and can call upon the right resources to fulfil the needs of the event and enable a matching of the expectations of the various stakeholders.

Goldblatt (2002) indicates that hundreds or perhaps thousands of elements must be evaluated to produce a foolproof event. Coordination is critical to successful organization and management of any project, and no more so than for an event, which is distinctly time constrained and must be delivered and executed on time. Watt (1998) believes that good coordination comes from having a shared goal and common objectives, within an appropriate culture and structure.

O'Toole and Mikolaitis (2002) believe that one solution to reduce costly inefficiency is to introduce 'systematic methods for researching, designing, planning, co-ordinating and evaluating every event'. They argue that a systematic approach will improve efficiency and offer a higher rate of return on the investment of time, money and people. The event operations management model, which this book is based around, builds on some of their ideas and incorporates much from the general project management literature.

Dealing with a network of suppliers and multiple customer and client needs requires a total quality management approach to ensure a successful event. Crosby first proposed Total Quality Management (TQM) in the early 1980s. Before this, Total Quality

Control (TQC) and Company Wide Quality Control (CWQC) (Juran, 1969) had gained acceptance throughout the USA and Japan. Crosby (1979; 1984) proposed that work should have zero defects – i.e. total absence of failure. This approach, understandably, had a major impact on general management at that time, attracting attention to quality and influencing managers to commit themselves to quality (Kandampully, 2002).

Each event that is staged can be considered as a quality project, which requires the skills of a project manager to keep it on time and within budget while satisfying the expectations of clients and customers. Indeed, Getz (1997) identified that one-off events have a definite start and end date, and he advocates the use of project planning methods to create and launch an event. Once an event has started there are no second chances (Allen, 2000). This book looks at how an event manager can successfully manage the event process, and each chapter is dedicated to each stage in the process.

Mature industries such as building and construction have used a project management approach for many years (Webster, 1994; Cicmil, 1997). With these approaches comes a bank of tools and techniques that have been adapted and refined to meet the needs of the project manager, satisfy quality issues and enable all practices to be completed in a safe manner to budget and to time. This book will investigate some of the most relevant of these approaches and their associated techniques, and will apply them, within the proposed event operations management model, to the event industry.

Event Operations Management Model: Tum, Norton and Wright 2005

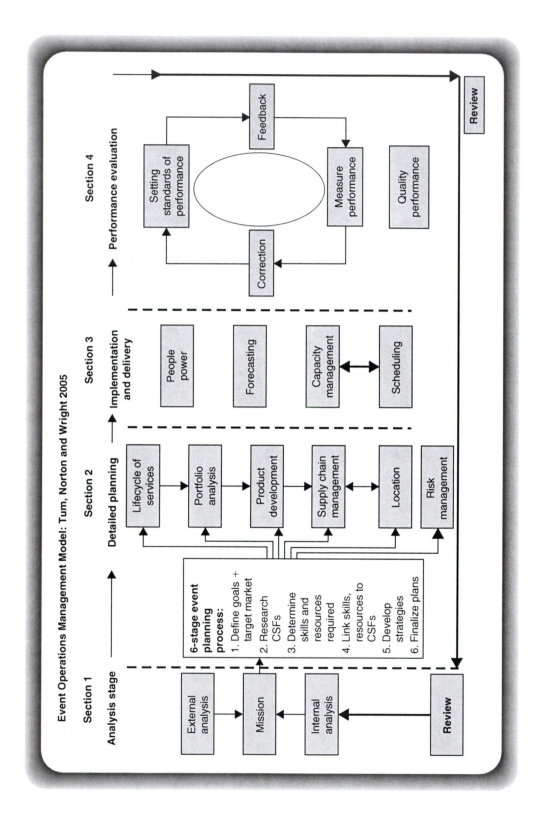

Section One

Analysis

Introduction

Within Section 1, the event operations management model is introduced and explained. The event operations management model provides the structure for the entire book, and the four sections within the book relate to the four stages of the model.

The importance of analysis is stressed in Chapters 1–6. An event manager must work with eyes, ears and mind open to activities that are going on around the organization – not only those that are close to the organization but also those that are thought to be remote and of no direct importance to the event. The concept that everything has a knock-on effect somewhere is very difficult to challenge.

This book identifies how, by using conventional operational management theory and project planning techniques, the event manager can be better equipped to manage events in the twenty-first century.

The chapters in Section 1 therefore concentrate upon internal and external analysis to identify the environments in which the event manager is working.

Chapter 1 introduces the development of the event operations management model. This model is proposed as the ideal process for an event manager. It is based on extensive research, and brings together aspects of previously published models. The model embraces all the aspects of managing an event, from concept through to implementation and review.

As alluded to in the preface, today's environment is dynamic, competitors are aggressive, and customers can be fickle and demanding. Many events organizations are small entrepreneurial companies, others are part of large companies often seeking to promote brands and excellence, and others are charitable or community based. None of these organizations can afford to make financial errors, lose reputation or fail to meet agreed objectives.

The event operations management model seeks to explore all the elements and issues that an event manager should be aware of as the event is considered from concept to completion.

Chapter 2 identifies some of the major terminology used within the operations management and the project management literature, which can clearly be applied to managers within the event industry. These previously very well researched and documented approaches are relevant and can be appropriately transferred to the event industry.

Critically, the importance of having a clear mission and objectives is discussed, as is the importance of knowing who the customers are and how their needs can be satisfied.

The notion of transformation of resources is introduced. This is the process whereby both tangible and intangible resources are utilized to create, and be consumed by, the event. Often creation and consumption is simultaneous.

The chapter concludes by examining the different formats that events can take. It is very important for an event manager to be able to consider the impact of these variances on costs, training needs, standardization and flexibility.

Chapter 3 considers in depth the external environment. It offers various techniques that can be used to appraise external factors, and explains the importance of both creating and understanding objectives set by and expected by a diverse range of people. In order to cover these points succinctly the importance of business policy is introduced, since this will have an impact on the event operations management model.

The chapter explores in depth many of the external issues and groups that influence organizations, and it offers a technique that can be used by an event manager to explore and analyse the impact of stakeholders on an organization.

Chapter 4 considers some aspects of marketing. This chapter provides a bridge between the internal and external environments. The main aim of the chapter is to demonstrate the importance of knowing what the customer wants and values. This is a significant aspect of the event operations management model.

The chapter considers specifications, consistency of provision, timeliness, flexibility, price and added value. The issues within this chapter are of considerable importance to the event manager.

Chapter 5 covers in depth the needs of the customers and the various stakeholders. It examines the amount of interaction between the organization and the customers, and the effect that different levels of contact can have on the management and control of the different elements of the event. Similarly, the chapter considers the degree of influence on the organization from the different stakeholders, and analyses the influence and impact that stakeholders can have on an event and how the event manager can aim to control this.

The concept of critical success factors is introduced and various techniques are explored to evaluate how well an organization is meeting the needs of its customers. This section culminates in exploring the concepts of gap analysis.

Chapter 6 focuses on the internal environment. This is an important part of the event operations management model. The chapter examines the culture of an organization and how this can influence quality decisions, what information systems are required and the importance of financial strength.

The chapter explores the efficient use of resources and the varied competencies of employees. A technique is offered which will enable the event manager to make efficient use of resources so as to provide the best possible customer satisfaction – i.e. the critical success factors (CSFs). The chapter closes with a discussion on the different management structures that organizations can create, and their varying advantages and limitations.

Hence, Section 1 offers a set of tools and techniques for events management, using a logical and clearly described event operations management model.

Chapter 1

Development of the proposed event operations management model

Learning Objectives

After reading through this chapter you will be able to:

- Define a project, and understand the various approaches to event operations and the management of a project
- Explain the importance of project management and its application to event operations management
- Appreciate how the event operations management model has been created
- Understand the four stages within the event operations management model.

Introduction

Tukel and Rom (2001) have researched various definitions of what a project is, and cite the work that has been put forward over a period of time by Kerzner (1994). Initially he offered three objectives for a project – that it should be:

1. Completed on time
2. Completed within budget
3. Completed at the desired level of quality.

[handwritten: Objectifs internes de l'organisation]

It can be seen that these are only internally focused objectives, and are concerned with the success of the project from the organization's point of view.

By the late 1980s, after the introduction of Total Quality Management (TQM) into academic literature, Kerzner (1994) added a further two performance measurements:

4. Customer satisfaction and acceptance of the outcome
5. Customers allowing the contractor to use them as a reference.

[handwritten: Objectifs externes de la clientèle]

This is an example of a trend by researchers to integrate customer involvement as a factor in determining project success.

[handwritten: satisfaction des consommateur determine aussi le succès d'un projet.]

Turner's (1999: 8) definition of a project starts to reflect some of the known and expected constraints and characteristics of a project:

> *… an endeavour in which human, financial and management resources are organized in a novel way to undertake a unique scope of work, of given specification, within constraints of cost and time, so as to achieve beneficial change defined by quantitative and qualitative objectives.*

This development of the definition is supported by Cicmil (2000), who argues that traditional project management had developed a range of specific techniques for planning, monitoring and control which used to be applied to industries such as construction, aerospace and defence. However, he also recognizes the limitations and challenges of modern projects. It is precisely those challenges that can often be present within virtual teams in the event industry – i.e. there exists complex and diverse customer–supplier chains and multiple stakeholders who have a complexity of expectations of an event.

It can be seen that project management is becoming more common and necessary as stakeholders and the business environment are demanding professional and commonly agreed standards. Bowdin *et al.* (2001) note that project management methodology is being used in fields as diverse as software management, business change management and event management.

Other work (Bubshait and Farooq, 1999) has focused on the person who is in charge of a project. This person is vital in providing, and often *being*, the main focal point. Gray and Larson (2000) advise project managers to innovate and adapt to changing circumstances in order to maintain control. Even well-planned projects in the event industry are likely to face unexpected challenges – customers' changing needs and numbers, variable weather conditions, road access closures, failures of suppliers etc. Cooke-Davies (1990) notes that any one of these changes may result in significant modifications being made to the project schedule and resource requirement. In the event industry, however, no changes can be made to the end time of the project, since this is the start time of the event. No slippage is possible, and there is only one opportunity to get it right. To quote from O'Toole and Mikolaitis (2002):

> *What separates the corporate event contract from others is the overriding importance of time.*

The dynamic nature of events and the way that the functional areas are so closely linked means that a small alteration in one area can result in crucial changes, and may affect the whole event (Bowdin *et al.*, 2001). Since an event has a start and an end point, it can also be defined as a project. It has a life expectancy, and the time from its inception to completion can be termed 'the event project life cycle'.

The work of Robbins and Coulter (1998), Cicmil (2000), Ibbs and Kwak (2000), Wright (2001), Grundy and Brown (2002), Wild (2002), Czuchry and Yasin (2003) and Slack *et al.* (2004) has been analysed in preparation for the following chapters regarding what they propose as an ideal project management methodology. The major elements, which are constantly highlighted as being essential, are to:

- Understand the external environment
- Establish a vision
- Define the nature and scope of the project and formulate clear objectives
- Plan, organize and manage the project
- Monitor and evaluate as the project develops
- Implement and control
- Take corrective action, review and learn.

Similarly, the works of Getz (1997), Goldblatt (1997), Watt (1998), O'Toole and Mikolaitis (2002) and Shone and Parry (2004) present ideal event management processes. There are no major differences between them and, as before, although the words may differ, the essential concepts remain the same:

- Research
- Clarify aims and objectives and feasibility
- Design and present preliminary plan
- Organize and coordinate
- Implement
- Close down
- Review and evaluate.

Shone and Parry (2004) show that there are considerable similarities between the management of projects and the management of events, and they believe that there are techniques from the project management literature that can be adopted by event managers. These include:

- The use of work breakdown structures
- Identification of critical tasks and external dependencies
- Gantt charting, related to critical path analysis
- Risk assessment.

We will come to these techniques and others as we work through the event operations management model used in this book, and through the various sections. There are four stages within the event operations management model (see Figure 1.1), and hence there are four sections to this book:

1. Analysis
2. Detailed planning
3. Implementation and delivery
4. Performance evaluation.

The process presented in Figure 1.1 shows a linear progression through four stages. This is a useful method of presentation, as it enables us to see and understand each stage clearly. Each stage will be covered within the relevant section of the book.

Figure 1.2 shows the same event operations management model, but it is presented in an iterative format – i.e. where each stage is dependent upon another and *vice versa*. Using this model, the event manager should be flexible enough to return to any one stage and re-investigate changes as they occur. Due to the dynamic and changing nature of the external environment, analysis cannot be static and plans need to be constantly revisited to verify original assumptions.

Each of the four main stages is split into sub-sections, and each of these is discussed and applied to the event industry in the relevant sections and chapters within this book.

Analysis

The analysis stage is covered in Section 1 of this book, and it looks at both the environment external to the organization or specific event and the internal environment of the organization itself. Section 1 is concerned with introducing the event industry in greater depth, and examines the background of operational management theory in an event management context. All organizations should have clear objectives and goals, and these should be encompassed within the mission for that organization or for a particular event.

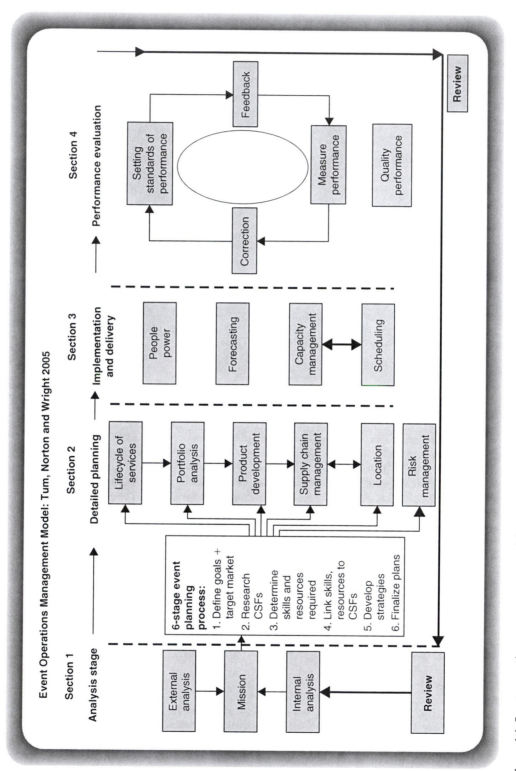

Figure 1.1 Event operations management model

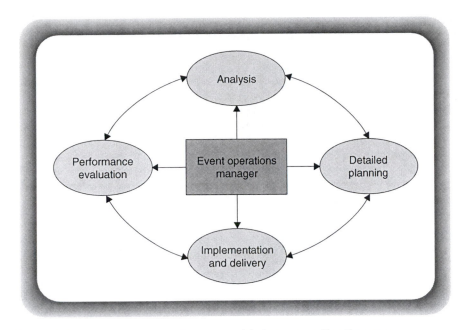

Figure 1.2 Event operations management model, shown as an iterative process

An analysis of both the internal capabilities, values and resources of the organization, and the external environment in which it operates, assists in determining the objectives for an organization. It is essential that a full analysis be undertaken prior to launching an event in order to move towards success.

Detailed planning

Section 2 looks in detail at all the planning activities that must be undertaken in order to stage an event. In some instances planning may take many years, as in the Olympics, and in other cases the planning may take just a week or even less. In each case many of the stages and techniques are the same, and these are detailed in the chapters. The topics cover the detail of the planning process and the management of the supply chain. Also within these chapters you will find work on choice of location for both the event organization and the events themselves. An important topic covered here is risk management. Although it sits within this section of the book, it should be understood that risk management should be considered throughout the life of the project.

Section 2 provides a basis for implementation, which is the next stage in our event operations management model.

Implementation and delivery

As its name suggests, Section 3 is concerned with the allocation of resources against the specifications designed for an event. Amongst other topics, this section of the book looks at motivation and the management of people, forecasting and planning for optimum capacity, and scheduling and coordination of all of the activities that bring an event to fruition.

Performance evaluation

Section 4 covers the last stage of the event operations management model, and it looks in detail at how the standard specification can be used in order to monitor and correct any stage of the operation both during and after the event. It is important that for future events, managers develop and learn from successes and mistakes of the past. The section also looks at how events can be evaluated, and offers various techniques to aid the event manager.

The important topic of quality is critically analysed within the last chapter. Although it is investigated here, quality should not be considered as a separate subject; it pervades every action and every stage of an event. Quality management is a fitting topic with which to conclude this book on event operations management.

Chapter summary and key points

This chapter has explored the varied definitions of a project that have developed over the years. In tandem with this investigation, the chapter has explored the various operations management models from both the general literature and the event management literature. It has been possible to consider the most relevant aspects of all these models and create a model that is appropriate for the management of an event operation. Incorporated into that model is an ideal model for managing an actual event, based on the project management literature.

The outcome is portrayed in this chapter, and is called the event operations management model. This has been shown in two formats; one linear and the other iterative. The linear approach is ideal to use as a structure for this book; the other is what will really happen in practice – i.e. as soon as one element of the model has been achieved and completed, before moving onto the next stage the event manager will invariably have to return to some earlier decision since the marketplace and the customer will be always changing. The model identifies that the event manager has to be nimble, and it also identifies that the event manager should be well organized and methodical.

Chapter 2

Event management: characteristics and definitions

Learning Objectives

After reading through this chapter you will be able to:

- Appreciate the growth of the event industry and its different characteristics
- Understand a range of useful definitions used within the operational management and project management literature
- Explain the importance of having a clear mission and how this must translate in to 'making it happen' for the customer
- Evaluate the need to match the environment, values and resources (i.e. EVR congruence)
- Understand the transformation process and appreciate the use of resources, which are the inputs into the process, and services and products, which are the output of the process (i.e. the event itself).

Introduction

We are at the start of the event operations management model, and as such it is important to take stock of all that is happening around the organization and the event. This chapter identifies some basic definitions that are essential to understand before we proceed through the rest of the chapters. In particular, the chapter introduces terminology from the events industry, general management theory and operational management theory. It establishes the framework in which event managers work, looks at the constraints of policy, and shows how events are limited and affected by resources and the nature of the event. The chapter serves as an explanation for the need for external and internal analysis which is required for any event organization that is in the process of creating an event and having sustained business success. The analysis of these two environments is covered in depth in Chapters 3 and 6.

The different types of event operations are discussed, and also their implications for decision-making and event design.

Important definitions

First we will define the terms *industry, market* and *strategic group*. Evans *et al.* (2003) make an important distinction between markets and industries, and other competitors within the same strategic grouping. They believe that a *market* refers to the needs of the customers and potential customers, whereas the *industry* refers to a group of products linked by common technology, supply or distribution channels. A *strategic group* refers to those organizations that are identified as being the major competitors.

Modern organizations may operate in more than one industry, and in more than one market. For example, in the event industry, ThemeTraders is a vertically integrated UK-based art, design, and production company specializing in creative parties, themed events, road shows and motivational events. Its vertical integration within the *industry* comes from its own services and production of props, costumes and equipment. Each of these affiliated services can be hired separately to clients if wanted. It has clients in a variety of *markets*, including banks, media, car manufacturers, universities, retail establishments, television shows, hotels and airlines.

Each industry and market has its own distinctive structure and characteristics. Industries are centred on the supply of a product, while markets are concerned with demand.

Campbell *et al.* (2003) define the two concepts clearly:

- Industries *produce* goods and services – the supply side of the economic system
- Markets *consume* goods and services that have been produced by industries – the demand side of the economic system.

The event industry

A variety of authors (Getz, 1997; Goldblatt, 1997; Watt, 1998; Bowdin *et al.*, 2001; Shone and Parry, 2004) identify the extent of the event industry and create typologies in order to consider, in more manageable groupings, the diversity of the event industry, its sectors and its markets.

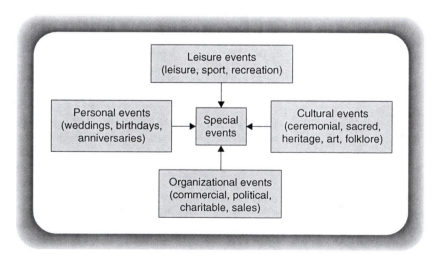

Figure 2.1 Shone and Parry typology of events (Shone and Parry, 2004)

Shone and Parry (2004) suggest a particular typology (Figure 2.1) which we use as a starting point in order to understand the breadth and variety of events. This approach is not offered as the definitive approach, but it does serve to highlight the diversity of event provision.

Getz's typology (Figure 2.2; Getz, 1997) is not dissimilar, but does include more detail within business and trade events, and also identifies educational and scientific events.

Another way the event industry could be split is into three sectors:

1. Public
2. Private
3. Voluntary.

Unlike commercial industries, events are not always driven by the need to make money, but may include a large number of personal, voluntary and charitable events. It is not difficult to think of worldwide examples for these categories but even in small communities illustrations of these three sectors can be found (see Case study 2.1).

All events are unique, and it is this uniqueness that makes them special and creates a challenge for the manager. Four different characteristics of events that are important to the event organizer are:

1. Size and volume of output
2. Complexity and variety of services/products offered to the consumer
3. Uncertainty of numbers attending, cost, time schedule and technical requirements
4. Interaction with the consumer, and degree of consumer and customer contact.

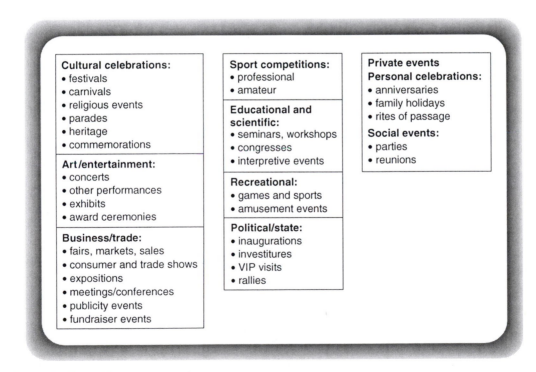

Cultural celebrations:
- festivals
- carnivals
- religious events
- parades
- heritage
- commemorations

Art/entertainment:
- concerts
- other performances
- exhibits
- award ceremonies

Business/trade:
- fairs, markets, sales
- consumer and trade shows
- expositions
- meetings/conferences
- publicity events
- fundraiser events

Sport competitions:
- professional
- amateur

Educational and scientific:
- seminars, workshops
- congresses
- interpretive events

Recreational:
- games and sports
- amusement events

Political/state:
- inaugurations
- investitures
- VIP visits
- rallies

Private events
Personal celebrations:
- anniversaries
- family holidays
- rites of passage

Social events:
- parties
- reunions

Figure 2.2 Getz's (1997) typology of events

Case study 2.1

Skipton

Skipton is a small, busy market town in North Yorkshire, England, situated on the southern edge of the Yorkshire Dales and with a population of 16 000. It has a castle, a canal, a bustling outdoor street market and many festivals and events, some of which are illustrated below.

Public sector event

Skipton Local Produce Festival was organized by the North Yorkshire County Council, Craven District Council and other local organizations as a method of promoting local produce.

The event was held over two days in October at the local Auction Mart, and included cookery demonstrations, music theatre, performance tent, roving performers, workshops, over ninety local produce stalls, and also producers from the Netherlands and Norway.

It was supported by the URBAL project, which is funded through the European Union INTERREG programme. The INTERREG project was launched in the Netherlands in June 2004, and includes partners from the Netherlands, Belgium, Norway, Germany, Sweden and the UK.

URBAL is designed to allow local producers to showcase their products at regional festivals with partner countries.

(Information printed by kind permission of Jochen Werres, Funding and Strategy Manager, Economic Development Unit, North Yorkshire County Council.)

Private sector event

Broughton Hall Country House Estate, Skipton, is still occupied by the Tempest family, and it is used in film and TV dramas. Besides being a country house it is a prestigious business park set in 3000 acres of parkland, and it holds events annually.

The 2004 annual fireworks and laser symphony concert held in July was entitled 'More sounds of the 70s'. This included a sixty-piece symphony orchestra and a vocal group. Audience members were invited to take their own picnics, although hot and cold refreshments as well as hospitality were provided.

(More information re. Broughton Hall Estate can be found at www.broughtonhall.co.uk.)

Voluntary sector event

The Skipton Charities Gala is held annually in July at Skipton, North Yorkshire. A gala – pronounced 'gayler' – in Yorkshire terms consists of a parade followed by activities for all the family, usually in a park; these would include games, funfair, demonstrations in an arena etc. There follows an extract from the Chairman's letter, cited in Skipton's Charity Gala programme.

As usual we pray for dry weather, leaving the rest up to us. We as a committee work so hard trying to put everything into place for the big day. We would like to thank our volunteers who excel themselves each year, without them our gala would not exist. Last but not least to you our public who support us each year come rain or shine, making Skipton Charities Gala nothing but the best.

Because of all this wonderful support we were able to donate over £1000.00 to local causes and charities so far this year. 'A Great Achievement', our sincere thanks go to you all.

Mr and Mrs Dawson (Fred and Doreen), who have been the backbone of Skipton Gale for over seventy years, are going to do us the honour of opening the 2004 gala.

Many thanks go to Marshall Waddington for the splendid firework display, which he donates year after year.

Also a special thank you to Skipton Police for all their hard work and support, on and before gala day.

(More information on Skipton Gala can be found at www.skiptonweb.co.uk)

These four characteristics are based on those proposed by Slack *et al.* (2004), and will be discussed more fully later in this chapter. However, it is important to understand the following concepts in advance.

Companies and organizations existing within the event industry

Event managers may work within a small or large event companies, or they may be employed within much larger organizations. The organization may be a multimillion-pound enterprise such as John Lewis, which employs social secretaries to organize anything ranging from small interview panels to their Annual Fun Day for 20 000+ Partners and their guests. Whatever their size, organizations and major events such as Children in Need (a charity fund-raising initiative in the UK) should have a mission – their *raison d'être*.

Mission

In event terms, the mission can be broadly separated into four areas:

1. The organization's task
2. The reason for staging the event
3. The event's stakeholders
4. The event's overall objectives.

These are usually defined by those who feel that the event should fulfil a need within their community, region, organization or company. The mission should then become the focus of the event, but be flexible enough so as not to stifle creativity and flexibility (see Case study 2.2; Getz, 1997; Bowdin *et al.*, 2001).

Different levels of management and decision-making

If we consider a company as being triangular in shape (Figure 2.3), we can see three different levels – strategic, business and operational. This approach is useful to improve our understanding of the different levels of decision-making – i.e. a long-term approach versus day-to-day management.

NYC & Company

NYC & Company (formerly known as the New York Convention & Visitors Bureau) is New York City's official tourism marketing organization. It lists among its goals the coordinating and/or facilitating of major promotional activities such as Restaurant Week, Paint the Town, CultureFest, OpSail, Broadway on Broadway, and the New York Marathon. It facilitates the expansion of convention and hospitality facilities, and provides support and resources to assist in obtaining major events, such as the 2012 Olympic Games, Grammys, and MTV Awards, for the city.

NYC & Company has the following mission statement:

NYC & Company, the city's official tourism marketing organization, is a private, membership-based non-profit organization dedicated to building New York City's economy and positive image through tourism and convention development, major events, and the marketing of the city on a worldwide basis.

(Information supplied by courtesy of NYC and Company. For more information, see www.nycvisit.com.)

Reflective practice 2.2

1. Consider NYC & Company's mission statement in Case study 2.2, and discuss how it corresponds to the four areas of mission noted in this chapter.
2. What changes would you make?

Evans *et al.* (2001) believe that decisions taken at each of these levels differ from one another in terms of:

- Focus
- The level in the organization at which they are made

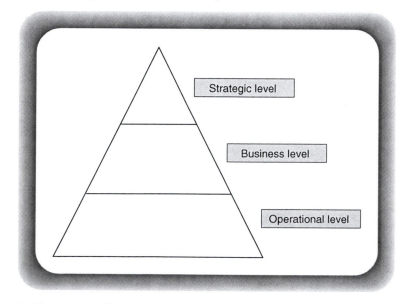

Figure 2.3 The triangle of management and decision-making

- Scope
- Time horizon
- Degree of certainty or uncertainty
- Complexity.

Strategic level decisions

Strategic level decisions are made by senior managers, and are concerned with long-term corporate objectives (i.e. a timescale usually greater than three years). These senior managers will create and evaluate strategies to achieve those objectives. Often these are incorporated into the mission statement.

Business level decisions

Within many companies there are specialized functions, and in many instances specific markets are sought and provided for.

The business decisions are dependent upon the strategic decisions, but only affect one part of the organization. They are medium-term in timescale – i.e. usually one to three years.

Operational level decisions

These are concerned with day-to-day management. It is where the implementation of the months of planning occurs, and where control and administration takes place.

The event manager is a decision-maker. As the event manager is at the hub of, and responsible for, making it happen, it follows that the most pressing decisions are of a day-to-day nature.

Certain influences will affect the decisions made by the event manager. The influences include the objectives of the organization, what is feasible with the resources available, the *structure* of the system, and the influences of the external environment, as our event operations management model shows.

Operational decisions are influenced by what is:

- *Desired* by the organization (mission and policy of the organization)
- *Feasible*, i.e. the availability, amount and quality of resources, both tangible and intangible, and the nature (in particular the structure) of the operating system being used
- *Possible*, due to the influence and impact of the external environment.

Figure 2.4 shows the constraints for an event manager. The mission and policy of the organization set the scope for the event manager; however, both the external and the internal environments influence the mission and, subsequently, any policies.

Once the policy has been decided, then what is desirable is expressed as the objectives of the organization, and the resources and structure of the organization may limit what is feasible. In Chapter 3 we will consider other external factors that limit what the event manager can provide – for example, the power and influence of the stakeholders.

The aim of the event manager will be to use resources as efficiently as possible to achieve the highest level of customer satisfaction within the constraints of policy objectives, available resources and the structure of the organization.

EVR congruence

Thompson (2001) indicates that a manager should fully appreciate the dynamics, opportunities and threats present in the external environment, and that these should match the organization's resources – both its strengths and its weaknesses. This concept can

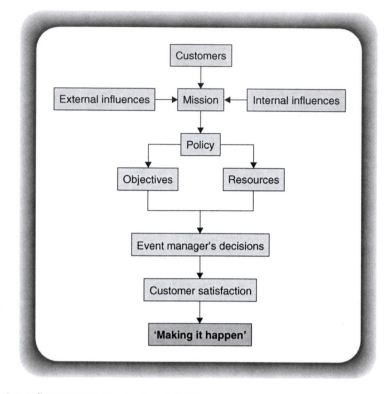

Figure 2.4 Influences on organizational decisions

also be expressed by saying that there should be a match between what the customer sees as being critical and the core competencies and resources being provided. However, it is also important that the values of the organization match both the needs of the environment and the critical success factors as determined by the customers. It is both the values and the culture that determine whether the environment and resources are currently matched, and whether they stay matched – i.e. congruent – in changing circumstances (Thompson, 2001). This is the notion of EVR congruence. There should be an overlap between the environment (critical success factors), the resources (tangible and intangible), and the values of the organization and its commitment to sustain this overlap (Figure 2.5).

If there is no overlap with any one of the three elements, the event manager should be in a position to address the situation and to achieve a suitable match that best addresses the organization and business.

Figure 2.6 shows an organization that has the desire, the skills and competencies, and the resources to move in a particular direction, but a direction that is not needed or valued by the consumer.

Figure 2.7 shows an organization that has the desire to move in a particular direction, and one that is appreciated and needed by consumers in a ready market. However, the organization does not have the skills and/or resources to deliver this particular product.

Figure 2.8 shows an organization that has the resources and skills to move in a particular direction, and one that is needed by the consumers. However, the culture and values of the staff within that organization do not want to move in that particular direction and with that product.

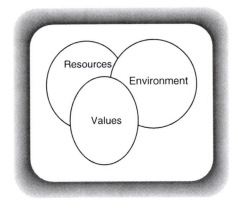

Figure 2.5 EVR showing an overlap of the three elements

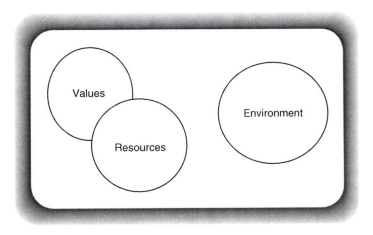

Figure 2.6 EVR showing an overlap of only the elements of values and resources

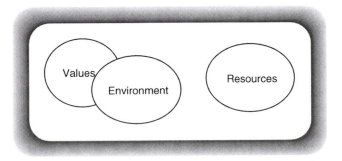

Figure 2.7 EVR showing an overlap of only the elements of values and the environment

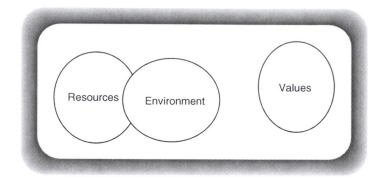

Figure 2.8 EVR showing an overlap of only the elements of the environment and resources

Important definitions

There are three further definitions that must be understood before proceeding further.

Service operations management

Service operations management is the function within a service organization that interacts with and delivers services to customers. Consequently, efficient operations management is crucial to the success of the organization. The role of a manager of an event operation is to manage an event and to provide customer satisfaction within the framework of the organization's policy, and to use resources as efficiently as possible.

Simply put, the event manager makes it, the mission, happen.

A further definition is provided by Wright (2001):

> operations management is the ongoing activities of designing, reviewing and using the operating system, or systems, to achieve service outputs as determined by the organization for customers.

Getz (1997), who has created a planning process for event operations, believes that it is the event manager who translates all of the key elements into the reality of an event (see Figure 2.9).

Campbell *et al.* (2003) see the operations function as being at the centre of the organization. It is that part of an organization which produces the output – the event itself. For example, for a product launch of a new perfume the operations function arranges coordination of an appropriate venue, reception staff, technical facilities and special effects, presentation scripts, an appropriate and relevant database of people to whom the product should be launched, and invitations to the relevant media. The actual launch and presentation is the output.

Service organization

A service organization is one where two or more people are engaged in a systematic effort to provide services to a customer. The objective is to serve a customer. For any service to be provided there has to be a customer. Without a customer, and interaction between customer and the service organization, the objective of providing service cannot happen. According to Wright (2001):

> A service organization exists to interact with customers and to satisfy customers service requirements.

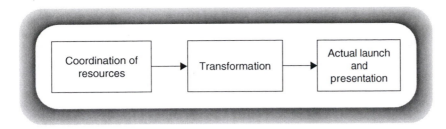

Figure 2.9 The transformation of resources into an event

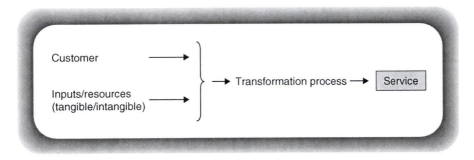

Figure 2.10 The transformation process

Service operating system

Slack and Lewis (2002) refer to a service operating system as the 'transformation process'. Wright (2001) defines it as follows:

> *A service operating system is the manner in which inputs/resources are organized and used to provide service outputs.*

Slack *et al*. (2004) recognize that there must be inputs to achieve an output. Within an operation, inputs/resources are transformed into outputs – for example, inputs could be raw food ingredients being transformed into a conference dinner (the output), or details about venues, room size and AV equipment availability being added to stored information to create a new improved database giving detailed information about the range of venues which are suitable for conferences (the output). The transformation process is the manipulation of the inputs/resources to produce an output i.e. service (Figure 2.10).

Inputs/resources

For ease and greater understanding in the events industry, we refer to the inputs as the resources needed and the outputs as service, or the event itself. Inputs can be tangible or intangible. Tangible inputs are physical, they can be seen and touched, and the amount or rate of use can be measured in quantifiable terms. Intangible inputs, which cannot be seen or touched, include:

- Time
- Information
- Innovative design

- Ideas
- Skills
- Sound, etc.

Measurement of the effective use of intangible resources is much more difficult than for the tangible resources. However, the amount of time and the information available are important issues for the event manager.

Without a customer the objective of service cannot be delivered, and therefore the customer must also be regarded as an input into the system that provides the service.

These inputs will be discussed in greater depth in Chapter 6.

Outputs

Service outputs include the following examples:

- A courtesy bus-shuttle service at an outdoor sculpture event taking passengers to different parts of the park, or 'Park and Ride' at an air show. A bus can travel on its advertised route, but until a passenger is picked up the function of the bus service is not carried out. Without a passenger the mission of the bus (i.e. to carry passengers) cannot be fulfilled. An empty bus travelling on the route is nothing more than an un-utilized, or 'stored', resource. Apart from the bus itself, other resources such as fuel and the time (wages) of the driver are being used.
- A hotel room. Until a guest checks in, the service function of the hotel cannot be performed. True the room can be 'serviced' and prepared in advance, but until a guest arrives there is no service output.

Case study 2.3

Royal Ascot, Ascot Racecourse

Royal Ascot is held annually in June at Ascot in Berkshire, UK.

The importance of intangible resources can be demonstrated by reactions to changes brought about by new management at Ascot Racecourse. In three years the Clerk of the Course and Chief Executive transformed attendance by concentrating on customer care. Richard Evans of the *Times*, quoted in *Ascot History*, said of the Royal Meeting that 'Ascot has gone out of its way to make customers feel welcome and wanted. Tradition and custom have not been sacrificed in the process and an air of relaxed formality has returned to the royal meeting'. Prior to these changes attendance had been faltering and information to customers on site had often been headed with the words 'By Order'.

(Magee, 2002)

Reflective practice 2.3

Consider Case study 2.3.

1. How could the terminology within signage affect the customer service of an organization?
2. Why would it?
3. What intangible resources are being affected here?

- A restaurant. With a restaurant it is possible for the chef to make up salads, and even to prepare and cook meals in advance, before any patron is seated. This may not be the policy (strategy) of a top-class restaurant, but nonetheless the decision (strategy) can be changed – i.e. it is not essential to have a customer before a meal is prepared. However, the mission of the restaurant is not to *prepare* meals, the mission is to *serve* meals, and the delivery of service cannot take place without the customer – it is not possible for the meal to be served unless there is a customer and the customer has placed an order.

In these three examples – the bus travelling on its route, the prepared hotel room and the partly prepared meal in the restaurant – there are stored resources waiting for the customer to arrive. However, without customer input no service output will be delivered.

The triangle of investigation

To summarize so far, we have:

- Noted the difference between industries and markets and strategic groups
- Considered the extent and diversity of the event industry
- Considered the importance of having a mission and appraised the three levels of decision-making within an organization
- Analysed the definitions and meanings of operational management, service organization, service operating system, and the transformation process.

It can be seen that in this chapter we ourselves have followed an inverted triangle of investigation (Figure 2.11) and moved from the general to the specific.

Now we are at the apex of the triangle. Who do we meet there? The customer!

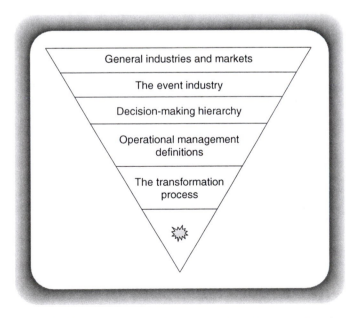

Figure 2.11 Inverted triangle of investigation, moving from the general to the specific

Who is the customer?

In events, customers can be the audience, a group of spectators, visitors, delegates or sponsors, or the individual client. From a commercial point of view, customers are the people who pay for the service. Kandampully (2002) categorizes customers into four groups:

1. External customers – a firm's end users
2. Internal customers – employees and managers of the firm
3. Competitors' customers – those the firm would like to attract
4. Ex-customers – those who have chosen to leave.

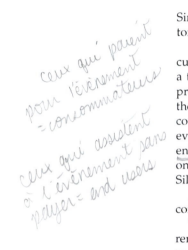

Similarly, in the events industry a distinction should be made between the paying customer and the end user.

In the majority of events the customer *pays* for the 'service' received – e.g. a paying customer at the Olympic Games in Athens, i.e. a spectator. Another example would be a ticket holder for a Pavarotti Concert. In fact, you might think you would be hard pressed to find a customer who does not pay. However, what about the audiences at the Queen's Golden Jubilee Celebrations, the audiences at major free outdoor local council events, and invited hospitality guests at annual dinners? What about incentive events and fabulous trips abroad? The distinction is that those who have attended and enjoyed these free spectaculars are 'end users'. In these instances, the customer is the one who pays for the service – so in the first example the customer of the Queen's Silver Jubilee is the Queen, or at least whoever holds her purse.

At local council events, is the customer the council, or perhaps the taxpayer or the consumer of the extravaganza?

Throughout this book, the term *customer* will be used. However, it should be remembered that this includes both the paying customer and the end user who does not pay but merely receives. Either way the customer is extremely important, and the customer's needs and impact on events feature heavily in this book. Chapter 5 analyses further the interaction between the customers, the stakeholders and how a company can start to measure its success in delivering all their diverse needs.

Different characteristics of operations and events

By now, you should understand a little more about the different characteristics of events. We know that, although the event operations management model (Figure 1.1) can be used for all different styles of events and is therefore transferable, decisions that are made about the characteristics and nature of the event have far-reaching consequences for the event operation manager.

We now consider these different characteristics and the different relationships we have with our customers.

We have seen that all operations involve a transformation process, where inputs are transformed into desired outputs – i.e. resources become transformed into services delivered; the event itself.

It is important to note the differences between types of operations and then to discuss the impacts that these differences have for the event manager and the organization.

Slack *et al.* (2004) believe that there are four important characteristics which can be used to identify different operations, and these distinctions are also useful and valid within the event industry:

1. The volume of service delivered at an event
2. The variety of the service delivered at an event
3. The variation in demand for the service delivered at an event
4. The degree of customer contact involved in producing the service delivered at an event.

Similar attributes to these were discussed earlier, although slightly amended. We remind you again of these four, adjusted by ourselves, to take into account the peculiarities of the event marketplace:

1. Size and volume of output
2. Complexity and variety of services/products offered to the consumer
3. Uncertainty of numbers attending, cost, time schedule and technical requirements
4. Interaction with the consumer, and degree of consumer and customer contact.

Size and volume of output

As an example, we can consider the thousands of applications from the public and many different charities to run in the annual London Marathon. The volume of enquiries and degree of processing of these enquiries enables a high degree of repeatability of actions for those staff who are concerned with the replies.

At the other end of the scale, imagine an event manager being involved with reviewing tender applications for extra seating for an indoor concert for 200 people from preferred suppliers. It can be seen that the volume of the similar task is very much lower, and the chance of employing more than one person to cover the second activity is remote. The staff involved in this small volume of administration will be employed to cover a wide range of other tasks, and therefore need to be much more flexible and highly trained in a variety of tasks. This may be more satisfying to the individual, but is less open to systemization.

With high-volume output, the task can become specialized and systematized and possibly warrant capital expenditure to enable the task to become more efficient – for example, by the use of computers and registration systems at a large exhibition.

The most important implication with high-volume activities is therefore that the unit cost can be much lower, since it can be spread over a large number of transformation processes/transactions.

Complexity and variety of services/products offered to the consumer

This dimension considers the variety of activities and tasks that the event manager can be called upon to perform during an event. In large events, different groups of staff are assigned to specific tasks – low variety, for example, being a steward at a particular entrance for an outdoor concert. (See Chapter 11 for more work on staff motivations.) However, at a small event – such as fifty-delegate seminar – the staff on duty could be asked a variety of questions regarding the provision of facilities and activities during the day, and be involved with a wide range of jobs.

A high degree of variety therefore determines the style of training required and the knowledge needed by individual staff. This means that flexibility comes at a price to the event manager.

Where variety is low, little flexibility is required and the tasks assigned can be standardized and regular. This lack of variety can result in relatively low costs, but may result in poor service if a member of staff becomes bored.

Uncertainty of numbers attending, cost, time schedule and technical requirements

Consider the demand pattern for a nightclub in a university town. When it is term time, the club will be full on certain nights and possibly would welcome even more space. However, during the summer months and at Christmas it may only use a fraction of its capacity.

If we consider a hotel close to a major road network and a tourist resort, it may be patronized by business conferences and business clientele during the week and by tourists at the weekends. It may find that its demand is virtually level. The consequence of this is that the hotel can plan its activities in advance and set out its staffing rotas.

Where there is low variation in demand, all activities can be planned in a routine and predictable manner. However, it may be that the range of activities varies between business and leisure guests.

The timeline does not have to be over one year, or over one week, but can show a variation in demand over one day. For example, can an event manager at an outdoor festival predict the demands on the bar over the course of a one-day event? How many staff should be employed for each hour of the day? Should it vary?

Would selling pre-paid tickets to a gala dinner confirm the number of diners? If so, the number of staff and amount of food can be pre-determined and this will ensure a high utilization of resources.

A low variation in demand enables routines to be established and for the required level of inputs to be predicted – whether over a one-day event or throughout a year.

A high variation in demand may prevent the organizer from knowing how many staff to employ and what capacity of space to make available, and may require greater flexibility from suppliers.

Case study 2.4 provides an example of a major annual event and the planning required.

Case study 2.4

The RHS Chelsea Flower Show

The RHS Chelsea Flower Show – the world's greatest flower show – is held annually for four days in May at the Royal Hospital, Chelsea. It has been held there since 1913, and the 2004 show was the eighty-second to be held at this site. Originally known as the Great Spring Show, it was first held in Kensington in 1862.

The Exhibitors

There are around 600 exhibitors in total. The 2004 show featured:

- Twenty-three show gardens
- Eight chic gardens
- Nine courtyard gardens
- Four city gardens

- Eight Sunflower Street gardens
- More than a hundred floral exhibitors.

International exhibitors came from countries as far away as the USA, Barbados, Kenya, Japan, Australia, Jamaica, South Africa and Trinidad & Tobago.

Some exhibitors, such as Nottcutt's, Kelways and McBean's Orchids, have exhibited at the show since its early days.

Exhibits are judged by specialist RHS Judging Panels before the show opens, and may be awarded Gold, Silver-Gilt, Silver and Bronze Medals.

Organization

RHS staff, exhibitors and contractors start planning for the show eighteen months in advance. Work is already underway for the show in 2005.

It takes 800 people three and a half weeks to build the show; construction includes 5 km of piping, 185 toilets, and enough canvas to cover 6 football pitches.

The floral pavilion covers nearly 12 000 square metres, and 7000 square metres of turf is relaid after the show. The showground covers 11 acres.

The visitors

There is a capped figure of 157 000 visitors to the show. This represents full capacity of the showground.

The RHS currently has over 300 000 members, and the Tuesday and Wednesday of the show are reserved for RHS members, although non-members may purchase tickets for the Wednesday afternoon and evening. Non-members can purchase tickets for Thursday and Friday.

Members of the Royal Family make a private visit to the show on the Preview Day (Monday).

Catering

During the course of the week, 6500 bottles of champagne, 18 000 glasses of Pimms, 5000 lobsters, 110 000 cups of tea and coffee, and more than 28 000 rounds of sandwiches are sold in the following restaurants:

- Ranelagh Seafood and Champagne – a large bistro-style restaurant serving seafood, salads, afternoon tea and strawberries; the champagne bar can also be found here. Open 10.30 am–7 pm.
- Ranelagh Restaurant – a large, seated catering area serving hot food, sandwiches, cakes and various beverages. Open 8 am–8 pm.
- Rock Bank Restaurant – a stylish seated restaurant offering full English breakfast, three-course lunches and late afternoon/early evening meals. This restaurant offers the best views of the show, overlooking some of the major gardens at the event. Tables in this restaurant can be pre-booked. Open 9 am–7.30 pm.
- Rock Bank Food Court – a large restaurant with some seating offering a range of hot and cold foods. This area includes a Pimms bar and a full bar facility. Open 8 am–8 pm.
- Thames View Restaurant – a small, seated restaurant overlooking the Thames, serving salads, pastries, baguettes, sandwiches and other cold foods together with hot and cold beverages. Open 8 am–8 pm.
- Western Avenue Food Court – this facility offers a wide range of hot and cold meals ranging from baguettes to jacket potatoes, crepes and ice cream. Open 8 am–8 pm.
- Champagne and Pimms – champagne and Pimms bars are located throughout the site. Open 8 am–8 pm.

(Reproduced by courtesy of the Royal Horticultural Society; more information can be found at www.rhs.org.uk/chelsea.)

Reflective practice 2.4

Consider the four characteristics of Slack *et al.* (2004)'s model, and outline the implications for The Chelsea Flower Show in terms of variety and volume of hospitality to customers and for employment of staff.

Interaction with the consumer, and degree of consumer and customer contact

Earlier it was noted that customer input is essential in any operation. Without the customer there would be no need for the operation. However, the event manager can make decisions on how much involvement the customer should have within the operation. For example, there are personal wedding planners who organize all of the details of the special day for the bride and groom – from organizing the flowers and photographer to discussing arrangements for the honeymoon, and booking hotels and transfers etc. On the other hand, the bride and groom may choose to use a wedding planning website and have no contact with a personal organizer.

With a high customer-contact event, the staff will need to have been trained in good customer skills and consequently the event will incur more costs than if it were a low-contact event.

In some events there will be a mixture of high-contact and low-contact activities – the event itself may have low contact with individual customers, but telephoning and reserving a seat will need high-contact skills from the operational staff.

Reflective practice 2.5

Looking at the table below, you should be able to give at least two examples of different events in the first and third columns for both the low and high dimensions of each of the typologies described.

High ⟶ Low

Event example	Typology	Event example
	Size and volume of output	
	Complexity and variety of services/products offered to the consumer	
	Uncertainty of numbers attending, cost, time schedule and technical requirements	
	Interaction with the consumer and degree of consumer and customer contact	

This exercise makes you realize the different types of events and their different characteristics.

However, more important is the next table, where you use the examples you have just cited and note the implications of these differences for the event manager. You will then see how making different choices regarding the design of the event and the customers' involvement has cost and planning implications for your organization. The types of implications that you should consider will be among the following alternatives:

- Repetition
- Systemization
- Unit costs
- Capital costs
- Flexibility
- Complexity
- Closely matching customer needs
- Flexibility of capacity
- Forecasted capacity
- Queuing
- Customer contact skills
- Standardization
- Centralization
- High staff utilization.

High ➝ Low

Implications for your event example	Typology	Implications for your event example
	Size and volume of output	
	Complexity and variety of services/products offered to the consumer	
	Uncertainty of numbers attending, cost, time schedule and technical requirements	
	Interaction with the consumer and degree of consumer and customer contact	

Chapter summary and key points

This chapter has covered the importance of analysis and how it can be executed within an organization. It is the first chapter of the book to describe this process, and its importance within the first section of the event operations management model. We have noted the difference between industries and the markets, and considered the extent and diversity of the event industry.

Within an organization it has been shown that there are three levels of decision-making, and we appraised the importance of having a mission. This concept was illustrated by examining three living applications of companies within the event industry and how they use the concept of mission as a communication tool.

The chapter has considered the definitions and meanings of several key phrases used within the general literature:

■ Operational management
■ Service organization
■ Service operating system, internal and external constraints, and the transformation process.

We have also considered who the customer is.

These resources will be discussed in much greater depth when we progress to analysing internal resources in Chapter 6.

The chapter concluded with an overview of the four different types of organizations characterized by four different dimensions – volume, variety, variation in demand, and degree of customer contact – and the impact of these differences was the subject of an application exercise.

Chapter 3
Analysis of the external environment

Learning Objectives

After reading through this chapter you will be able to:

- **Understand the importance of objectives, and how event managers can cope within a changing and evolving environment**
- **Appreciate the importance of the customer**
- **Identify all other influencers on business policy**
- **Apply techniques that can assist event managers to understand and control their environment more objectively and effectively.**

Introduction

The content of this chapter is from the first stage of the event operations management model. It considers the external environment, and introduces the analysis process. In Chapter 2 (Figure 2.4), analysis of the external environment was considered an essential part of the overall process as outlined in the event operations management model (Figure 1.1). In this chapter, we can break that analysis down into various sub-headings.

In Chapter 2 we said that the role of the events manager is to arrange and use resources efficiently and effectively so as to achieve the goals or mission of the organization. We also said although events managers may not always be involved in determining goals and objectives, nevertheless they are the people responsible for turning the goals and objectives into realities, and 'making it happen'. Every business is now competing on the world stage, and to survive must strive to reach world-class standards. National and geographic boundaries no longer afford a protective barrier for competitors. Customers today are well travelled and well informed, and are quick to make value judgements on performance.

This chapter will consider how business policy is created, and how it often changes due to external influences.

Objectives of the event manager

Event managers have three key objectives:

1. To achieve the strategic objectives of the organization. For example, an event management company working within a local authority may have as its main objective to stage events, which assist

in achieving the overall aims of the authority. If the local authority wants to promote inclusiveness of all the community, then 'free street events' would be one way of bringing all of the community together.

2. To satisfy customers' wants. In this instance, the customers are those people who attend the event. Without customers, the organization will cease to exist.

3. To achieve efficient use of resources. If an organization cannot afford the level of service it is providing, it will soon go out of business. We will analyse how to use resources efficiently in Chapter 6.

All these objectives must be achieved simultaneously.

Tensions and issues for an event manager

An event manager with a changing and evolving business policy will have various tensions and issues to deal with. An events manager may be involved in shaping the corporate policy and objectives of the organization, establishing and acquiring resources, and setting specific operational targets. However, organizations seldom operate in an ideal fashion. The reality is that in many cases the event manager will inherit an existing structure. Problems may include the following:

- An event manager may be working within a small organization which has grown and expanded, so its structure is no longer ideal and may now be less than adequate.
- The principal objective, be it customer satisfaction or efficient resource utilization, may not be clearly defined in the business policy. Indeed, most organizations will have customer satisfaction and resource utilization as twin and equal objectives, without realizing that inherently there is a conflict between the two.
- Some organizations may have a clear mission and objectives, but the needs of the customers have changed. Some employees may reflect these changes in their work and others may not.
- Some organizations have tension occurring between the event manager and the person who secures future business and promises the impossible.
- Other states of tension exist between customer needs and what the stakeholders of the organization feel are appropriate or desirable.

The event manager has the task of making the seemingly impossible, possible. Consequently, the manager needs to be an optimist and adept at applying structured thinking as well as unstructured or lateral thinking to problems, so as to achieve the goals imposed on him or her.

Business policy

The business policy for an organization sets:

- The objectives of the organization
- The service to be provided
- The market to be served
- The way in which the service will be provided
- The level of quality to be aimed for
- The quantity and quality of resources that will be employed.

Business policy does not happen by accident; it is a conscious attempt by organizations to provide long-term goals and to plan resources to achieve those goals. As De Wit and Meyer (2004) explain, one of the difficulties for managers in today's environment is that both the business environment and the individual firms are constantly in flux, and achieving a match between the two is an ongoing challenge. Business policy may start with the purpose of the organization – the very reason it exists (the *raison d'être*), and this is often referred to as the *vision* of the organization.

As explained by Dulewicz *et al.* (1995):

> *A vision depicts the aspirations of the company, a desired and attainable picture of how the company will appear in a few years' time, which can capture the imagination and motivate employees and others. The mission is to achieve the vision, expressing the commitment and will to do so. On the way decisions will have to be made according to the values of the company, as indicated in the decision-making behaviour of the board – according to what the board believes is good or bad, right or wrong from the company's point of view.*

Similarly, Thompson (2001) differentiates between vision and mission statements. He believes that vision statements should focus on those values to which the organization is committed, and that there should be appropriate measures in place to indicate progress towards those ideals. He sees the mission statement as addressing not what the company should do to survive, but what it has chosen to do to thrive.

Mission statement

As referred to in Chapter 2, the purpose of the business is often articulated in a mission statement. However, frequently what the mission statement says may be at variance with the true mission of the organization.

For example, we know of no organization with a mission statement that says 'our aim is survival, and to survive we will reduce our work force by 25 per cent', or 'we will aggressively advertise our service levels, but we will not spend any money on training our staff'. Such organizations are more likely to publish missions that proclaim 'we value and respect the importance of our highly trained and dedicated staff, and 'our aim is to provide outstanding world-class service'.

It is important for the event manager to understand what the true mission is, irrespective of what might be stated in the published mission. For instance, if survival is the mission (and this could well be a legitimate mission), this has to be understood and thus will shape the strategies to be employed.

Ackoff (1986) suggests that a good mission statement has five characteristics:

1. It contains a formulation of objectives that are measurable
2. It differentiates the company from its competitors
3. It defines the business that the company wishes to be in
4. It is relevant to all stakeholders and not just shareholders and managers
5. It is exciting and inspiring.

Case study 3.1 provides some examples of mission statements.

Holistic management

We should be aware that an organization does not operate in isolation. The event operations management model shows in the first stage that there are different environments that have an influence on it and should be analysed. These are the internal and external environments. Following analysis of these, it is then possible to develop the planning process. All organizations should work in partnership with their suppliers, customers and competitors (Thompson, 2001). An immediate impact is made on an organization by suppliers and customers, on whom it depends, and its competitors – both existing

Case study 3.1

Mission statements

The examples in these case studies illustrate mission statements from three different types of organizations involved with events. As can be seen, not all organizations use the word 'mission' when articulating the purpose of their business.

Melbourne Food and Wine Festival, Victoria, Australia

The Melbourne Food and Wine Festival is a unique event which operates on a not-for-profit basis. It commenced in 1993 with a simple programme of twelve events. It has grown annually, and the 2004 Festival included more than 120 events over a 3-week period from 19 March–4 April. The Festival is managed by a Board of Management and supported by a small team who are responsible for the successful coordination of its events.

Its mission is as follows:

> *The Festival's charter is to promote the quality produce, talent and lifestyle of Melbourne and the State of Victoria, and to reinforce Melbourne as the pre-eminent culinary city of Australia.*

(Printed by courtesy of Melbourne Food and Wine Festival. For more information see www. Melbournefoodandwine.com.au. Student information is also available on this site.)

Euro RSCG Skybridge, London, England

Euro RSCG Skybridge is an award-winning marketing solutions agency that works with the world's top companies to help them to achieve optimal performance. Their work includes experiential events and travel, communications strategies and innovative creative concepts. Information and video clips of events can be seen on their website (www.skybridge.com).

The events division consists of twenty full-time events professionals who organize and operate events on a global basis.

Their mission is as follows:

> *Our vision is to be the best international provider of marketing solutions, creating and adding value for our clients, employees, shareholders, business partners and the communities within which we work.*
>
> *We will achieve this through working in partnership with our clients to produce transformational performance and customer experiences that are appropriate to their needs, practical, easy to implement and that have a measurable impact on results.*

(For more information on RSCG Skybridge, see www.skybridgegroup.com.)

Clear Channel, San Antonio, Texas, USA

Clear Channel is a multinational organization started in 1972 by Lowry Mays and Red McCombs. They acquired their first Clear Channel radio station in 1975, entered television in 1988, and by 1995 owned 43 radio stations and 16 television stations. By 1998 they owned or programmed 204 radio stations, and had a worldwide outdoor advertising presence in 25 countries through the acquisition of More Group PLC. In 2000 they acquired SFX entertainment, one of the world's largest diversified promoters, producers and presenters of live entertainment events. They now either own or programme 1376 radio stations and approximately 700 000 outdoor advertising displays.

In 2001, Clear Channel Entertainment produced and marketed the three top grossing concert tours, and collectively Clear Channel divisions were operating in 65 countries worldwide.

In the UK, the music group exclusively runs six live entertainment venues and operates in nine European countries through the acquisition of concert promoters and other live entertainment producers. It is also a dominant force within theatre and sports management of professional athletes.

Clear Channel's mission is as follows:

The Clear Channel Creed – It's What We Believe!

We are in the business of helping our customers grow their businesses. We do this effectively with our wide variety of media and entertainment products.

We believe in maximizing our customer's satisfaction, we will deserve and will earn their continued loyalty. Our goal is to have long-term, mutually profitable relationships.

We believe in providing superior value to customers through high quality, technologically advanced, fairly priced services designed to meet customer needs better than all the possible alternatives.

We believe Clear Channel's people are our most important asset. Our teams make the critical difference in how we perform, and their skills, talents and determination separate us from our competitors. We also believe people can achieve their full potential when they enjoy their work, so it is a priority to provide a workplace where growth, success and fun go hand in hand.

We believe we have an obligation for the well being of the communities in which we live. We further believe the future success of our communities and the industries where we do business is dependent upon the responsibility we feel, the high standards we set and the positive impact our actions have.

We believe excellence is the standard, and we seek to achieve excellence by encouraging and nourishing these core values:

- Respect for the individual
- Honest, open communication
- Individual development and satisfaction
- A sense of ownership in Clear Channel's success
- Participation, cooperation and teamwork
- Creativity, innovation and initiative
- Prudent risk-taking
- Recognition and rewards for achievement.

We believe success is measured by:

- Achieving leadership in the markets we serve
- Developing our own people to form the building blocks of our internal growth and expansion
- Maintaining the highest standards of ethics and integrity in every action we take and in everything we do.

We believe the ultimate measure of our success is to provide a superior value to our stockholders.

(Extracts from website. For more information on Clear Channel, see www.clearchannel.com.)

Reflective practice 3.1

Consider the organizations described in Case study 3.1.

1. How do the three examples given conform to the five characteristics that Ackoff (1986) says should be present within a mission statement?
2. Use the Internet to research the above organizations and determine whether they are practically applying their mission statements in the production/organization of their current events.
3. Are there any discrepancies, and if so, what criteria would you use to measure these?

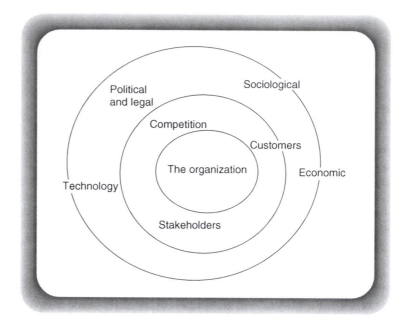

Figure 3.1 Environmental forces

ones and new ones joining the industry (see Figure 3.1). The influencers in the inner circle of the figure may be easier to control and manage than those in the outer circle.

Those in the outer circle are the wider environmental forces. These are commonly grouped together as PEST (political and legal, economic, sociological and technological) forces.

It is useful to think of all these forces in concentric circles, since they impact on every aspect of the organization and upon each other – sometimes equally and at other times with varying emphasis.

This chapter will seek to explore these environmental factors in greater depth, and to place them into context within the events industry.

A further diagrammatic representation of the influences within organizations is shown in Figure 3.2. This figure shows the customer firmly in the centre.

The importance of the customer

At the centre of Figure 3.2 is the customer. Without a customer, the organization will cease to exist. However, without suppliers the organization will not have sufficient resources, and without transforming those resources into a service an event cannot exist to be consumed.

Although the importance of satisfying the customer cannot be denied, it is important to appreciate that customer satisfaction is only one determinant of business policy.

As Wild (2002: 11) points out, 'many organizations have gone bankrupt despite having loyal and satisfied customers' (see Figure 3.3).

A company cannot achieve sustainable profits without the customer being satisfied. Sustained profits are totally dependent on customer satisfaction, but the reverse is not true (Kandampully, 2002). The event company equally should focus on the customers and improve their total experience. The whole organization should unify its approach in order to match, if not exceed, customer expectations, whilst organizing supply and use of resources in an efficient and controlled manner. In short, the level of customer

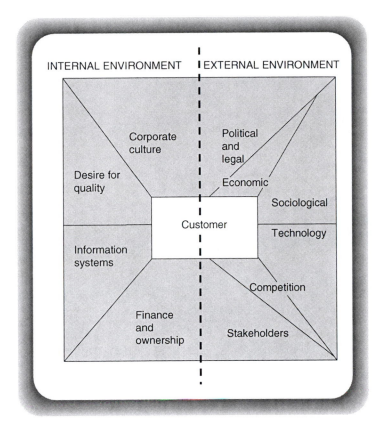

Figure 3.2 External and internal factors on the customer

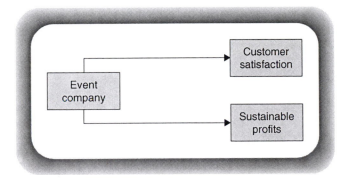

Figure 3.3 A company requires customer satisfaction and sustainable profits

satisfaction provided has to be *affordable* and *sustainable*. This will entail having an efficient and reliable supply chain – i.e. suppliers who provide the right resources, at the right time, to the right place, at the right cost and in the right quantity.

Most organizations can provide a high level of customer satisfaction for a short period, but the level offered has to be sustainable. In service industries customers will be very aware if service levels drop or are inconsistent with what they expect based on past experience.

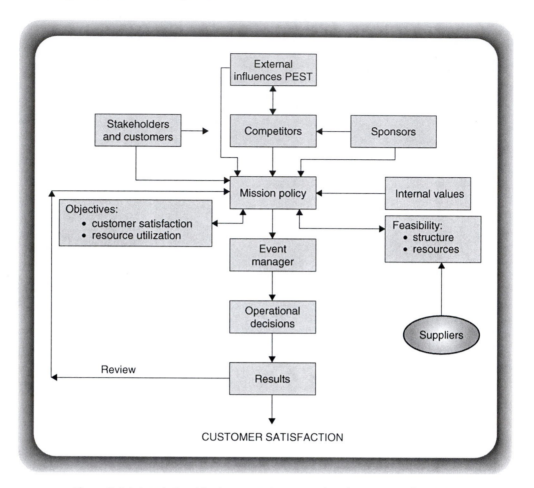

Figure 3.4 Interrelationships between the external environment and their impact on the mission of the company

Figure 3.4 above should be studied and understood, since it shows at a glance the interrelationships between the external environment and their impact on the mission of the company, and also the impacts from the customer and the suppliers on the desired structure of the operation and the resources available. It can be related to the first stage of the event operations management model.

Policy influencers

Figure 3.2 has an outer band, which includes (on the left-hand side):

- Corporate culture
- Desire for quality
- Information systems
- Finance and ownership.

These are certainly influenced by external factors, but they can be managed by actions from *within* the organization. You could think of these as being the *strengths* and *weaknesses* of the organization. Internal factors are covered in Chapter 6.

The other factors, shown on the right-hand side, are:

- Political and legal
- Economic
- Sociological
- Technology
- Competition
- Stakeholders.

These are all factors external to the organization, but which affect customer expectations and also, at another dimension, may limit what the organization is able to do. Often these influences are known as PEST factors. This handy phrase does however miss out the influence of competitors, which in no circumstances should be forgotten, and the importance of stakeholders.

You could think of PEST and competitors and stakeholders as providing *opportunities* or *threats*. To complicate this notion, some stakeholders may be internal to the organization.

In a traditional SWOT (strengths, weaknesses, opportunities and threats) analysis, the opportunities and threats are 'external' to the organization, and the strengths and weaknesses are 'internal' issues. Hence you can see that strengths and weaknesses are going to come from those aspects shown on the left-hand side of Figure 3.2, and the opportunities and threats from those aspects on the right-hand side of the figure.

Knowing the organization's own strengths and weaknesses will help determine feasibility, and will also indicate areas where corrective action should be taken. For the external factors, the aim is to determine opportunities and threats, and to determine how the organization is (or might be) affected by these external factors.

The work in this book will allow us to investigate how strengths can be used to maximize opportunities and reduce threats, and how opportunities can be used to minimize weaknesses. Griffin (2000) sees SWOT analysis as one of the most important steps in formulating strategy. Using the organization's mission as the context, managers can assess internal strengths and weaknesses as well as external opportunities and threats (Griffin, 2000). The goal is then to develop excellent service, which exploits opportunities and strengths, neutralizes threats and avoids weaknesses.

In Chapter 6 we will look at the internal factors as they might affect a company, but in this chapter we consider in detail the external factors (i.e. the opportunities and threats) facing an organization. To remind you, from Figure 3.2 these are:

- Political and legal factors
- Economic factors
- Sociological factors
- Technology
- Competition
- Stakeholders.

Political and legal factors

In the home market, laws and regulations might be seen as limitations; however, laws and regulations also serve to protect an organization. Whatever the laws are, it is important that an organization is aware of how they will affect the operations of the organization. Laws could limit the number of hours that staff work, the amount of maternity leave people are entitled to, and so on.

For our home market we should have a reasonable idea as to what is legally possible, what our health and safety responsibilities are, and how current fire regulations may affect our events. When providing services in other countries, or using performers from other countries elsewhere, it is essential that the organization makes the effort to find out what legal restraints exist and what is socially acceptable before committing to any actions. These should be communicated to all concerned.

Generally laws are for the benefit of people as a whole, and are enacted as the result of pressure from the people to add a safeguard. Thus it is useful to be aware of popular issues and to make adjustments to operations so as to be seen to be a responsible organization within the pervading culture, rather than waiting for legislators to take action as a result of public pressure. When a safeguard is made the subject of rules and regulations, it is likely to have more stringent conditions than when organizations or industries abide by their own self-imposed safeguards.

When we place this into the event context, the event manager should be considering (among other factors) the following:

- Health and Safety Executive
- Laws and regulations
- Licences
- Changes in politics and regimes across the world
- Different laws in countries where events take place, or from where suppliers originate
- The labour market, as affected by government training initiatives
- Financial opportunities and the cost of borrowing
- Alternative funding arrangements.

There is no limit to the list of factors that will influence organizations. However, it is essential that during the analysis only those aspects that could have a direct influence or indirect influence on your organization or on your competitor be considered. Organizations should spend time considering this list and expanding it in order to really delve into changes that are occurring, which are imminent or just remotely possible, and which could affect the organization.

Case study 3.2 provides an illustration.

Economic factors

The economy, exchange rates, interest rates, population growth and demographics, student population, the average wage, unemployment and other statistics relevant to the event industry are all areas of vital information when considering business policy (see Case study 3.3).

Economic conditions are influenced by politics and governments (Thompson, 2001). Governments decide who will be inside or outside the European Union; governments decide rates of interest, education policies and training schemes, and the power of trade unions; and governments may affect the expectations of shareholders.

The problem is to identify what is relevant to your event and locality, and to be aware of where to find information. It is essential to gather intelligence of all of the above, and to understand how you can manipulate the changes to your advantage. It is also useful to observe how your competitors are coping with the changes.

Sociological factors

Sociological trends and the sociocultural environment encapsulate demand and tastes, which vary with fashion and disposable income (Thompson, 2001). Over time, fashion and trends change and what was once a novelty becomes essential or no longer

Case study 3.2

Edinburgh Hogmanay Festivities, Scotland

The Edinburgh Hogmanay Festivities are held annually in Scotland on New Year's Eve. There follows an excerpt from an article published following its cancellation.

Edinburgh Hogmanay Party Cancelled

By Russell Fallis and Victoria Mitchell, Scottish Press Association

One of Britain's biggest New Year's Eve street parties was cancelled at the eleventh hour tonight, due to 'adverse weather conditions', organizers announced.

The high point of Edinburgh's Hogmanay celebrations was cancelled for public safety reasons after the Scottish capital was hit by bad weather.

An estimated 100 000 people had been expected to gather in the city centre for the focal point of the four-day festivities.

First, 8000 ticket-holders for a sell-out gig in Princes Street Gardens were informed that the concert, being headlined by pop duo Erasure, was cancelled as the strong winds had rendered the stage unsafe.

A spokeswoman for the event said: 'The Concert in the Gardens has been cancelled because of the high winds. The structure is starting to disintegrate and it is a dangerous situation.'

Reflective practice 3.2

Consider Case study 3.2.

1. What external factors influenced the organizers in their decision to cancel this event?
2. What cost implications are there?
3. How could these reasons affect other events in the future?
4. Could this have a lasting influence on large public events?

required. When this happens, pricing policies will need to change. Similarly, a particular style of event in the UK may not be appreciated elsewhere, or *vice versa*, dependent upon local fashion and trends.

Event organizations should be aware of demographic changes as the population changes in terms of age distribution, ethnic origins, affluence, numbers of people employed and leisure trends. As the changes occur, events should reflect the changes or be marking different products to changing markets. Threats to existing service styles might be increasing, and opportunities for differentiation and market segmentation emerging.

Technology

Customers will often be beguiled by technological promises and computer wizardry in virtual conferencing or laser light shows. On the other hand, an event organization will be limited by the technology that it has at its disposal. Keeping up to date with technology for the sake of keeping up is expensive. Companies may consider leasing or hiring in expensive and specialist equipment and know-how. It is best to be aware of changes and of what the competition is doing, and to offer a good service with the

Case study 3.3

Economic factors that can influence event costs

Below are listed the minimum hourly wages in the US, UK, Australia and New Zealand at press.

USA: The minimum wage in the US is $5.15, although Senator Kerry has proposed increasing this to $7.00. However, there are nine states where the current minimum wage is higher than the official US minimum, seven states where there is no minimum wage at all, and three states where the minimum wage is lower than the official US minimum.

UK: The minimum wage in the UK as of 1 October 2004 is as follows:

- Main (adult) rate for workers aged 22 and over, £4.85 (increased from £4.50).
- Development rate for workers aged 18–21 inclusive, £4.10 (increased from £3.80). **NB**: The development rate can also apply to workers aged 22 and above during their first 6 months in a new job with a new employer and who are receiving accredited training.
- For 16- and 17-year-olds, £3.00 (a new rate).

Australia: The adult minimum wage is $11.35, but an increase is wanted by the trade unions (Australian Council of Trade Unions).

New Zealand: The adult minimum wage is $9; that for 16- and 17-years-olds is $7:20.

(More information can be found on www.dol.gov, www.epionline.org, www.dti.gov.uk/, www.actu.asn.au/, www.worksite.govt.nz.)

Reflective practice 3.3

1. What implications do minimum wages have on the events industry?
2. Check the current exchange rates and calculate which of the countries listed in Case study 3.3 has the most favourable rate for employment if you were choosing the location for a new event.
3. What supplementary information do you need?

expertise that you have or can have available. The use of technology may be one way to secure competitive advantage.

Technology external to the organization may be captured and used. This may be influenced by government support and encouragement (Thompson, 2001). However, could your existing technology be rendered useless by breakthroughs used elsewhere? It is important to consider how costly new technology would be to install, and whether it requires extra investment in the form of training. However, it may be that the technical providers at many events are your own suppliers. In this case it is essential to be aware of the changes and to have good relationships with the suppliers.

The concept is rather like being on a treadmill at a gym (Figure 3.5); no sooner do you reach a comfortable speed than the trainer wants you to run faster. As you reach that new speed, you cannot keep up and you start to slide backwards. No sooner has a company or an event come up with a good idea than a competitor copies it. This can be more easily achieved by the competition if what is being copied is tangible (e.g. a desirable venue for a large conference, with varied and relevant facilities). However, it becomes more difficult to copy intangible resources (or competencies), which rely on staff values and corporate culture and a desire for quality.

The treadmill moving forwards →		
Tangible resource (e.g. venue, lighting, sound system)	Easy to copy	What can we provide next?
Intangible resource (e.g. relevant training, eye for detail, networking and contacts)	Harder to copy	How can we deliver closer to specification and still sustain profits?

Figure 3.5 The treadmill of change and competitor action

Competition

Competition is often a major threat. In the determination of the service and the level of quality to be offered, at the very least the organization has to meet the service provided by the competition. Today, competition is worldwide. No matter that we believe we are providing a service to a local market; people today are well travelled and very well informed, and our customers judge us by their perceptions of world-class standards. For any organization, competition, although not yet present, might only be days away. Technology and innovation provide no protection; technology can soon be copied, and new methods and systems are readily available to anyone (see Case study 3.4). Often customers are influenced by what the immediate competition *says* it can or will do. This might not be quite the same as what actually happens. Nonetheless, it is the perception of what the competition is offering that sets the market standards. Knowing what the competition is offering is only possible if it is known who the competition is, and who the likely new competition might be.

The factors described indicate only a selection of the external influences, and individual managers need to appreciate how these external forces affect their organization. The analysis is extremely useful in picking out emerging opportunities that your company could take advantage of, and the threats that could just affect your own company and not your competitors.

These external influences will affect different organizations in different ways, sometimes more forcefully than others and sometimes insignificantly. You must be aware which.

Stakeholders

Stakeholders are very much part of the external environment, and are therefore in the first stage of the event operations management model. They should be thought of as part of the external analysis. However, there are some internal stakeholders (for instance, the employees and the managers). Stakeholders are groups of people or individuals who have an influence on, or are influenced by, the activities of the organization. Shareholders form one group of stakeholders. It used to be part of economic theory that shareholders should be given first priority (Thompson, 2001), because there was a belief that owners (i.e. the shareholders) and managers were synonymous. Event managers are paid employees and, whilst concerned about profits, they also regard growth and

Case study 3.4

Internet technology

Internet technology allows businesses and individuals to access information worldwide at the touch of a button. The following information was taken from the websites of The Conference Centre at Church House, London, England; The Banff Centre, Banff, Canada; and The Melbourne Exhibition and Convention Centre, Melbourne, Australia. All are open all year round.

The Conference Centre at Church House, London, England
Inspiring people

You need to know what's inside our conference centre if you are considering holding an event here. But it's also the people at a conference centre that make an event successful; so we're going to tell you about the people inside ours too.

Many London-based conference centres suffer from the perpetual sound of traffic. Church House doesn't. It's position in the shadows of Westminster Abbey, within the tranquil setting of Dean's Yard, is a protection, and the noise of London simply fades away.

And it's a great location, close to both Charing Cross and Victoria Stations, allowing easy access via train and tube.

Whilst our building and its surroundings are steeped in history and tradition; our events draw on the latest equipment and the skills of an enthusiastic team. This refreshing combination creates a unique environment and is the reason for our many industry awards.

On-the-day success of every event is assured with the help of our dedicated Client Hosts. It is their job to manage your event as it happens, ensuring down to the finest detail that it unfolds in the way it was planned to.

We have seventeen spacious function and meeting rooms and can accommodate every type of event. Most of our rooms benefit from natural light and all enjoy the elegance and sophistication expected from a building of the 1930s.

The Conference Executive is responsible for event planning. This is a meticulous job that takes concentration, and requires faultless organization. The Conference Executive is the sole contact for the clients, liaising with them regularly on each facet of their event, booking rooms, preparing menus, briefing audiovisual staff, meeting suppliers, agreeing table layout and room decoration – the list can seem endless, the end result is seamless perfection.

We have advanced sound and lighting technology permanently on-site. All rooms are fitted with a network of Cat 5 cabling and ISDN. An infrared interpretation system to aid in international meetings is accessible to all halls and many of the small meeting rooms.

Lights and sound can make a room come to life. Our in-house technicians ensure they always do. They often manage major high-profile events, from clients as diverse as government to the media. They will work with you, carefully planning every stage of this critical aspect of your event, offering guidance and advice, to ensure the show you want is the show you get.

We are one of only a handful of conference centres that hold the Meetings Industry Association's accreditation, Hospitality Assured – Meetings, which ensures a commitment to the highest standard, and is a testament to the dedication and hard work of our people.

Committed people do not make an event successful; they make it outstanding. Only when people from all levels work together with a common purpose can the service delivery we offer be achieved. For us, success isn't when our clients notice the hard work we do, it's when their event works so well and runs so smoothly that our role appears simple. After enjoying the day, they reflect and realize our efforts. This is when we are truly inspiring people.

(Extracts from website. For more information on Church House, see www.churchhouseconf. co.uk.)

The Banff Centre, Banff, Alberta, Canada

Experience The Banff Centre, offering unparalleled facilities with over 400 guest rooms, 60 exceptional meeting spaces, lecture theatres, and auditoriums to accommodate groups from 5 to 1000 people. It is an incubator for creativity that inspires and empowers artists, the mountain community and business leaders. The Banff Centre has a longstanding tradition of fostering innovation and new thoughts.

As experts in fostering fresh thinking, we realize the importance of your surroundings. That's why we offer over 60 exceptional meeting facilities, lecture theatres, and auditoriums to suit groups from 3 to 1000 participants. You can easily experience the full splendour of the Canadian Rockies from each meeting space, and you won't find a better sanctuary for your mind, body and spirit.

The Banff Centre welcomes you to the Business Centre, located in the main foyer of The Donald Cameron Hall. We handle guest and participant requests for faxing, photocopying, and computer use. The Business Centre respects copyright. The Banff Centre is licensed with Access Copyright (The Canadian Copyright Licensing Agency).

The Banff Centre provides free wireless access for individual browsing and email checking in several buildings on the property. To take advantage of this service, you must have wireless capability in your laptop that is preconfigured for DHCP.

Dedicated high-speed service for large groups, either via wireless access or by physical wiring, is also available. This must be prearranged with your Conferences Services Manager, who can provide you detailed information on computer requirements, locations and costs. Dial-up service can also be made available with advance notice.

A computer lab is also available. Featuring eleven new computers as of November 2003, each station is equipped with standard software including Windows XP, Norton Anti-Virus, Office XP Professional Suite, Adobe Acrobat Reader, Internet Explorer and QuickTime.

The Conference Management Package has been developed over a number of years and is designed to assist conference planners and organizers by assuming responsibility for several key components of the conference process. The emphasis is on a base package of services which are generally recognized as being the most timely or logistically challenging for many organizations. Complementing this base package is a shopping list of additional services that The Banff Centre offers to any clients who wish to incorporate them into their Conference Management Package for an additional fee.

Banff Centre Conference guests benefit from our graphic design capabilities and our partnership with The Document Source-Xerox. Consider using our on-site facilities to assist you with your production needs – from presentations, proposals and signage to a complete range of customized conference materials.

The video conference equipment located at The Banff Centre is a Tandberg Vision 5000 (ISDN based H.320 unit, capable of a six-channel, 384 kbps connection). The TELUS Video Conferencing Room is located in the Professional Development Centre and can seat a maximum of seven people at the table. For larger groups, the equipment can be moved to a larger meeting room, dependent upon available space. A document camera, VCR, and PC connection are available for use with the video conference unit. Fax and photocopy services are available at the Reception Desk in the main lobby of the Professional Development Centre. Water service is provided, and additional food and beverage service is available upon request. Further details and booking information is available, Monday to Friday, during regular office hours. A technician will be provided for any video conference booked on any day, or time of day.

(Printed by courtesy of Banff Conference Centre; further information can be obtained from www.banffcentre.ca.)

The Melbourne and Exhibition Convention Centre, Melbourne, Victoria, Australia

A consistent winner of many prestigious 'Awards for Excellence', the MECC is renowned for providing national and international convention and exhibition organizers with the highest standards of personal service and event facilities.

The Centre was the very first to earn the distinction of being named the World's 'Best Congress Centre' by the principal professional body for congress centre managers – the Association Internationale des Palais de Congress (AIPC). Domestically, the MECC has also been a recipient of the Meetings Industry of Australia's highest accolade many times over.

The MECC offers a level of Quality Controls and flexibility that has made it popular with exhibition organizers and meeting planners alike. Whether it is the ease of access and loading dock facilities or the state-of-the-art theatres and meeting rooms, the Centre more than meets expectations – it exceeds them.

Few venues are better equipped to cater for your event requirements than the MECC. Our rooms all offer the highest level of sound, video and staging technology, as well as the latest telecommunications.

Our commitment to excellence also extends to Food and Beverage, where our team of highly skilled chefs, led by Executive Chef Frank Burger, prepare and serve meals that reflect the Centre's overall reputation for excellence.

The Melbourne Exhibition and Convention Centre offers a wide range of audiovisual and communications technology, including voice and data cabling, ISDN and Internet capabilities, a 750 extension PABX system and state-of-the-art fibre optics, all of which are discreetly linked to every area in the entire complex. So you can 'plug in' from any point.

The MECC has three theatres which are all fitted out with the latest audiovisual technology including high bandwidth video and data cabling infrastructure, and some meeting rooms feature built-in screens, electronic whiteboards and complete data and signal cabling for presentations and data transfers.

The Bellarine Rooms have a series of large-diameter conduits beneath the floor linking all existing cable trenches at each of their ends and at their midpoint.

With 30 000 sq m (322 500 sq ft) of single floor, pillarless space on offer at the Exhibition Centre, exhibitors also have access to a wide range of telecommunication services via floor pits, plant areas and a basement tunnel running the entire length of the building.

Essential services include single- and three-phase power, telephone, fax, computer and communication outlets. Each of the floor pits is fitted with six voice/data jacks that enable voice and data traffic at speeds of up to 10 Mb/s, web broadcasting and ISDN. Audio, voice and data cabling also runs throughout the Centre, allowing room-end to room-end connectivity.

At the Melbourne Exhibition and Convention Centre, we are committed to offering our clients the highest standards of personal service and support. We know that organizing events is not always easy, so our staff will be there every step of the way to offer their advice and experience to ensure everything goes smoothly.

Our staff are all highly trained in their particular field of expertise. Whether it is food and beverage, event planning, technical services or sales and marketing, you can be assured of receiving the very best service and attention to detail.

(Printed by courtesy of Melbourne Conference Centre; for more information see www.mecc.com.au.)

Reflective practice 3.4

1. Consider Case study 3.4, and compare the information contained in each example with the following criteria:
   - Presentation style of their message
   - Availability of the latest technology
   - The conveyance of intangible benefits to the customer.
2. Now rank each conference centre in order of preference for each of the criteria, and state why you have made these decisions.

security as important, and they will have their own agendas for success. Competitors and governments may have a restraining force, and companies should also create good relationships with their suppliers and partners.

A technique for considering the varying strengths and influences of the different stakeholders will be introduced in Chapter 5. This analysis is essential since the needs of the different stakeholders may not be consistent with each other, and they are extremely likely to vary in consideration of different factors and within different situations.

Sponsors

Sponsors form a further group of people from the external environment, and they should therefore be analysed within the event operations management model. They are stakeholders, but should be considered separately because they can have a major impact on an event company. Historically, sponsorship had its earliest modern origin in professional sport events (Goldblatt, 1997). Sponsorship allows different groups of people to reach certain markets, and assists event organizers to have access to additional funding to offset costs. However, events do not always easily attract sponsorship. Potential sponsors have to 'get something out' of the event. It is extremely unlikely that they will provide money or supplies unless there is a payback.

Shone and Parry (2004) have developed a list of those aspects that sponsors will be hoping to benefit from:

- Relevant market exposure
- Publicity and increased public relations
- Media exposure
- Free admission to the event/hospitality
- A heightened image, by association.

Sources of sponsorship identified by Shone and Parry (2004) are:

- In-kind arrangements, exchange of goods or activities
- Grants from local, regional or national governments, or the European Union
- Grants from charitable bodies, development agencies, arts, leisure or heritage bodies
- Lottery grants
- Fund-raising activities related to the event
- Commercial bank borrowing
- Trust funding.

Sponsors are very useful to an event manager, but may also be a source of limitation or inconvenience. One might wish to be the main sponsor, and cause confrontation with other sponsors or limit or change your own plans.

The sponsors may wish to influence the event in a way that is against your original objectives; you may have to adapt your event, and this might not be suitable. Also you should consider whether the sponsor has a reputation that will enhance your event, or whether it might endanger your project. In some instances a partnership should not be entered into.

Reflective practice 3.5

You are the organizer of a marathon in a large city, such as the New York Marathon.

1. What competitive, economic, political, legal, social and technological influences affect its organization?
2. How do you keep abreast of what is happening?

Chapter summary and key points

This chapter has covered in detail the external analysis of an organization. This is within the first stage of the event operations management model. The chapter has considered the importance of business policy, which sets the long-term objectives for an organization. The chapter has taken an organization-wide perspective and is concerned with the setting of goals and targets for the whole enterprise and the importance of determining the best use of the available resources. Business policy must take into account several factors, as shown in Figures 3.1–3.3.

The effective event manager will maintain a keen interest in all facets of the organization, and be aware of external trends and factors that could influence it. The manager, to be effective, must be aware of policy changes, and these should not come as a surprise. Ideally, the event manager should be sufficiently well informed of external pressures to make policy suggestions. Chapter 4, still within the first stage of the event operations management model, is concerned with the bridge between the external environment and the internal environment. As depicted in the event operations management model, both of these environments should be analysed and the next chapter looks at the relationship between the two.

Chapter 4
Defining service provision

Learning Objectives

After reading through this chapter you will be able to:

- Understand the importance of the knowledge bridge between the analyses of the internal environment and the external environment
- Know how to define the service that is to be provided
- Discuss how to promote an event
- Analyse the operational feasibility of an event.

Introduction

This chapter is essentially the interface between the external analysis and the internal analysis of the organization. It rests within the first stage of the event operations management model. Before an organization can attempt to satisfy the customer, it must first know the customer wants – i.e. the Critical Success Factors (CSFs) that make them purchase from one organization rather than another.

With regular scanning of key sources of information, it is possible to build a market intelligence database. This is a relatively cost-effective way to gain useful insights, and a precursor to an accurate forecasting system (Wood, 2004).

The primary function of marketing is to bring together buyers and sellers with the intention of exchanging products and services of mutual value (Kandampully, 2002). To be successful, the marketing department should analyse the expectations of each party. The three questions below constitute a knowledge bridge between the customer and the producer:

1. What does the customer want in terms of the service being offered (product)?
2. What price will customers be prepared to pay (price)?
3. Where will the service be provided (place)?

To complete the 'knowledge bridge', the marketing function will have the responsibility of promoting (advertising) the service. Traditionally, the marketing mix is made up of product, price, place and promotion – the 4Ps. However, these 4Ps do not address the distinctive characteristics of services and events; nor do they take into account the importance of the customer or the members of staff supplying the service. Other authors have added:

- People
- Process

- Physical evidence
- Performance
- Profit.

Event managers may focus on exciting and well-executed events, but neglect other areas such as quality, visitor satisfaction and evaluation before, during and after the event (Wood, 2002). A survey by the Meetings Industry Association (MIA) found that only 40 per cent of venues solicited the event organizers' opinions on their service, and fewer than 15 per cent of organizations and venues thought to ask the delegates or attendees (Tum, 2002; unpublished papers).

Defining the service to be provided

Service should be provided to conform to the following factors:

1. Specification
2. Consistency
3. Timeliness
4. Flexibility
5. Right price
6. Added value and little extras.

In many instances these different characteristics will have different weightings to different groups of people – to the customer, to the organization itself and to the stakeholders. It is this different emphasis that provides a daily challenge to the event manager.

The first and crucial issue is the specification. Unless the service fulfils the requirements of the customer, it will not be used. In Chapter 2 we discussed the courtesy bus service at a sculpture park, and we said that if the bus is not going from a to b then it would be of no use. The service offered might include other 'nice to have' attributes, but unless the basic service is right, the extras, the 'nice to have' features, become irrelevant. Therefore no matter how clean and comfortable the bus, or how polite the driver, unless the service is right (i.e. the bus stops somewhere close to the exhibits or the picnic spot) it is of no use and all the 'nice' extras are meaningless.

The second important issue is consistency. Customers expect service to be at the same level, or better, each time it is experienced. With the bus service we would expect the bus to arrive as stated on the arrival boards, and to follow the correct route. At an outdoor music event, the audience would expect the sound system and video screens to be working effectively throughout the event. Promoters of music events would expect their suppliers to be consistent throughout all of their events.

Once a level of quality of service has been promoted or actually provided, customers will be quick to notice if it is not achieved or sustained. There is no point in setting a high standard of service if the operation cannot consistently meet the standard.

The third issue is timeliness. Unless the tea and coffee is ready at the agreed coffee breaks at a conference, the delegate and the conference organizer will become disenchanted and may not return to that venue. Some conference venues for smaller meetings have break-out rooms adjacent to the seminar rooms where delegates can make their own coffees throughout the day. Here, exact timing for provision of hot drinks has been exchanged for total freedom for the delegates. However, timing for the venue is still important since the raw commodities (e.g. milk in a refrigerated environment and coffee and clean cups) should be available whenever needed.

Timing is of lesser importance when customers make appointments in advance. For example, for services from a wedding planning consultant, customers may be prepared to wait in order to see whoever is considered to give the best service, be it for advice, venue availability, or for a reputable and innovative lighting expert. It is past experience, promises and advertising that raise customers' expectations.

Fourth, flexibility is important in the service industry; there is no time for checking quality, no time for rehearsing the wedding photography – it has to be right first time. The moment the event is delivered it is consumed. Immediately, of course, we come across difficulties – customers can change their minds and want a slight change to the wedding arrangements, or rain will stop play at the Test Match at Lord's Cricket Ground, London, or there is a bomb threat in the outskirts of London and half the guests arriving for a major Annual Dinner and Ball are 45 minutes late so the meal and the entertainment have to be rescheduled. In all of these scenarios the event manager has to be flexible and to accommodate the changing situations. Customer expectations still have to be fulfilled despite changes in circumstances.

Fifth, determination of the right price can be agreed once the marketing team is satisfied that they know what the customer wants – the specification. This will determine the price that can be charged. What can be charged depends, of course, on what the customer is prepared to pay. The issue for the event manager will be 'can the service be provided to the given specification, including all those extras added by marketing, within the price set and still provide a profit?' Thus the event manager in achieving a defined level of customer satisfaction will simultaneously be required to minimize the use of resources and their costs to an affordable level.

In sixth position is 'added value and little extras'. Once the courtesy bus has met the basic requirements, then all the other 'extras' – such as cleanliness, comfort, plenty of seats, polite driver, waiting shelter, and perhaps even music interspersed with announcements from the driver – will add to the perception of quality and could provide the edge in a competitive environment.

Some specification issues are taken for granted by customers. Examples of this in the bus service are that the bus is roadworthy and the driver is licensed. Often what the customer takes for granted will be crucial to the whole operation, and will take a good deal of effort on behalf of the event manager to achieve – such as keeping the fleet maintained and roadworthy. These aspects are expected, and are not seen by the customer as added value extras.

Other 'requirements' of customers can be traced back to the marketing team 'selling' features that the customer had not previously considered important but which once sold will become to be expected by the customer. Carlzon (1989) calls this 'the olive in the martini'. In some service industries, for many customers the appearance and status will be every bit as important as the actual service received.

Case study 4.1 describes a major festival held in Miami, Florida.

Where the event will take place

The next issue to decide upon is where the event will take place. You may have a choice, and where you eventually choose to host your event can have an enormous effect on its success. This concept is explored more fully in Chapter 10, which is within the planning stage of the event operations management model. The location for the service provision is a marketing issue, and the decision will be affected by where the customers are and where the client wants the event to take place.

Case study 4.1

Carnaval Miami, Florida, USA

Carnaval Miami is the largest global showcase in the Hispanic Market with a festival that attracts the local community as well as people from around the world. For two weeks in March, the City of Miami transforms itself into the City of Carnaval. People from Europe, Asia, Central and South America all make the trip to participate in the festivities. The Kiwanis Club of Little Havana hosts a grand party with events full of colour, Latin music and international foods for the enjoyment of residents and tourists alike. Carnaval Miami's Calle Ocho is the culmination of many concerts, sports, culinary competitions and a Latin Jazz festival.

Calle Ocho celebrates its 26th Anniversary in 2004, inviting the entire community as one. The 'marquee' event of Carnaval Miami is 'the' largest celebration of Hispanic culture in the United States. 'El Festival de la Ocho', as commonly known to many, closes down SW 8th Street from 27th to 4th Avenues for twenty-three Little Havana city blocks. Over 40 stages are placed on intersecting avenues, featuring merengue, salsa, pop and Caribbean music. Ethnic food kiosks line the North and South sides of the street, while intersecting avenues showcase musical stages, youth sites, sampling pavilions and more. It offers a world of opportunities to show, test, taste and sample products.

The Kids Pavilion has become a 'festival within a festival', inviting children from all over Dade and Broward counties to be part of the celebration. Four city blocks between 8th and 4th Avenues are host to this kids' village of entertainment.

To celebrate the 'funtastic' party, the Guinness Book of Records record for the 'World's Largest Street Party' will be broken in the streets of Little Havana. Media blitzes and press conferences will be held prior to and on the day of event at a designated location. Major television networks, local Hispanic radio stations and newspaper partners will all be part of the festivities. Photographers from international newspapers, magazines and film-makers, visitors come from all over the US, Europe, Central & South America, a myriad of Latin music continuously performing throughout the 7 hours of Calle Ocho, all culminating with fireworks to say goodbye to another great year.

(The above comes from the Carnaval Miami website; for further information see www. carnaval-miami.org or search for 'Calle Ocho'.)

Reflective practice 4.1

Consider Carnaval Miami, described in Case study 4.1.

1. As an event manager responsible for the stage constructions, what logistical considerations are there?
2. How would you deal with these?
3. What problems could there be associated with the Guinness Book of Records attempt?

The location of services will have a great impact on operational decisions concerning supply, choice of suppliers, distribution, logistics, and health and safety issues.

Promotion of the event

Obviously marketing will advise on promotional strategies, but the overall thrust and philosophy of the promotional drive is very much a business policy decision. No promotion activity should ever take place without the full involvement of the event manager. Marketing is not just about getting people in through the door, but also about ensuring that they get the kind of satisfaction from the event that they have been led to expect (Shone and Parry, 2004; see also Case study 4.2).

The more detailed the knowledge of each customer's requirements, the closer the organization can get to a customized offering, creating greater satisfaction and long-term customer relationships (Wood, 2004).

Case study 4.2

The golf club

A golf club advertised a free open day for prospective new members; the day chosen was a non-competition day when the course would be relatively free of club players. Noting that no play was scheduled for that day, and unaware of the open day, the green keepers made an early start on coring and re-sewing the greens, and temporary rough greens were cut. The overall impression gained by the prospective new members was not good, and the time and money spent on the promotion was to a large extent wasted.

Marketing mix and operational feasibility

It can be seen that the marketing team has a great influence on business policy. The team determines who the customer is, what the service offered will be (specification, time, place and price), and promotes the service and added value little extras. The event manager has to determine the overall feasibility – in other words, does the organization have the capacity to consistently provide the desired service and meet the expected demand and quality attributes within the price set and still return a profit? If not, what extra resources are required and what else could be done to make the impossible possible? In short, can the service, with all the desired features, actually be provided at the cost marketing suggests?

Case study 4.3 suggests a possible scenario.

Case study 4.3

Product launch

An important customer has tasked you with arranging an event for the launch of a new product. You plan a creative launch. In the lead up to the big day, starting six months in advance, you book a conference centre, arrange a lighting specialist (including lasers etc.), organize a sound system, hire a jazz band, and agree the guest list with your client – including local members of parliament, the mayor, sporting personalities and 500 other guests. You send out the invitations, arrange a television personality as the guest speaker, and contact the media to get as much coverage as possible. You arrange caterers, and spend much time agreeing the menu. The client is responsible for providing gift baskets featuring a selection of their fine products for each of the guests. The event is timed to begin at 7 pm and to run through to about midnight. Two weeks out from the big day only 50 per cent of the guests have replied, and of those who have replied only a few have accepted the invitation. You find that the local sports team has got to the final of the league, and that the deciding match will be played in a neighbouring town starting thirty minutes after your scheduled event begins. The match will last at least ninety minutes. The excitement in the town is immense; never before has the local team got to the final. People are either going to the game, or watching the live broadcast on television. No one expected that this could happen six months ago when planning for your event began.

Reflective practice 4.2

Consider what you could do, bearing in mind that the television personality is only available for the night you booked. Likewise, the conference centre is also pre-booked for the next three months; however, you have it booked for three days – Friday for preparation, Saturday for the big event, and Sunday to clean up etc.

Chapter summary and key points

This chapter provides the bridge between external and internal analyses. In particular, the importance of an understanding of the marketing mix is discussed. The main focus of the chapter is the importance of knowing what the customer wants and values. Above all, if the end delivered product/service does not meet the basic specification, then other 'nice to have' features will not matter. Thus meeting specification is the first and overriding objective. Secondary objectives are to maintain consistency, to be on time, to be flexible, and to provide extras that delight the customer. All this has to be provided within the constraints of a given price. Finally, what is promised and agreed has to be feasible. Chapter 5, still within the first stage of the event operations management model, will examine more closely the needs of the customers and the stakeholders. This is an essential element within the event operations management model, since it is necessary to analyse the impact that these groups have on your future planning of the event and the shape and design it will have.

Chapter 5

Customers, stakeholders and gap analysis

Learning Objectives

After reading through this chapter you will be able to:

- Understand who the customer is, and appreciate the customer's needs, perceptions and what gives satisfaction
- Determine the stakeholders to the event and identify the challenges they present
- Undertake an analysis of what you can provide and what is expected by the stakeholders and customers
- Create competitive advantage using quality of service provision.

Introduction

This chapter pulls together some of the concepts in the earlier chapters and offers techniques regarding how to manage the interface between the needs of the customers, the impact of the stakeholders and the goals of the organization. It is within the analysis stage of the event operations management model, since it is not possible to start the planning stage until all the influences upon the event have been analysed. The chapter considers who our diverse customers are, the dimensions of customer satisfaction, resource utilization, and how by using the right resources it is possible to satisfy the needs of the customers and the varied stakeholders, keep within the strategic objectives of the organization and make a profit.

Wild (2002) notes that operations management is concerned with the achievement of both satisfactory customer service and resource utilization. He suggests that both of these objectives cannot always be maximized, and hence a satisfactory performance must be achieved on both and sub-optimization avoided. It is this conflict that often provides the challenge to event managers.

Who is the customer?

In Chapter 2 we established that the customer is an input into the process. Quite simply, without a customer no service can be performed. Kandampully (2002) believes that service quality can be defined as the extent to which a service meets the expectations of customers. But who are our customers?

Kandampully divides customers into four broad groups:

1. Internal customers – employees and managers of the firm
2. External customers – a firm's end customers
3. Competitors' customers – those who the firm would like to attract
4. Ex-customers – those who are now going elsewhere (and therefore are no longer our customers).

Internal customers

In Chapter 16, within the implementation stage of the event operations management model, we discuss the philosophy of Total Quality Management (TQM) in greater detail. Proponents of TQM consider the importance of the customer to be vital in the operating process. For example, with TQM an event organizer passing a lighting specification to a lighting company would consider *that company* to be the customer. Consequently, the specification should be well written and unambiguous so that the lighting company knows exactly what to provide and when.

Some people believe that the TQM concept of the internal customer was always a contrivance, initially aimed to get factory workers on an assembly line to reduce waste and pass on a good job to the next operator in the process. It was easy to say that without customers we will not sell our goods, and without sales the factory will close, but for the operator wielding the screwdriver and faced with a seemingly never-ending assembly line, the customer was remote and faceless. Making the next person on the line the customer gave the 'customer' a face.

We applaud this approach, since anything that serves to make work more meaningful, gives people more esteem, and reduces costs has to be recommended. However, in reality it has to be accepted that the event steward has very little control over the quality of the event – the steward does not decide on the appropriateness of the lighting rigs used or decide on the sound system installed.

In the event industry we could engage with all participants of the supply chain – i.e. all the specialists who are providing part of the service that contributes to the final delivery of the event to the end customer. By encouraging them to deliver a service that will enable the delivery to be in line with the customer specification, it will help to achieve competitive advantage. The supply chain is covered further in Chapter 9, within the detailed planning stage of the event operations management model.

It can be argued that all staff engaged on an event receive and offer services to one another. The concept of all participants being both suppliers and customers within the process will encourage all 'actors' to consider the quality of the entire event. It will create an understanding of interdependency between suppliers and staff (Kandampully, 2002).

The degree of intensity of interaction between the customer and people of a service organization varies, and depends on the type of service offered. For example, an event manager providing advice to the Managing Director of a large company whilst organizing a touring product promotion will have a high degree of face-to-face interaction with the customer. Further down the scale, an event manager organizing a team-building day for twenty employees of a car dealership, or an event manager taking a small group of visitors around a pharmaceutical company on an induction programme, would have less face-to-face contact.

At the bottom of the scale, an example is where customers buy their own theatre tickets from an automatic machine point; here, customer interaction is purely with a machine.

Figure 5.1 shows a reducing degree of interaction between the event organizer and the customer. These different activities consequently have different influences for the

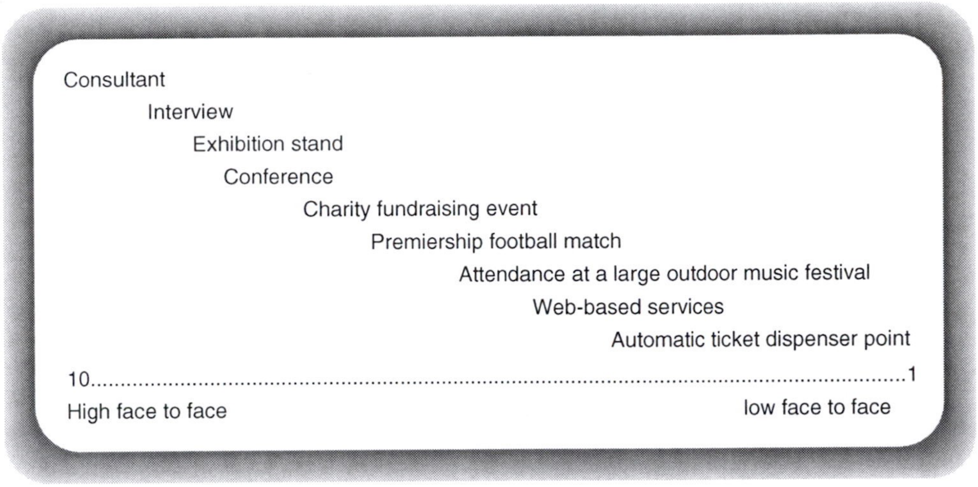

```
Consultant
        Interview
                Exhibition stand
                Conference
                        Charity fundraising event
                                Premiership football match
                                        Attendance at a large outdoor music festival
                                                Web-based services
                                                        Automatic ticket dispenser point

    10.....................................................................................................................................1
    High face to face                                           low face to face
```

Figure 5.1 The varying amounts of customer interaction

event manager in terms of customer relations and training, usage of time and opportunity to maintain standardization procedures. The greater the interaction with the customer, the greater will be the variances and the need for training in customer relations.

Irrespective of the level of face-to-face interaction, without some customer interaction service cannot be provided. Note, this does not mean that the customer always has to be present when the service is being provided. For example, when a stage is being erected for a classical outdoor concert the customer need not be present, but nonetheless without discussion with the relevant suppliers and without knowing the size of the audience, the acoustics available and the amount of set-up time, the staging company cannot provide a service.

External customers

External customers are sophisticated. Never before has the customer been more travelled, better informed or had higher expectations. Event customers now take it as a matter of right that they will get a reliable, high-quality product and courteous, well-informed service. World-class organizations know that new products or services and technological improvements are quickly copied and improved upon, and thus may offer only a short-term advantage in the marketplace. They also know that the 'competitive edge' comes from providing a higher level of customer satisfaction than does the competition.

It is therefore imperative, during this analysis stage of the event operations management model, to ascertain what the customers want at an event, since expectations have a great effect on subsequent levels of satisfaction. High expectations may sell more tickets for one event, but if those expectations are not met then future business will be lost (Wood, 2004). The expectations also need to be gleaned from those who did not attend, as market perceptions help to create an event's relative competitive position.

The quality of product and the level of service provided in a competitive market must at least equate to what the competition is providing or is perceived to be providing. Customers' expectations are influenced by what they have previously experienced, by what the competition is claiming to provide in advertisements, by what we are promising in our promotions, by what the media is saying, and sometimes by the promise of technological improvements.

Customer satisfaction

When introducing the concept of customer satisfaction, it has to be understood that the basic requirement of any service, for customers, is that the service must meet their specifications, secondly that it will meet cost expectations, and thirdly that it is timely.

Specification – providing customers with what they expect to receive or are prepared to accept – is the essential requirement. In consideration of Wild's (2002) dimensions, customers will also be concerned with the reliability of the service. For example, will it be as experienced before, does its reputation live up to the reality? Is the design of the event relevant and appropriate?

Regarding cost, the customer will evaluate the product or service received in terms of its overall expected costs, including any additional expenses.

As for time, is the timing of the event appropriate? What is the duration of the event? Is there a delay between agreeing on a brief for an event and it being confirmed in writing? Delay is often unacceptable to a customer, and reduces overall customer satisfaction.

Wild (2002) breaks down these three attributes into further dimensions, which are shown in Table 5.1 (opposite).

Assessing critical success factors

What is acceptable or reasonable will always be open to question, and will depend on how important the service is to the customer and the alternatives available.

Thompson (2001) says that one element of success is for an organization to meet the needs and expectations of its stakeholders. Therefore an event manager needs an understanding of what those needs are, and a mixture of common sense and competency in order to satisfy these needs. The critical success factors are those aspects that external customers consider essential in fulfilling their requirements.

Reflective practice 5.1

You are a conference company, planning events for a range of clients using a variety of venues across the country to match your clients' requirements. You have ascertained in detail what the client wants from an appropriate venue. These are the critical success factors (CSFs):

- Conference room availability for 300 people, theatre style
- Responsive staff willing to be flexible
- Audiovisual facilities including video conferencing and Hi-Fi
- Closeness to road and rail network, 10 minutes maximum
- Price within budget of client
- Good reputation.

As the event manager, you should ask the client to rate these CSFs on a scale of 1–5 as to which is the most important (5 being the most important). This cannot always be done quickly and may take a lot of research, but nevertheless it is a very useful exercise.

Next, plot the results of the research onto a chart as shown in Figure 5.2.

Usually customers will accept, or tolerate, a service that does not perfectly meet their requirements. The amount of tolerance will be dependent on what the competition is offering or, if there is no immediate competition, what the alternatives are. Customers might be prepared to trade some specification for cost or availability for specific dates.

Table 5.1 Customer requirements with subdimensions

Basic customer requirement	Further dimensions
Specification	Design Performance Reliability
Cost	Price Expenses Cost reliability
Timing	Delay Duration Timing reliability

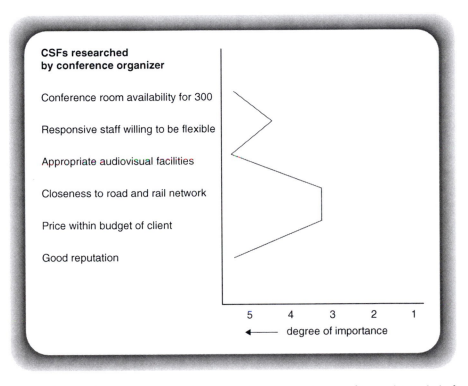

Figure 5.2 Identification of the relative importance of critical success factors demanded of a venue by conference delegates

The chart in Figure 5.2 can then be used further, by adding on the varied attributes of the various venues that are under consideration. This will show which venues match the desired characteristics, or critical success factors, demanded by the customer. Use different colours to highlight the client's requirements and the facilities of the different venues. This technique can be shown to the client so they can make an informed decision as to which venue to choose.

Case studies 5.1 and 5.2 illustrate various CSFs.

Case study 5.1

Edinburgh International Conference Centre (EICC), Scotland

Client: OSCE Parliamentary Assembly
Event: Thirteenth Annual Session
Date: 5–9 July 2004
Number of delegates: 650
More information: www.oscepa.org

Security is an issue for any conference, but when the conference is itself one of the world's leading forums on international security issues, special measures are obviously required.

When the Thirteenth Annual Session of the Organization for Security and Cooperation in Europe Parliamentary Assembly (OSCE PA) came to the EICC in July 2004, it also meant the arrival of 650 delegates, many of them parliamentary members from numerous nations around the globe.

The EICC made an ideal venue for this event for many reasons and, as a past venue for events such as the Commonwealth Heads of Government Meeting (1997), good security measures were clearly amongst its benefits.

During the five-day OSCE PA conference, visitors to the EICC had the reassurance of passing through airport-style screening. 'The delegates expect it', says Tracey Garratty, Delegation Secretary at the Overseas Office of the House of Commons. 'The UK approach is fairly low-key compared to parliamentary assemblies held elsewhere in the world, but it's very much about reassuring without intruding.'

With such an international audience – the OSCE PA prides itself on a membership ranging from Vancouver to Vladivostok – language and translation was also a key issue. 'The organization uses six official languages and the OSCE PA office in Copenhagen arranges the interpreters,' says Tracey, 'but you also have to find somewhere that has the capacity to allow six languages in simultaneous translation, and the EICC is able to do that.'

The conference, which involved fitting the entire Pentland Suite with desks for all the delegates, featured a busy programme, including a keynote speech from the Rt Hon. Peter Hain, Leader of the House of Commons and Secretary of State for Wales, and a wide range of committee and plenary sessions. The event culminated in delegates signing 'the Edinburgh Declaration' – a series of resolutions covering issues such as terrorism, racism and human trafficking.

Delegates also had the opportunity to continue networking over a busy social programme, including a reception at Holyrood Palace hosted by HRH the Duke of Kent and a dinner at the Museum of Scotland hosted by the Rt Hon. Michael Martin, Speaker of the House of Commons.

In 2005 the assembly moved on to Washington DC, but memories of Edinburgh remain warm, with the EICC's central location proving a major plus point.

'The size of Edinburgh gives it a big advantage,' says Tracey. 'Everything is within walking distance. There's a very good selection of hotels and they are all fairly close, which gives delegates the freedom to pop out and not feel isolated.'

'The feedback we have had about the EICC is also very positive,' she adds. 'People seem to like the set-up, the professionalism and the way it's been run. The staff are very helpful. They know what they are doing.'

(Case study printed by courtesy of Edinburgh International Conference Centre (EICC) and Whitel Light Media, Edinburgh. For further details of EICC, see www.eicc.co.uk.)

Reflective practice 5.2

Consider Case study 5.1.

1. What do you consider to be the CSFs for the delegates at the OSCE PA conference?
2. Go to the Edinburgh International Conference Centre website at www.eicc.co.uk and, using the criteria in Figure 5.2, plot the suitability of the EICC against the criteria.

Case study 5.2

Dolce International Corporate Headquarters, Montvale, New Jersey, USA

Dolce International specializes in the meeting experience, and it is one of the leading global companies within the conference centre niche of the hospitality industry. It currently has twenty-six properties throughout the United States, Canada and Europe.

The Dolce brand of Conference & Resort Destinations includes properties in all six categories defined by the International Association of Conference Centres (IACC). The venues include:

- Executive conference centres
- Corporate conference centres
- University conference centres
- Resort conference centres
- Ancillary hotel conference centres
- Day meeting centres.

While the portfolio is varied in terms of location, type, and physical structure, they all offer Dolce's branded standards of service with meeting environments and service designed to provide the best meeting experience in the world.

One example is the Dolce Hayes Mansion, San José, California. This is an award-winning conference centre offering groups and individuals a unique blend of tranquillity, service and productivity.

The website describes the mansion in the following terms:

Opened to the public in 1994, the property quickly became the region's premier facility for meetings and events. An expansion and renovation programme, completed in 2002, enhanced the distinctive architectural characteristics of the original structure, and created even more additional meeting and event space.

Thoughtfully removed from the distractions of every day, Dolce Hayes Mansion is a place where absolutely no detail is left to chance. With over 33 000 square feet of dedicated meeting space, 22 specially designed and equipped conference rooms, and advanced multimedia capabilities, Dolce Hayes Mansion is the perfect destination to hold your next meeting. All meeting rooms are equipped with high-backed, fully adjustable executive conference chairs, individual lighting and heating/cooling controls and on-site audiovisual equipment. Skilled technicians and dedicated meeting professionals are always on hand to make sure your meeting runs smoothly from start to finish.

Vital statistics
Meeting facility details: 33 000 sq ft
Meeting rooms: 22
Board rooms: 1
Breakout rooms: 22
Ballrooms: 6666 sq ft and 3000 sq ft

Rear screen capabilities: 1
Front screen capabilities: 22

Other facilities available:
  Stage
  Sound system
  High-speed Internet access
  Video conferencing
  Basic LCD projectors included in the CMP
  TV and video playback equipment
  Overhead projectors
  Lapel microphones
  Handheld microphones
  Ergonomic chairs
  Hardtop work tables
  Dolce e-café with computer workstations
  Natural lighting in meeting rooms
  AV staff on site
  Whiteboards

(Printed by courtesy of Dolce International; further information can be obtained from www. dolce.com.)

Reflective practice 5.3

Consider Case study 5.2. What do you consider to be the critical success factors of Dolce International within the conference market?

Figure 5.3 compares the critical success factors and alternative providers. It can be seen that those venues that are closest to the customer's line may become the successful choice of the organizer.

Venue A did not have a conference room for 300 people; it is close to the rail and road networks and was less than required cost. Venue B exceeded the clients' needs, and was very expensive.

This technique is useful to measure how well a supplier or location can match the needs of the customer or the organization. Another technique is discussed in Chapter 10; which although shown as being very useful for choosing ideal locations for offices or for the event itself, could also be used to choose the sourcing of ideal resources.

The providers' perspective

From the perspective of a services provider, what is provided has to be what can be afforded, and must be at least up to the same standard as the competition. The determination of what to provide is based on economic considerations rather than altruism. Customers are needed for income, and in the long term the organization cannot afford to run at a loss. Many an organization has failed to survive although customers have received excellent service. The efficient use of resources is covered later in this chapter.

The technique of using the range of critical success factors demanded by your clients and plotting these against the resources available can be adapted by any organization that has undertaken extensive research into what the customer most desires and what is considered as being critical. As discussed earlier, the chart's use can be

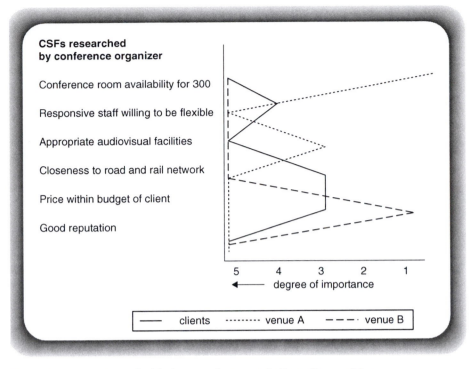

Figure 5.3 Comparison of critical success factors and alternative providers

extended and the attributes of the facilities changed and plotted to see the match (or otherwise) with the customer's requirements.

Further market research as to what the customer wants from an event company can also be plotted onto a similar graph. The organization should be highly critical and objective regarding where its own service and attributes would sit on the same scale. These attributes should also be plotted onto the same graph. To answer the question 'how well are *we* doing?', it is clear that the closer the organization's line to that which defines the customer's needs, the more the organization is in tune with those needs.

It can be seen that if the line drawn for an organization is to the left of what the customer wants then it is over-providing, and possibly spending more money and resources for a less valued attribute. If it is to the right, it is falling short of what the customer wants.

The next stage for the organizer is to analyse, in a similar way, what the competition is providing, and plot that onto the same chart.

The chart will now have a variety of lines, showing:

- What the customer wants
- What you believe you are providing
- What competitor A is providing
- What competitor B is providing
- What competitor C is providing.

Competitive advantage by using quality of service provision

As described earlier in this chapter, there is a need to emulate world-class standards in order to serve sophisticated customers. New services are quickly copied and improved upon by the competition, and often the only competitive advantage will come from the level of service provided. Thus customer satisfaction goes past the basics of specification, time and cost to include the *quality* of service.

Quality has two dimensions, customer satisfaction and efficient use of resources. What constitutes quality, how it is judged and controlled, and the culture of quality is detailed in Chapter 16. However, in light of the importance of the quality of service in gaining a competitive edge, our discussion on customer service would be incomplete if we were to ignore the rudiments of what can be done to enhance the basic attributes of specification, time and cost.

In our example of choosing a conference venue, having offered a service that attracts customers and which meets the researched critical success factors, it is possible to look at ways of adding a perception of increased service without adding to the cost.

Adding value

Generally, some perception of added service can be provided at very little cost.

Using our conference venue as an example, and assuming that the CSFs meet the customers' basic needs, additional quality service attributes could include well-organized coffee and lunch breaks, cleanliness of the car park, friendly and well presented reception staff, and useful and meaningful signage. Well-organized service can be achieved by good planning, and should not cost the company any extra. Keeping the car park clean might add marginally to the cost (cleaning facilities and wages). Issuing the staff with smart uniforms will obviously be a cost, and training them in customer care will also incur some cost.

All such costs are minimal when compared to the overall operating cost of the conference venue. However, the general perception will be an improved service, although the critical success factors have not changed.

It is important to recognize that above all customers expect a reliable and a consistent service. A service that is sometimes excellent and sometimes indifferent will only confuse the customer. Once a service level has been established, then that standard must be maintained.

For any organization, increased service at little or no cost will require a special culture. The workforce has to be enthusiastic and must have some authority to make limited operational decisions. Creating a quality organizational culture, resulting in staff motivated to reduce inefficiencies and to give friendly and consistent service, is covered in Chapter 11, within the implementation stage of the event operations management model.

Summary

To recap, customer satisfaction involves several points:

- The service provided has to match the customers' expectations, but not always exactly.
- The company that exactly matches the critical success factors required by the customer will have the highest rating – providing the customer has found that company and knows exactly what is required in the first place.
- The perception of an improved quality service can be achieved at very little cost, and involves cleanliness, consistency, reliability, friendly and helpful frontline staff etc.
- If you provide attributes that are to the left of the line on your CSF matching chart, you may be spending more money and time on provision of service and facilities that the customer does not believe are important. If you are providing attributes that are to the right of the line, you are underachieving.
- What is offered has to be affordable and maintainable.

Wild (2002) reminds us that customers will have expectations, even to an extent that is in excess of their original specification, if that is what is being offered. Failure to meet these expectations will cause dissatisfaction, but matching these expectations will give rise to satisfaction, and exceeding them may result in delight.

What are stakeholders?

We will now concentrate on determining who the stakeholders are, and how to rank the relative importance of the various requirements of customers and influential stakeholders. These were discussed briefly in Chapter 3, since many of the stakeholders are external to the organization. However, not all of them are, and it is essential to understand different techniques that can be used to assess their importance and influence.

Freeman (1984) defines a stakeholder as any person or group who can affect, or is affected by, the performance of the organization.

The word 'stakeholder' was coined in an internal memorandum at the Stamford Research Institute in 1963, and it referred to 'those groups without whose support the organization would cease to exist'.

De Wit and Meyer (2004) propose two definitions of stakeholder:

> *a wide sense, which includes groups who are friendly or hostile (trade associations, competitors, unions, employees, customer segments) who can affect the achievement of objectives or be affected by them ... and a narrow sense, which aims to identify specific individuals or groups on which the organization is dependent upon for its survival (employees, certain suppliers, key government agencies, Health and Safety Executive and financial institutions).*

Wright (2001) believes that knowing who the stakeholders are and how their concerns might affect the operation of an organization is becoming more and more critical. He defines a stakeholder as anyone who has an interest in what an organization does. This might seem a very broad definition, and indeed it is.

Funds for an event may come from local authorities or charities initially investing in a fundraising event, or sponsors, racecourse venues etc. The body that provides the funds obviously has a stake in the efficiency of the operation. These stakeholders – the fund providers – should and increasingly do seek value for money. In their eyes, value for money includes not only providing a level of service to the customer, but also the efficient use of resources.

There are other stakeholders who do not directly provide money – for example, taxpayers – and who are also concerned that their money is being spent wisely (see Case study 5.3).

Determining who the stakeholders are

It can be seen that for any business, a stakeholder is anyone with a pecuniary interest in the organization (such as shareholders, banks, financiers, investors, suppliers of goods and services, the people who work in the organization and their families). Other more general stakeholders include investors in the share market, local bodies in the district of the operation, the venue/location where the event is being held, people who live and work in the general neighbourhood, and the Green movement. For government and quasi-government organizations, charitable trusts and other like bodies, stakeholders are fund providers, bankers, suppliers, people who work in the organization and their families, and the community at large. We should even include the competitors and the whole event industry.

Whereas before you thought you had to satisfy only the customers' needs and their CSFs, you can now see that all the stakeholders have different CSFs and priorities. What a challenge!

Case study 5.3

Carnival parades

Carnival parades are held worldwide, all the year round. In community-sponsored carnival parades, the end-users are those people who attend. A major stakeholder is the community itself (the major source of funds), which is concerned that there will be value for the money invested. However, do not forget the taxpayer who is funding the community. Other providers of funds may include product sponsors of branded goods (e.g. Coca-Cola™). All these groups are stakeholders, and they have a stake in the *quality* of the outputs.

There are still other stakeholders who do not directly provide funds for the event, but who will have a very real interest in its quality and safety. These might include shopping enterprises in the vicinity, local communities that may be affected, police, and road transport bodies.

Each stakeholder group is likely to have different priorities in judging the service provided, and will have varying levels of interest in the event. Some fund providers and taxpayers will be anxious that resources are being efficiently utilized (money is not being wasted), while others will be more concerned with the disruption that is being caused and still others with the safety and security of the event. Further groups might be interested in the content of the carnival parade and that it matches their expectations, or that it should bring more trade and economic value to the region.

Reflective practice 5.4

Choose a carnival and make a list of the different stakeholders, their needs and their priorities.

Case study 5.4 describes the Glastonbury Festival, which has many stakeholders.

Adaptation of matrix

Pareto analysis is a useful tool. Wilfredo Pareto was a nineteenth century Italian economist who concluded that 80 per cent of the wealth was held by 20 per cent of the population. The same phenomenon has often been found in businesses, where, for example, 80 per cent of the sales come from 20 per cent of the customers, or 20 per cent of the stock held accounts for 80 per cent of the inventory value. In other areas, 80 per cent of road accidents occur in localized areas (20 per cent of the roads have 80 per cent of the total accidents). In the early twentieth century, Lorenz produced a graph for demonstrating the cumulative dominance of the 20 per cent. Juran (1988) refers to the 80/20 phenomenon as the 'vital few and trivial many'.

When considering stakeholder satisfaction, Pareto analysis may indicate that a vital few of the stakeholders have a greater influence on the business. It may therefore be the case that the event organizer needs to take greater notice of these stakeholders.

Stakeholders such as banks and creditors (suppliers of goods and services) will generally only be interested in the financial security of the business. Other stakeholders (such as people living in the neighbourhood of the operation) will have different concerns (such as pollution, noise, and perhaps even heavy traffic flows). If local concerns are known in advance, then action can be taken to prevent offence. Actions that have to be taken as a result of protests or legal initiatives not only taint an organization's reputation, but also prove more costly than if the operation had been set up correctly and stakeholders' concerns addressed in the first place (see Case study 5.5).

Case study 5.4

The Glastonbury Festival, Somerset, England

Glastonbury Festival began on 19 September 1970, by Michael and Jean Eavis at Worthy Farm, Pilton, in Somerset. Attendance was 1500. The Glastonbury Festival of Contemporary Performing Arts – to give its full title – is now an institution, being the largest green field and performing arts festival in the world, with 150 000 people attending the 2004 event. It creates a city under canvas with distinct districts, and is located in over 900 acres in the Vale of Avalon – an area some 1.5 miles across and with a perimeter of over 8 miles.

The Festival, held annually in June, is unique, with over 30 different performance areas on site and some 2000 different performances over the weekend. The site is divided into the following areas: Acoustic Stage, Band Stand, Cabaret Tent, Cinema Field, Circus Big Top, Circus Field, Craft Fields, The Crown, dance fire stage, dance tent, Fields of Avalon (incorporating the Avalon Stage, the Avalon Café Stage and the Little Massive Stage), The Glade, Green Futures Field, Green Kids, Green Road Show, Greenpeace Field, Healing Fields, Jazz World Stage, Jazz Lounge, Kidz Field, Left Field, Lost Vagueness, John Peel Stage, Other Stage, Permaculture, Poetry and Words, Speakers Corner, Theatre Tent, Tipi Field and, of course the main stage, called the Pyramid Stage. There are also the traders' areas, food and merchandizing, and then there are medical and welfare centres, security, all the emergency services, a bank, places of worship – the list is endless.

The Glastonbury Festival pays over £1 million each year to charities and good causes, with the main beneficiaries being Oxfam, Greenpeace, Water Aid, and local good causes. It also supports the Fair Trade Foundation and Future Forests, and looks to operate in a way that reflects the values of the environmental and humanitarian charities it supports.

The Festival runs an unsigned performers' competition for new performers, which in 2004 generated over 2000 entries, several of which were subsequently signed to major labels.

The Licensing Authority is Mendip District Council.

The Festival has a small permanent staff and employs experienced event industry specialists on short-term contracts in the main, augmented by thousands of volunteers.

(Information supplied by the Glastonbury Festival Office; further details can be found at www.glastonburyfestivals.co.uk.)

Reflective practice 5.5

Consider Case study 5.4.

1. Prepare a list of the stakeholders for the Glastonbury Festival, and against each group or individual annotate their concerns about the festival. Identifying the stakeholders and determining their *concerns* should prove to be an interesting exercise. Remember to include the festival customer in this analysis.
2. Against this list, rank their importance on two dimensions: first, their interest in the event on a scale of 1–5 (5 being high); and second, the influence they could have on the event on a scale of 1–5 (5 being high).
3. Plot these dimensions onto Figure 5.4.
4. Analyse what this exercise has told you.
5. Consider a scenario where too many tickets have been sold for Glastonbury and more people attend the event than estimated. Would any of the stakeholders move from where you have put them in the earlier exercise? Comment on this movement.

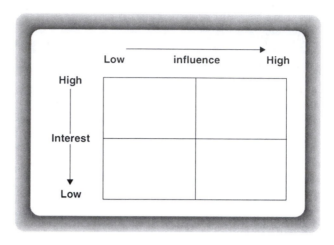

Figure 5.4 Influence and interest of Glastonbury Festival stakeholders

Customer/stakeholder challenges to the event organizer

Customer satisfaction has two elements. First, we have to know exactly what the customer wants. Secondly, we have to ensure that what is being offered and the manner in which we operate, in order to satisfy the customer, does not conflict with the interests of other stakeholders. Is this always possible?

Further methods of determining the requirements of the different stakeholders are discussed below, these include surveys, composite customer service ratings and gap analysis.

Surveys

To establish what is wanted by the direct customer and by any other stakeholders, an events operations manager could undertake a survey. The survey will determine first what the customers and stakeholders want, and secondly their perceptions of what they are currently getting.

For example, the results of an imaginary survey at a large national exhibition are reproduced in Table 5.2 (rated on a scale of 1–3, where 3 is highest).

Table 5.2 Desired service compared to perceived service

Some of the stakeholders	Accurate exhibitor directory	Good layout/flow	High-quality food facilities
Desired service (using three random CSFs)			
Attendees	3	3	3
Exhibitors	3	3	2
Caterers on site	1	1	3
Perceptions of received service (from the three stakeholders)			
Attendees	2	2	2
Exhibitors	2	3	3
Caterers on site	1	1	3

Case study 5.5

Jagger beats sore point to wow fans

(by Sarah Bell, 29 August 2003, *This is Local London*)

TWICKENHAM *was rocking and rolling in more ways than one as the Rolling Stones went back to their roots at the RFU stadium on Sunday after the planned Saturday concert was cancelled because Mick Jagger had a sore throat.*

The delayed opening night of their UK tour saw the band playing to 50 000 fans, including 5000 local residents, at the first concert to be held at the stadium. Taking to the stage, Mick Jagger said: 'No one has ever played in the Twickenham Rugby Club before, so we're very privileged. We started off playing at the Richmond Rugby Club up the road so it's not very far really from there to here.'

Richmond upon Thames Council, who helped man a helpline for residents and monitored noise levels, said they received just six complaints during the sound checks and concert.

Many residents also listened to the concert from their gardens and one complaint came from a resident who said that they couldn't hear and asked for it to be turned up.

Richmond police said they thought the event had gone well with no major incidents, and just a 'few people who were a bit worse for wear'. PC Nigel Cox, responsible for the police operation, said: 'It was very good really, from our side of things. All the crowds got there and away from the station safely, there was some traffic congestion at the end, and the A316 was very busy. We had a few problems with ticket allocation, but it was handled well.'

He added that the rescheduled date was not a problem, saying: 'If anything it has given us an insight into what it is going to be like and we will plan it the same as we have for this one.'

Businesses in the town thrived with the crowds. Frank Dupree, landlord of the Cabbage Patch, said: 'It was very good. I was choked about Saturday because I was meant to be going myself. It was a lovely crowd and no problems whatsoever. It was a much older crowd and less boozy than for the rugby. All gentle really.

It was a shame the concert wasn't earlier, as we could have got another bash afterwards. It was quite surprising how early they were in town, we were busy at 2 pm, a lot of people were just wandering around the town. It was great for Twickenham and I wish we could have more.'

Managing director Edwin Doran of Edwin Doran's Travel World said: 'The town was buzzing. Every pub, bar and restaurant was full with visitors spending money and looking forward to the return of two local residents to the borough where they started their musical careers. Isn't it magnificent that our town got such magnificent positive national publicity?'

Residents living closest to the stadium said the noise was not as bad as they had expected and the main problem was the traffic, which took a long time to clear. Barbara Irvine of Whitton Road said: 'The noise was less than we expected, on the positive side. The thing we didn't like were the fireworks at 10.30 and although we were expecting them, speaking to elderly people and people with young children, it is difficult for them. The crowd control during the day was very good, while during the evening there were a lot of people just walking around aimlessly and causing problems with the traffic trying to get past. Between Chudleigh Road and Palmerston Road there were 29 cars parked illegally.

Traffic didn't dissipate quickly and there was still heavy traffic at midnight and the fumes are horrible. They need to pay more attention to how they are going to evacuate people in their cars.

The cancellation was good for us because on Saturday we were able to leave our houses, otherwise you are in all day because it is impossible to get through the crowds.'

Yet the cancellation saw both hotel and restaurants losing trade. The Bremic Hotel on Russell Road was fully booked for both nights with 25 per cent cancelling, which was described as 'not good', but many rebooked for September.

There were also some fans and workers milling around the stadium, who had not heard the news of Jagger's sore throat on time. Ron Donovan from Durham, New Hampshire, ordered tickets last December from lastminute.com and said that he had had to collect them in person. He was philosophical, saying: 'I travel a lot and nothing ever goes to plan. If you get upset then you will go on getting upset. I try to take things in my stride.'

(Article printed by kind permission of the *Richmond and Twickenham Times*, part of the Newsquest Media Group.)

Reflective practice 5.6

Consider Case study 5.5.

1. Identify stakeholder concerns and suggest ways these could be alleviated for future events.
2. Identify areas that could have caused concern if preventive action and planning had not been carried out.

In table 5.2 the results of the survey showed that:

1. Attendees' requirements are an accurate directory of exhibitors, an excellent layout and flow, and high-quality food facilities
2. Exhibitors' requirements are an accurate directory of exhibitors, an excellent layout and flow and good food facilities
3. Caterers' requirements are high-quality food facilities; they are not really concerned whether the directory of exhibitors is totally accurate or whether there is an excellent layout and flow.

Regarding the perceptions of the service, the chosen stakeholders in this scenario all saw the directory as having some inaccuracies. The attendees did not believe that there was a good layout and flow, although the exhibitors themselves judged this more highly. Similarly, the attendees were not totally impressed with the food facilities. The event manager needs to rethink the priorities of the exhibition and look at the requirements of other stakeholders to see who can be satisfied, and to assess who it is most critical to satisfy.

Composite customer service rating

Christopher (1992) gives another method of rating customer service. This is illustrated in Table 5.3, using an example of an event management company preparing a brief for a seating company to provide 3000 chairs at an outdoor concert.

In this example, the key criterion for the seating company (as the customer of the event management company) has been established as a clear, unambiguous specification. This is the most important criterion, and has been given a rating of 50/100. On-time delivery of that specification is the next most important, and other important criteria (but of lesser rating) are preparation of the area for receipt of the chairs, and timely payment of the final invoice. This is shown in column 'a'.

Column 'b' shows that the specification received was only 70 per cent accurate, the timeliness of the specification to the suppliers represented only 80 per cent of their expectations, the area was only 90 per cent ready for receipt of the chairs, and the invoice was only paid at 95 per cent of their timely expectations. The exercise showed that on this one transaction the company was falling short of expectations and only achieving a composite customer service rating of 78 per cent.

Ideally, internal measures should be set against targets established by the customer. What might seem trivial to the business could, in the customer's eyes, be seen as a major problem.

Table 5.3 Customer service rating

Service required	Weighting % (a)	Performance (b)	Weighted score (a × b)
Clear specification	50	70	0.35
On time	25	80	0.20
Preparation for receipt of delivery	15	90	0.135
Timely payment of invoice	10	95	0.095
	100		0.78

Gap analysis

The level of service offered by an organization stems from the business policy or objectives. These were referred to at the start of Chapter 2. Objectives may, to a large extent, be driven by what the competition is doing or is threatening to do. When deciding upon and specifying a level of service, management tends to rely on the advice of the marketing function. If the marketing function does not correctly interpret the requirements of the customer, then there will be a gap between the level of satisfaction the organization believes it is providing and what the customer believes is being achieved. The concept of service gaps arose from the research of Berry *et al.* (1988) and his colleagues (Parasuraman *et al.*, 1985, 1991; Zeithaml *et al.*, 1990). Their SERVQUAL model is discussed in some detail in Chapter 16.

As Lewis (1994: 237) says, referring to Parasuraman *et al.*:

> They defined service quality to be a function of the gap between consumers' expectations of a service
> and their perceptions of the actual service delivery by an organization; and suggested that this gap
> is influenced by a number of other gaps which may occur in an organization.

The magnitude of the gap will be compounded by the number of steps in the service process and by the distance of the operational function from the customer. This is illustrated by the following examples.

In our first example, let us suppose that the marketing department at an International Folk Festival on the south coast has interpreted what the customer wants only 90 per cent correctly. Straight away, this means that the actual performance can never be better than 90 per cent of what the customer really wants. If, however, business policy is such that it is deemed sufficient to provide resources to meet only 90 per cent of the customer's requirements (this 90 per cent being set on the understanding that marketing is 100 per cent correct), then at best the customer will only get 81 per cent of what it wants.

In our second example, let us assume that an event management company slightly misinterprets what a major charity wants for a fundraising event, and that also it sets itself an internal target of 90 per cent. If we further suppose that the operation is so resourced that to the best of their ability they can only achieve 95 per cent of the standard set, this means the final result will be that customer satisfaction is at best only 69 per cent. The calculation is as follows:

- Customer requirement 100%
- Misinterpretation of needs 90% (i.e. they get it 90% right)
- Business policy sets target at 90% of 100, but this now actually equates to 90% of 90 = 81%

- Due to being under-resourced, the back of house team sets an internal standard of slightly better than 90% of target. However, owing to slight ambiguity and misunderstanding of the management target, this means that even when 92% of internal target is reached, it is only 90% of what was set by management – i.e. 90% of 81% = 73%
- The front of house team, also under-resourced, is 95% on target – 95% of 73% = 69%.

From the above examples, it is clear that unless gap analysis is understood, management will firmly believe that the overall result is somewhere near 90 per cent of what the customer wants. Each department, when queried, will also fervently believe that it is reaching between 90 and 95 per cent of the required performance levels. However, in the second example above it can be seen that the customer's expectations are only being matched to 69 per cent.

If an organization is close to its customers and aware of what the competition is doing, then a gap of this magnitude should not happen. The larger the organization and the greater the delineation of responsibilities between departmental functions, and the further the operations function is removed from the customer and from consultation in business policy decisions, the greater the likelihood of gaps occurring between what is provided and what the customer really wants. This concept is explored further in Chapter 16.

Reflective practice 5.7

You are an incentive travel company called 'Travel to Success', offering your services in providing packages to blue chip companies for their high-flying sales staff.

Typically you provide one- to two-week breaks in Thailand and China, linked with further promotional events to stimulate further sales among the workforce. Your unique selling point (USP) for your company is that you provide an evaluation of the effect of the incentives on the workforce over the following year. Armed with excellent qualitative research you are able to advise companies on the best methods of incentivizing their workforce with a high return on investment.

Imagine that you have done extensive research in the marketplace, and now construct a chart as in Figure 5.2.

1. Identify the critical success factors (CSFs) as determined by your hypothetical in-depth customer research, and list them on the vertical axis.
2. Assign values to the importance of each factor from the point of view of your customers.
3. Trace an unbroken line onto the chart for each CSF.
4. Estimate your own company's performance (hypothetically) and plot this on the chart (using a different colour).
5. Similarly, create two further imaginary companies ('Incentive Holidays R Us' and 'Outperform') and plot their scores onto the chart, again using different colours.
6. What do the results tell you?

Reflective practice 5.8

Return to the earlier section on critical success factors.

1. If you were to take into account the feelings of the major stakeholders, would the line you plotted for the Incentive Travel Company, 'Travel to Success', change with regard to how you could measure its attainment of the weighted critical success factors demanded by your customers?
2. You could now plot the needs of your customers and also the needs of your prominent stakeholders on the chart. You will see that the lines do not match. What does this tell you? How will you manage the gaps and the tension between your stakeholders?

Chapter summary and key points

This chapter is the penultimate chapter in the analysis stage of the event operations management model. It began by looking at who the customer is, and distinguishing between stakeholders and customers. The importance of determining critical success factors, not only for customers, but also for stakeholders has been stressed.

To summarize, generally an organization will aim consistently to achieve certain standards or levels of quality as determined by business policy. The decision as to the level of service to provide will be an economic one, and may be driven by what the competition is doing or is likely to do. The intention should be to define accurately what the customer wants. Normally an organization will not be able to meet all the requirements of the customer completely, and some trade-off will be possible. It is also wise to understand who the stakeholders are and what their concerns might be, and how they can affect your performance.

> *Where a strong organizational culture exists, enthusiastic and helpful staff, at very little extra cost to the organization, can enhance the perception of service level.*
>
> (Wright, 2001)

> *Given infinite resources any system, however badly managed, might provide adequate customer service.*
>
> (Wild, 1995)

Many an organization has failed to survive although the customers have been more than satisfied with what they have received. Thus customer satisfaction is not the only criterion by which an operations manager will be judged. Customer satisfaction must be provided simultaneously with an effective and efficient operation. The level of customer satisfaction offered must not only be affordable to the organization, but also consistent and sustainable. The events organization, if it is to survive, has to make a profit. Profit is not a dirty word.

Chapter 6 will look in detail at how to analyse the internal environment – i.e. the organization itself. This is the last and essential element in the analysis process prior to the detailed planning stage.

Chapter 6

Analysis of the internal environment

Learning Objectives

After reading through this chapter you will be able to:

- Analyse the internal environment and consider the efficient use of resources and their appropriate prioritization
- Consider the customers' needs, and appreciate the potential conflict of resource utilization and how to balance objectives
- Understand different company structures and how these styles can influence the success of an event and its organization.

Introduction

This is the last chapter within Section 1. It brings together the preceding chapters, and enables the event manager to understand and make sense of all of the analysis that has taken place. As shown in Chapter 2, without input from the customer the function of providing service will not happen. Figure 6.1, which is reproduced from Chapter 3 for ease of reference, shows that there are two distinct forces that have to be analysed and appraised before a successful mission can be formulated: the external environment and the internal environment of the event company. In Chapter 2 we discussed the importance of having a clear mission and goals for the event or the organization itself.

Chapter 3 looked at the task of analysing the external environment, and Chapter 4 led into the bridge between the external environment and the provision of resources, and how the event was going to be managed.

Chapter 5 picked up some of the main players within an event organization, i.e. the customers and stakeholders, and introduced the concept of analysing whether their varied needs are being met or whether there is a gap in the service.

This chapter looks in detail at the other elements of the internal environment within an event company as identified in Figure 6.1:

- Corporate culture
- Desire for quality
- Information systems
- Finance and ownership.

The chapter also considers many of the tangible and intangible resources that an event manager has to coordinate and control.

The internal environment

First we will discuss those elements within an event organization as identified as being in the internal environment as in Figure 6.1.

Corporate culture

Corporate culture is the amalgam of beliefs, norms and values of individuals making up an organization – i.e. the way we do things around here. For a business policy to be successful it has to be accepted by the members of the organization and mirror their goals and aspirations. The chief executive might be the one who articulates the vision, but unless there is a cultural fit and the people working on the events buy into it, it won't happen.

Culture and values are deep-seated and may not always be obvious to members and to newcomers to the organization.

Thompson (2001) sees culture as being the way staff behave and the importance of their values, and how this dictates the way decisions are made. Culture can also dictate

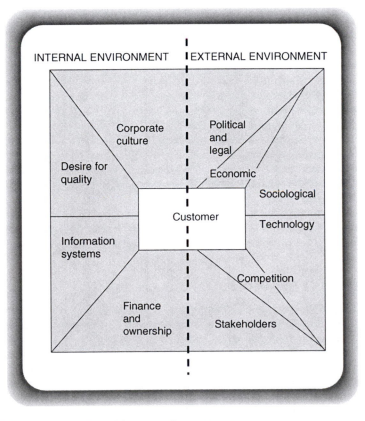

Figure 6.1 External and internal forces on the customer

the objectives of the company structure and systems, and its attitudes towards managing people (Thompson, 2001).

If the event organization has a strong culture, then each individual will instinctively know how things are done and what is expected. Conversely, if the culture is weak, then the individual may not react in the manner that management would hope.

Desire for quality

The level of quality offered is very much a business policy decision. It has been said that quality is free. Certainly doing things right the first time and every time should cost us nothing apart from training our people to know what is right and what corrective actions that they can take.

If we refer to our earlier example of a courtesy bus service in Chapter 2, we will see that a higher-level service and quality would not cost a great deal more. With the bus, the aim was to run a regular service, keeping to a defined route and a set timetable. In addition, the driver had to be licensed and the vehicle maintained to a roadworthy level. We could add the perception of extra quality at little (if any) additional cost by simply getting things right first time, every time.

Take, for example, a major exhibition in a capital city exhibition venue. If all the venue staff and exhibitors were to take pride in their appearance and be polite to customers, and if the venue were to be kept clean, the perception of a quality service would be enhanced at no appreciable extra cost to the organization. True there might be a minor cost in providing uniforms, and in the cost of cleaning, and perhaps in training in customer relations. If, however, we wished to increase the service by taking on extra work, such as our staff assisting in the erection and breakdown of stands, this would mean extra staff, more equipment, and extra scheduling.

Thus to increase the service is more expensive. Yet this might be what the customers have asked for. What determines our policy – is it the customer, or economic considerations? No doubt we would have to consider how many extra exhibitors the extra service would generate, and whether this extra income would offset the extra costs.

Quality is therefore also an economic consideration. At one level it is cheaper to do things right, and to do them only once, and it is also helpful to have happy and eager staff who will give customers friendly helpful service. This should not add to the costs; however, extra quality above these levels may increase cost. Thus the level of quality we can afford and sustain is very much a business policy decision, and to a large extent it will be driven not by what the customer wants but by what the competition is doing or threatening to do.

Any quality initiative has to have strong and overt support from management. Our contention is that quality is everyone's business, but unless management provide the vision and the drive any quality initiative has the chance of failing.

Information systems

With the information technology available today, there is no reason why every member of an event organization cannot be kept up to date with and have a clear understanding of what the current policy of the organization is. Few of us do not have a personal computer on our desk with access to electronic mail systems. Two-way communication is now commonplace, and many organizations go to great lengths with staff magazines, bulletin boards and so on to keep staff informed as to company policy as well as social events, work schedules and commitments. As we have said in previous chapters in the event industry many of our resources are external to the event organization and so it is imperative to keep in constant contact and to notify changes and revisions as they occur.

The old method of management was for the bosses to do the thinking, set the goals and give directions. The workers were not paid to think; their job was to obey orders. With such an approach it is no wonder that many people were reluctant to show initiative and thus few really had the interests of the organization at heart. This is often referred to Taylorism, after F. W. Taylor, a late nineteenth century American known as the father of scientific management. His philosophy was for management, by scientific means, to find the best way of doing a job and by using appropriate equipment. He believed in training the workers in the best way, and he offered incentives to increase productivity. Supervisors were employed to maintain the best method. Management did the thinking and workers were not expected to make suggestions; their job was to do what they were told. Chapter 11 covers many of the motivation theories, and Taylor's work is explained there.

Today, most of us work where we do because we understand the policies of the organization, believe in the product or service we are offering, and enjoy being involved, even in a small way, in helping to shape policy.

Finance and ownership

Most event organizations are limited by money. The necessary funding comes from the owners, profits (equity or shareholders' funds), sponsors and borrowing. Unless owners are getting a reasonable return on their investment, they are going to ask questions.

Owners, investors, the share market, sponsors and bankers will judge the event on the bottom line in the accounts. If the event organization is part of a government department, or is funded by the government or the public, the return will be seen in terms of value for money, and the persistent question will be 'can we do better for our money by going elsewhere?'

Financial strength, being profitable or getting value for money is a major shaper of business policy. More than anything else, lack of funds will determine policy.

The primary task when creating a budget is to outline the anticipated costs of producing the event (Harrison and McDonald, 2004). By identifying and documenting the costs involved in the production of an event, the event professional can establish the necessary income and possible sources of income.

As stated in Chapter 2, the event manager is the person who is responsible for using the resources of the organization as efficiently as possible to make goals and objectives happen. Central to the goals and objectives will be the need to make a profit, for without a profit a business will not survive. In not-for-profit organizations and charities, the goal is either to break even or to raise funds. Consequently, stringent financial systems are essential. Apart from mere survival, there will also be a need to satisfy fund providers (owners, shareholders, financiers) that their investment is secure and that they are receiving (or will receive) a satisfactory return on their investment. If an organization is a non-profit institution (such as government-funded), the central objective will be to show fund providers that they are getting value for money. The need to evaluate events in terms of success to all the different shareholders and in particular from a financial perspective is extremely important.

Many new businesses have a very short lifespan (over 70 per cent of small businesses fail within five years of beginning operations), and every month there are reports of medium and large businesses in financial difficulties. Like it or not, the continued success of any organization relies on financial stability. Often event managers see the accountants as soulless people devoid of imagination, interested only in short-term returns on assets. However, unless there is a positive cash flow, long-term business plans are meaningless. It is vital that any organization has a reliable accounting system in place to provide fast and accurate information. The minimum requirement is a budget and reliable feedback of actual results for comparison to the budget. These should be in time for corrective action to be taken where required. Rather than the accountants pressing operations for returns and figures, it should be remembered that the accountants are a support function, and it should be the event manager who is pressing the accountants to provide essential information.

Resources

In the event industry the major resource will probably be people, and we need to know what their competencies are – i.e. how skilled they are, their attitudes and dedication, and whether they are resourceful and capable of taking initiatives. Some staff will be full time, others part time and only for the duration of the event; some will be volunteers provided by other agencies, and some will come from suppliers.

Other resources include premises, information systems, time, equipment, materials and vehicles. The location of premises or where the event will take place, the reliability of the information system and other necessary equipment, the reliability of suppliers, and most importantly the quality of the people, will determine the overall capability or competence of the event. Establishing a quality of culture, how to motivate people and continuous improvement are covered in Chapter 12, and in Chapter 16 the topics are revisited when we discuss quality issues.

In the event industry the tangible and intangible resources available will consist of a mix of the following:

- People and their skills
- Information technology
- Equipment and machines (audiovisual equipment, registration facilities, materials movement equipment, seating etc.)
- Vehicles (leased, owned)
- Space (offices, warehouses, conference venues, green field areas, stately homes etc.)
- Materials (gifts, stationery etc.)
- Inventory (merchandise for sale, stationery, stock for later use)
- Time
- Information itself, and data.

Obviously not all events will have (or need) all of these resources at the same time. However, there will never be an unlimited amount of resources, and often they will be limited in quantity and quality. Any increases in their provision will be dependent on funds available. When funds are not an inhibitor there can be other constraints – for example, we may need specialized signage or advertising material, but it might be some weeks before delivery will be made and that time is not available to us.

Some of the more important of these varied resources are now explored further.

The customer

In some situations the customer is also an active input into the system – for example:

- When queueing whilst waiting for an event to start
- When inputting ideas
- When performing part of the activity – for example at teambuilding events and when self-serving at a buffet
- When completing a registration form on-line.

Materials

Materials used by the event include utilities such as energy, water and gas. Materials also include goods that are consumed by the event, goods that are transformed by the event, and goods held for sale and as inventory (i.e. in storage). In the events industry these materials would include lighting rigs set up to provide lighting at an outdoor concert, or giant jigsaws ready to be put together by the participants in a teambuilding activity, or merchandise, or data about possible venues or databases of potential customers. The hardware, the software and the data together form part of the inventory of materials that the event manager coordinates.

Machines/equipment

These include communication equipment, catering equipment, mobile seating stands, vehicles, and many other items of hardware.

Human resources

The human resource does not only include the number of people employed on the event, but also their knowledge and skill levels, and the intangibles of dependability and attitude.

The staff does not just include those who are employed, but also agencies who are subcontracted to the event for its duration, and volunteers. In fact, all staff working on the event from its conception to its delivery and breakdown, and all the emergency services, make up the human resource.

Buildings and space

In the event industry it is not only the brick-built venues for events that are essential, but also historic venues, exhibition venues and green-field sites.

Time

Time has to be made available to build an event and see it through right through to its breakdown and evaluation. In the event industry, time may be the most expensive resource and also one of the most constrained.

Information

With today's technology, information would seem to be readily available. The concern of the event manager, however, will be knowing what information is required, and then being able to interpret and use the information so as to achieve the event's operational objectives.

Reflective practice 6.1

List three resources for each of the six following headings (two of which should be tangible and one intangible) that could each be classed as a resource for a Wedding Breakfast and an evening function following a marriage ceremony:

1. The customer
2. Materials
3. Machines/equipment
4. Human resources
5. Buildings and space
6. Time.

Prioritizing resources

The list of resources may appear to be formidable, but generally the list can be reduced or modified to show the most *important* resources for the particular organization we are concerned with. The important resources are those that are most necessary to satisfy the customers' essential requirements, and these may change from one event to another, or indeed from one client to another.

Reflective practice 6.2

For an event organization to launch a new cosmetic product, the four most important resources might well be people, design technology, database of contacts, and space. Certainly stationery, transport and other equipment will be needed, but these may be of less significance. Likewise, you, as the event manager, might see your car as an important resource, but this will have a minor impact on the achievement of customer satisfaction.

Suppose that your event management company has determined that it is valued by its client for:

- Friendly service
- Useful advice on means of evaluating the success of the launch, accurate bookings and response to enquiries
- Courteous service
- Confidentiality
- Competitive prices and 'special' deals.

To achieve customer satisfaction as defined in this manner, you will need a reliable integrated computer system that gives on-line information, communication with relevant groups of people, and confirmation of bookings and tickets. Your company will need sufficient office space to accommodate several staff members, and a good network of reliable and loyal suppliers. Finally, your company will need reliable, well-presented and courteous staff, and well-devised evaluation procedures.

Using the product launch as an example, you can now extend the approach for customer satisfaction to include resource utilization (see Table 6.1):

1. First, create a chart with the customer's CSFs listed in the left-hand column.
2. In subsequent columns, identify those resources that are needed in order to deliver what the customer wants, their current standard of provision, and what should be done in order to improve and effectively deliver these resources.

It can be seen that this technique relates to the work completed earlier when looking critically at gap analysis regarding what the organization is currently achieving against the customer's needs.

Not everything can be done at once, and perhaps only those CSFs with high ratings should be considered.

This serves as an excellent tool when balancing out resource deployment and future costs, or when asking for more finance for a particular event.

Looking at the hypothetical example of the cosmetic product launch described above, let us assume that it has been established that customers rate 'accurate bookings and response to enquiries' as most important. It is upon this aspect that the event manager should then concentrate his or her efforts.

Competitive prices, although important, are a lesser consideration for this particular client, as are special deals.

Having established this rating, the next step is to determine the most vital resources needed to give the customers satisfaction. In this example it is found that accurate

Table 6.1 Identifying resources required to deliver the CSFs

CSFs	Degree of importance 1–5 (5 high)	Resources required	Quality of resource currently available	Action to be taken to improve delivery
Friendly service	4	Trained, customer orientated staff	High, but not sufficient numbers to meet every customer's needs	Deploy more trained staff for this particular event
Evaluation to determine success of launch	5	Clear objectives and evaluation system in place	Excellent, well designed survey instrument used on previous similar events	
Accurate bookings and response to enquiries	5	Database and efficient staff	Good database. Not insufficient phone lines for this number of enquiries	Increase temporary phone lines
Courteous service	4	Trained, customer orientated staff	High, but not sufficient numbers to meet every customer's needs	Deploy more trained staff for this particular event
Confidentiality	4	Secure systems and trained staff	Excellent loyal staff	
Competitive prices	4	Knowledge of competitors' prices, and efficient systems and suppliers	Some up-to-date knowledge	Employ extra temporary staff to research competitors
Special deals	3	Ability to add value	Flexible systems in place	Need to research competitors and what would constitute 'special deal'

bookings and response to enquiries is of paramount importance, alongside a system to evaluate the success of the launch. Hence an integrated computerized information and ticketing system is essential, and a clear survey instrument to measure success of the launch. When the system is 'down' little can be achieved – information on prices, schedules, and availability of seats cannot be provided; nor can bookings be made and tickets and vouchers issued. A back-up 'manual' system consisting of the telephone, bound books of pamphlets, and handwritten tickets can be unwieldy, slow and expensive due to mistakes being made through information not being current and bookings being incorrectly recorded.

Trained staff are important, but of lesser importance than the system, for without the system the staff can do little.

The efficiency factor

The discussion above concerning resource utilization has been from the stance of customer satisfaction.

Traditional production and operation management texts tend to suggest that the prime role of the operations manager is the efficient use of resources in transforming inputs into outputs, and that customer satisfaction is almost a subservient objective. While this might be so for certain types of capital-intensive operations where the customer is not an input into the system, such as a factory where goods can be produced irrespective of whether a customer order is held or not, we have concluded for events that resource utilization is *subservient* to customer satisfaction. That is not to say that efficient use of resources is unimportant; indeed, efficiency is vitally important. However, total efficiency would mean making the optimum use of resources – i.e. elimination of all waste, no spare space, no idle time, minimum of time spent with clients, customer queues so that service staff are fully employed and so on. This is not always possible where a degree of flexibility for customers is essential (see Case study 6.1), and where forecasting demand cannot be a guaranteed statistic (this is considered in further detail in Chapter 13).

Precedence of objectives

Some event organizations will concentrate on customer satisfaction at an affordable and sustainable level as being the overriding objective, and others will focus on

Case study 6.1

Christmas Concert in a cathedral

The concert begins at 19.30 and concludes at 22.00, with a 20-minute interval during which refreshments are served for corporate guests only. The cathedral can hold 700 people, of which 100 are corporate guests. Prior to the start of the concert there is a reception for the corporate guests. There are two choirs, one consisting of twenty singers and one consisting of forty sixth-formers from a local school plus a percussion group of ten.

There are six ladies' toilets and four gentlemen's toilets in the cathedral. These are deemed adequate for the use of the performers and the corporate guests. There is a refreshment area adjacent to the cathedral, which can be used for the corporate guests. As only the corporate guests are receiving refreshments it means staffing levels can be kept to a minimum, as half the total staff are required for the earlier reception for the corporate guests and they can leave once the concert begins. This will leave the others to serve interval drinks only. There is adequate provision of toilets in the adjacent area.

This makes operational sense, but what about the rest of the audience? If refreshments were to be served to them it would require more staff and facilities in order to cope with the numbers who may require refreshments, especially to supply 700 people in 20 minutes. It would require the building of a structure outside the cathedral, as refreshments are not allowed inside, and also the hiring of portable toilets.

Operationally these are extra costs that, on the face of it, are surplus to requirements – especially for just 20 minutes. However, what if this concert takes place in winter and the temperatures are forecast to be near freezing? Cathedrals are immense buildings and difficult to heat. Should the event manager reconsider the position regarding the audience? A hot drink at the interval, whether tea, coffee or a festive beverage, could promote and enhance the feeling of warmth offered by the concert's traditional Christmas repertoire. Event managers have to balance cost versus customer satisfaction, and tangible versus intangible benefits.

Reflective practice 6.3

Consider Case study 6.1.

1. If we believe resource utilization to be subservient to customer satisfaction, then how should the organizers effectively use resources and offer customer satisfaction?
2. List the optimum number and type of resources you would use.
3. If money were no object, list the minimum number you feel could be used.
4. Now compare these lists with colleagues and determine the compromise solution. Be prepared to argue your reasoning.

efficient use of resource utilization ahead of customer satisfaction. This is not to suggest that the organization that is resource-focused ignores customer satisfaction; often resource utilization will be in harmony with customer satisfaction.

For example, aircraft passengers will value getting to their destination (specification) on time and will be prepared to pay a certain price. If the airline meets these criteria (specification, time, and cost) customers will be basically satisfied, and if at the same time the airline has a full aircraft (no empty seats) and keeps its operating costs to a minimum then simultaneously efficient resource utilization and customer satisfaction will have been achieved.

In this airline example it is only when pre-booked passengers are turned away that the customers' objectives come into conflict. Suffice to say that passengers travelling first class, those who have been prepared to pay for extra service, will not be the ones to be offloaded. First-class passengers could well rate the service and all the personal attention that they get as being truly first class. Thus although some passengers will be less than happy – i.e. those who have been offloaded – the airline company could still claim in its mission statement, and in its advertising, to provide world-class service, although the overriding objective is clearly resource utilization.

Case studies 6.2–6.4 illustrate various aspects of the precedence of objectives, and these are considered in the subsequent Reflective practice questions.

Case study 6.2

The Bakewell Show, 4–5 August 2004, Bakewell Showground, Derbyshire

Glorious sunshine and record crowds helped make the 2004 Bakewell Show one of the most successful yet. The 174th Bakewell Show, known fondly as 'The Little Royal', registered a record number of visitors through the gates.

The show attracted around 60 000 people, some from as far away as Australia, New Zealand, South Africa and Uganda, as well as many visitors closer to home, who all enjoyed an action-packed programme of entertainment.

There were more animals on the showground than ever before, with numbers in the sheep classes up considerably and increases in cattle numbers too – a tribute to how the area has recovered from the foot and mouth crisis.

There were more than 6000 entries in 700 competitive classes, and a record number of animals on the showground. The livestock section had 130 classes featuring thousands of animals, including horses, donkeys, pigeons, poultry, rabbits, dogs, goats, cattle and sheep. Trade-stand numbers were boosted to 304 from 250 in 2003.

Centre ring entertainment on the first day saw a stunning medieval display from the Horses Impossible Team, featuring horsemen fresh from making the new King Arthur film. Dressed in colourful costumes, they demonstrated the amazing fighting skills of the period as well as amazing horsemanship.

On Thursday visitors were treated to fast and furious scurry racing, which proved extremely popular when introduced last year.

New, in 2004, were the Suffolks – the oldest breed of heavy horse in Britain, with a bloodline that traces back to 1768. Many of the older visitors were delighted to see the rare breed horses, which were in use on farms when they were children.

During the Show there was a chance for younger visitors to win a state-of-the-art computer in a special competition. The competition involved the children visiting every part of the Showground. The decision to make the children's area three times larger proved very popular.

Other attractions included a spectacular floral art show, scrumptious food and a farming exhibition where visitors could taste fine foods, see vintage vehicles and visit the village green, where traditional rural crafts were demonstrated.

(Printed by kind permission of Bakewell Show; further information can be found at www.bakewellshow.org.)

Case study 6.3

Royal Agricultural Winter Fair, 5–14 November 2004, National Trade Centre, Toronto, Canada

The Royal Agriculture Show (known as The Royal) in Toronto is the largest of its kind in the world, representing the best of Canada's livestock and agricultural produce. The show provides exhibitors with the opportunity to market their products through display and competition to 340 000 visitors from over 60 countries.

International Business Centre

To accommodate 3000 international visitors, The Royal provides hospitality in the International Business Centre, located at the south end of Hall B. This facility provides visitors with a comfortable place to do business, put their feet up, and mingle with other guests. Fax machines, telephones, photocopiers, computers with email access, printers, meeting facilities and complimentary coffee and snacks make doing business at The Royal easy and efficient.

National Holstein Show

The National Holstein Show is the second largest of its kind in North America, attracting more than 5000 enthusiastic spectators from over 60 countries around the world. Visitors line up at the Coliseum as early as 6:00 am to secure the best seats in the house for this exciting show. Exhibitors from across Canada and the United States will showcase more than 350 Holsteins at the day-long competition. Immediately following the Holstein show, the Grand Champions of all the National Dairy Shows – Jersey, Brown Swiss, Ayrshire and Holstein – compete for the title of Supreme Champion.

Three National Beef Cattle Shows

In 2004, The Royal is hosting no less than three National Beef Shows in the first weekend. The best-of-the-best Angus, Hereford and Shorthorn cattle will be crowned Canadian National

Champion under one roof, showcasing to an international audience that Canadian beef is some of the best in the world. Other shows hosted at the 2004 Royal are Salers, Maine-Anjou, Blonde D'Aquitaine, Charolais, Galloway, Highland, and Simmental.

The Royal Auctions

One of the most popular auctions, the Market Beef Cattle Auction, will be held on 6 November 2004 in the Ring of Excellence. Highlighting the top steers and heifers from the Market Livestock Show and the Syngenta Queen's Guineas Show, this auction generates significant earnings for breeders as buyers from restaurants and grocery stores battle it out for the best in beef. Other auctions are the Market Lamb Sale, Ontario Junior Barrow Sale and the Sale of Stars – selling the top Holstein genetics in Canada.

This year marks the 25th anniversary of the Scotia Bank Hays Classic, Canada's premier dairy youth event. This year, 4-Hers from EVERY province will compete for the coveted Grand Champion titles – Grand Champion Showman and Grand Champion Calf. Over 450 youths competed last year, and it's anticipated that an even greater involvement will take place in 2004 with the 25th anniversary celebrations.

Young Speakers for Agriculture will celebrate its 20th anniversary at the 2004 Royal. This year will be the best competition ever, with strong representation from all provinces in Canada. This is a real salute to all Canadian agricultural youth, as last year's competition attracted participants from Alberta, Manitoba, New Brunswick, Nova Scotia, Ontario, Prince Edward Island and Quebec.

Giant Vegetables

One of the most fascinating features of the Horticulture Show is the Giant Vegetable Competition. The 2003 champion pumpkin weighed over 1200 pounds, and last year's giant parsnip will be listed in the 2005 Guinness Book of World Records – weighing in at a whopping 8 pounds, 6 ounces.

(Further information on the Royal Agricultural Winter Fair can be found at www.royalfair.org.)

Case study 6.4

Perth Royal Show, 2–9 October 2004, Claremont Showground, Perth, Western Australia

At The Perth Royal Show there are literally countless things to see and do – all at no extra cost. It is the biggest WA community event, and it profiles agricultural attractions, exciting activities and around the clock entertainment.

The 2004 Show attracted record numbers, with 483 761 people, and had over 2000 volunteers helping to run the event plus 15 000 of the State's finest agricultural exhibits competing in over 42 competitive sections.

There are thousands of special animals and hundreds of exciting performers on show daily, including street theatre, marching band and live performances all around the grounds. All creatures great and small and WA's finest agricultural and domestic animals compete and are on display as part of the show.

For example, there are more than 160 alpacas, 200 cats, 1800 dogs and 120 pigs competing for attention, ribbons and trophies. Last year 16 emu chicks hatched in the Senses Foundation Animal Nursery.

The Swan Draught Sheepdog Arena Trials test the talent of WA's top sheepdogs as they herd three sheep through a series of obstacles into a pen. There is the Farmyard Favourites Petting Zoo, where children and adults have the chance to hold and feed baby rabbits, cuddly lambs, adorable piglets, tiny chicks and cheeky goats. There are more than 1000 pigeons, chooks, ducks, turkeys and water fowl on display at the John O'Meehen Pavilion, and there is the Novelty Calf competition where the calves and their junior handlers get dressed up.

The school holidays can start with a trip to the Perth Royal Show and there children can visit Kiddie Land and have a ride on the merry-go-round, the rockin' tug or the all new 'cup and saucer'. Parents ride for free when they accompany their young children.

Children can discover the magic of the Australian bush through songs and the didgeridoo playing of Wandering in the Bush performer, Greg Hastings.

For older children there is the chance to flip, spin and grind in extreme clinics. Grom sessions offer you the chance to ride with the Planet X Pro's on a purpose-built course. Get the latest tips and tricks from some of the best action sports riders in the country in freestyle BMX and skateboarding. Learn new skills from accredited coaches in a safe and supervised environment in sessions designed for three age groups, 6 to 10 years, 11 to 14 years, and 15 years and over. There is a participation fee of $10, with everyone involved getting a free show bag packed with stickers, magazines and a DVD. All equipment and protective gear is provided. You can register on-line at www.planetx.net.au or on the day.

Everything old is new again. At this year's Perth Royal Show, wedding cakes evocative of the 1950s, smothered in royal icing and generously decorated in gold leaf, will be the star attraction of the cookery competition.

WA cake decorators were invited to enter their 1950s-look wedding cakes in a special class of the popular cookery competition to commemorate 100 years of the Perth Royal Show at the Claremont Showground.

As well as a step back to post-war Australia, visitors will be able to get a taste of early Australian cookery such as Anzac biscuits, jam tarts, lamingtons, marble cake, lemon butter and damper.

This year the cookery competition attracted 540 entries in classes for scones, biscuits, muffins, cream puffs cakes, puddings, chocolates jams, preserves, decorated cakes including fairytale wedding cakes and gingerbread houses.

A special competition for the best decorated Royal Agricultural Society of WA birthday cake will be another highlight of this year's competition. In addition to the agricultural competitions and the animals, the daily events and entertainment, sideshows, thrilling rides and games, there are over 7000 square meters (indoors) of products and services of many businesses, government agencies and charities totalling over 600 commercial displays.

(For general information see www.raswa.org.au. Information supplied by courtesy of the agricultural shows above; edited versions of their websites have been used.)

Reflective practice 6.4

Consider the three agricultural shows described in Case studies 6.2–6.4.

1. What would limit the level of customer service provided, and how would this differ between the different 'Royal' shows?
2. In what aspects would resource utilization be the overriding objective, and when would customer satisfaction have first priority?

Balancing of objectives and the potential conflict

The two basic objectives for an event manager are customer satisfaction and efficient resource utilization. The examples given above show that, having understood the key requirements of the customer, it is then important to attempt a match with the resources available.

It will not always be possible to achieve an absolute balance between what the customer wants and what the organization is able to do. For the events manager, a further restraint will be the objectives of the organization. If the objectives are driven primarily by the need for efficient use of resources, then customer satisfaction will be more difficult to achieve.

As stated previously, given infinite resources any system, no matter how badly managed, might provide adequate service. The truth is that there will not be infinite resources, and often existing resources will not completely mesh with the achievement of total customer satisfaction. The event manager will be expected to achieve adequate use of resources and a reasonable level of customer satisfaction.

Matching customer satisfaction with resource utilization

If the overriding aim is to make the most efficient use of existing resources, it might mean that the service to be offered has to be rethought and re-promoted. Thus the service will be altered to meet the competencies of the organization, rather than extra resources being added to meet a higher-level service.

Before any change to the specified service is contemplated, the event manager should seek improved methods of operating and better ways of doing things using existing resources. Rather than saying 'it cannot be done', the positive approach is to look for ways to make the impossible possible with existing resources.

Company structures

Equally important in the management of resources is the structure of the organization. The successful implementation of an event can be influenced by the degree of decentralization, the way the event is coordinated, and the relative extent of formality and informality (Thompson, 2001).

Centralization relates to the degree to which authority, power and responsibility is devolved through the organization. As more responsibility is delegated, the organization becomes more decentralized.

Coordination of activities affects the way work has been divided up between functions, e.g. marketing, finance and operational, and how it will be managed. This is often shown on charts, and clear delineation allows for clarity of purpose and understanding of everyone's contribution to the final event.

Formality–informality. Formality is often represented by policies and reporting systems, whilst informality is required if managers and other employees are to use their initiative and innovate change (Thompson, 2001).

The organizational structure for an event forms a framework for all of the different activities and services that are to be provided (Shone and Parry, 2004). At any event, there is a mixture of products and services. For example, when Leeds City Council in the UK organize their summer city-centre celebrations, they combine into one operation:

- Artists, dancers and musicians, from this country or from anywhere around the world
- Sound and lighting systems and other technical services
- Security and stewarding
- Food and beverages where required
- Expertise from the Highways Department
- Police and fire services
- Administration and support services
- Financial services.

However, note also some differences:

- Some of these activities are in full view of the event attendee while other groups of people have very little direct contact with the attendees
- Some of the staff are paid and others are volunteers
- Some of the staff are responsible directly to the event manager and others are employed by agencies or subcontractors.

In many instances, particularly at community festivals, event committees employ an event coordinator for three to four months prior to the Festival, but the other staff may be volunteers working voluntarily on the Festival's committee – i.e. a virtual organization.

Within the event industry there is a great variety of different organizational structures. There is a great deal of past research and commentary on these alternatives, discussed by leading management authors such as Thompson (2001); Johnson and Scholes (2002), and Mullins (2002).

Bowdin *et al.* (2001) apply much of this management theory directly to event management companies. The main finding from Bowdin *et al.* (2001) is that the majority of event organizations have a small number of staff with relatively uncomplicated organizational structures. These authors identify three types of organizational structures:

1. Simple
2. Functional
3. Network.

Large organizations make use of further structures such as task forces/matrix structure, and committees.

Virtual organizations

Most events are of a limited duration. Even though their organizations may have simple entrepreneurial structures, matrices or functional structures, the event itself can be networked or virtual (see Figure 6.2).

Figure 6.2 shows an example of how a virtual organization could work within the events industry. Core activities such as marketing, operations and administration would be managed from within the company. Anecdotally, from within the industry, this could be by one person or several. Accounts and finance, although core and dependent upon the expertise of the company personnel, could be undertaken by an accountant.

The size of the virtual company and the interaction with suppliers will then depend upon the size or number of events. The organization may only employ four people, but during an event it can see its workforce increased many times over as staff are employed on an event-by-event basis. Similarly, contractors are used to provide the services that are not core to the organization, and with the development of these, relationships networks begin.

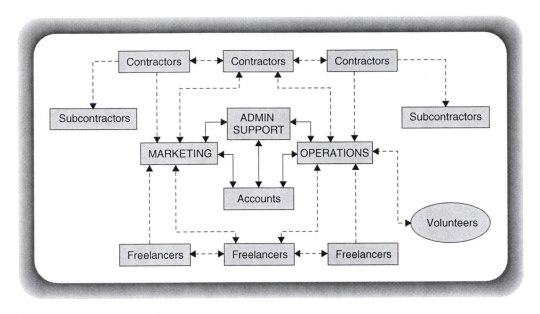

Figure 6.2 A virtual organization

Changes in technology and the ability to communicate fully and quickly have enhanced the effectiveness of virtual organizations.

The need to use specialist suppliers (e.g. caterers, seating and staging, sound and lighting specialists, the artists themselves) has encouraged the growth of small entrepreneurial organizations to use a network of suppliers.

Even with large organizations, such as charities and government, subcontracting and strategic alliances are very favourable.

Campbell *et al.* (2003) describe a virtual organization as being a network of linked businesses that coordinate and integrate their activities so effectively that they give the appearance of a single business organization. This removes the negativity that can be associated with being a 'one-man band', and provides the customer with a turnkey operation.

We would challenge the need to have the appearance of being a single business organization, but would emphasize the need for all suppliers and core organizations to be focused on the end product and service. The consumer is of utmost importance, and consistency with the individual goals and objectives of each and every company, employee and volunteer is required.

The net result is that the event should be flexible and responsive, specialist-driven and cost effective.

The structure shown in Figure 6.2 can have several key advantages:

1. It is more efficient because it has lower costs and greater outputs
2. Specialist firms with current expertise and experience can be contracted in on a needs-only basis
3. There can be clear budgeting with the costs known beforehand
4. It is flexible and relevant to each unique event
5. There is the opportunity for rapid communication and decision-making.

However, Bowdin *et al.* (2001) also identify disadvantages to this type of structure:

1. Quality control may be difficult as contractors provide much of the work
2. The reliability of supply may be compromised

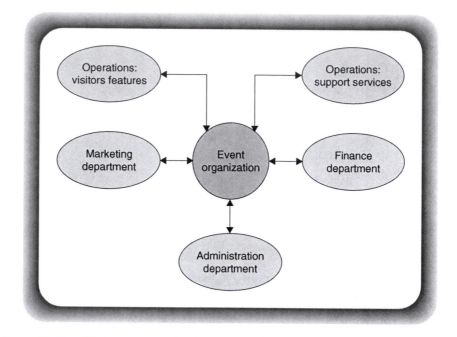

Figure 6.3 Simplified events organization structure (Shone and Parry, 2004)

3. Coordination of suppliers may be difficult
4. Deficiencies in contracts work may result in costly and lengthy legal proceedings.

We will look at the concept of virtual organizations again in Chapter 9, where we discuss in greater depth the advantages that can accrue from developing suppliers as partners.

Shone and Parry (2004) believe that event organizational structures will include five main functions (Figure 6.3):

1. Visitor services operations
2. Support services operations
3. Marketing
4. Administration
5. Finance.

These five functions can be further subdivided depending on the nature and size of the event. In some instances, the same people within one organization may be responsible for more than one function.

Hence it is clear that the many different organizational structures highlighted by Bowdin *et al.* (2001) are particularly varied within the event industry.

These different structures may occur within organizations ranging from a community event such as a town's Scarecrow in the Garden competition, to a Regional Agricultural Show, to a complex political party conference, to the Queen's Golden Jubilee celebrations, to the Olympics.

In each case it is essential that all people who are working together, in whatever capacity, know who is in charge and what is expected of them – i.e. their roles and responsibilities within the organization and the operation of the event.

As Shone and Parry (2004) say, there should be no ambiguity, so that safety and efficiency are not compromised.

You should undertake further reading of work that covers these different styles will help you to gain an appreciation of these different types of structures and their usefulness and impact upon the company which they house.

Chapter summary and key points

This is the last chapter of Section 1, and represents the end of the analysis stage. The chapter has determined that one of the prime objectives of an organization is customer satisfaction through the achievement of a consistent and sustainable level of service. The determinant of the level of service to be provided will be driven by the competition and demands of customers and stakeholders – i.e. by the external environment. To provide the necessary *affordable* level of service, the operations manager is vitally concerned with efficient and effective use of resources. We also noted that resources might be limited in quantity and quality, and therefore the event manager must balance the two, potentially conflicting, objectives of customer satisfaction and efficient resource utilization.

The chapter has also studied different company structures and how these can influence the way in which organizations operate. Conversely, how an organization operates can affect its structure.

Chapters 1–6, form the first stage of the event operations management model and have identified those critical areas that require analysis – i.e. the external and internal environments. The detailed analysis leads to the event manager being able to define the goals of the organization, having taken into account the varying needs of the stakeholders, the customers and the organization itself. The chapters discussed the importance of understanding the critical success factors of the customers and establishing whether their needs could be met from the resources and skills available within the organization. From the analysis, the objectives of the event and also the objectives of the organization should be reassessed to see that the mission is still in line with the overall needs of the organization.

Section 2 considers the detailed planning stage of the event operations management model, taking the analysis further in order to plan the event carefully and methodically. As discussed at the outset, it uses many of the techniques from project planning and operational management literature.

Event Operations Management Model: Tum, Norton and Wright 2005

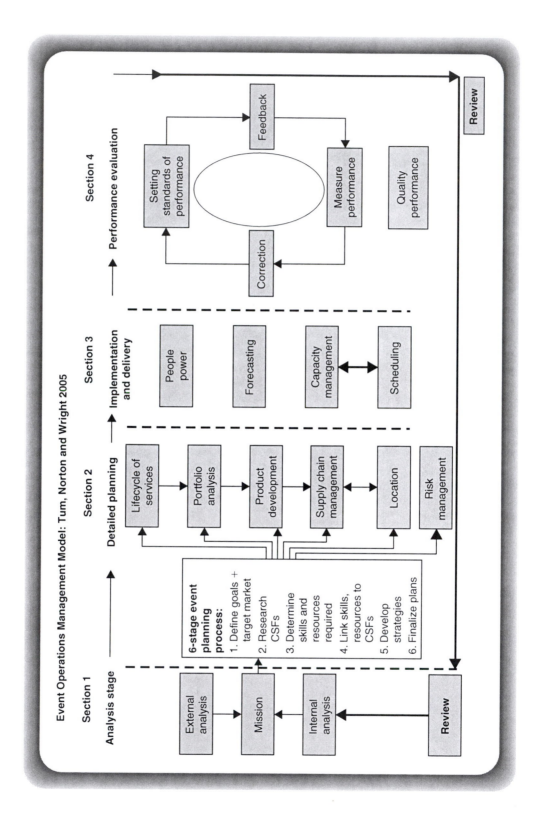

Section Two
Detailed planning

Introduction

The event operations management model was introduced in Chapter 1. The model is continuous, and includes subsidiary cycles within each stage. Section 1 of this book has identified and discussed the external and internal environments that require detailed analysis prior to the formulation of the mission for the organization or the event. This first stage, involving analysis, is imperative in order to understand the environment and situation in which the event is going to be implemented, and for the event manager to assess critically the customers needs and the resources required.

Section 2 is concerned with the second stage of the event operations management model, the detailed planning process that has to be undertaken prior to the implementation of the event. No event can take place without planning. The greater the amount of time taken at this stage, the better the event will be. As plans are made and worked through, many unprepared for eventualities will disappear, and the outcome will be smooth and well organized. Section 2 therefore covers a range of different activities. Some of these could easily have sat within the implementation stage, but it is the authors' view that if plans are made in advance and communicated well, then the event will be effective and efficient in its delivery. All the different elements provided by suppliers and staff, following clear and agreed consultation, will be appropriate for the event, and create a well-executed event in line with the event objectives.

The planning stage of the event operations management model is described throughout the following five chapters. You will see that the work and planning needed is shown in the event operations management model, and is clearly discussed and examined practically within each chapter.

Chapter 7 looks at the importance of planning for the future. This is essential for any event management company so that it can plan the resources required in the coming years, and plan activities and financial requirements so that it can achieve the long-term objectives of the company. The chapter therefore considers the need to plan for the future over long-, medium- and short-term time frames. Consequently, it is important that the work covered in Section 1 has been understood and completed by every event manager in order to use the objectives set and turn them into operational plans. There is much in general operational management literature that can be seen in this chapter, since the six steps of a detailed planning process are introduced. Following this the concept of product life cycles is explored, and why an event manager who is striving for sustainable success should consider market share, market growth and market attractiveness.

Chapter 8 develops the concept of product life cycles, and considers new product development and innovation. This is particularly important, since changes in society, customer needs and expectations have intensified the need for event managers to be creative and to establish new events and new ways of delivering events. Similarly, increasing competition means that event managers are never immune from change and the actions of others. This chapter gives some practical advice on how to analyse and plan for the future. It introduces flow chart symbols and ideas from the general operational management literature that should be of great value to an event manager when putting together an event.

Chapter 9 looks critically at the role and importance of suppliers, and how the purchasing function should be considered strategically. This chapter examines the relationships between suppliers, and the necessity for optimizing the sourcing of all resources. It considers the benefits of vertically integrated companies and the question of outsourcing or making use of resources within the company. In short, the chapter questions how competitive advantage can be achieved and raises the need to assess the use of every resource, including all human resources. The chapter does not end on a strategic note, however, but offers practical guidance on how to purchase resources more effectively and on the importance of having clear specifications.

Chapter 10 considers the location of the business premises. It is important to consider the overall objectives of the company, and hence the business policy, and how these will affect the location. It could be argued that the last section of this chapter, which deals with the layout of an actual event, should be included in Section 3 of this book, which deals with implementation and delivery of the event itself. However, all these aspects are intertwined. The chapter continues to look at aspects of layout and signage, and concludes with a section on health and safety at events, and ergonomics. The latter two aspects are considered here because they could both involve changes to the event layout and efficiency.

Chapter 11 links to the end of Chapter 10, discussing risk and hazard assessment in detail. This is an essential aspect if the event is to run safely and smoothly. There are many techniques from the literature that cover risk assessment, and the main principles and techniques will be covered in this chapter. This provides a very useful guide for event managers, as well as creating an understanding of the importance of aiming to create risk-free events.

Chapter 7

Planning, product portfolios, and product and service development

Learning Objectives

After reading through this chapter you will be able to:

- Understand the need for long-range planning
- Explain the six-stage detailed event-planning process
- Appreciate the development of the product life cycle
- Analyse portfolios using the Boston Consulting Group Matrix (BCG).

Introduction

In this chapter we are concerned with the formulation of a plan and detailed decision-making. These important concepts will be put into the context of the event industry and its peculiarity of having set deadlines from which all planning works backwards. In particular, this chapter creates a six-stage detailed event planning process that can be used by event practitioners. Further work is clarified so that the event manager can understand how the range of different services and events that are offered by the organization should link together to create a harmonious whole, supporting each other.

In order to illustrate this, the life cycle of services and the Boston Consulting Group Matrix (BCG) are introduced. The other aspects of operational management that are shown in the event operations management model are covered in subsequent chapters within Section 2 of the book.

The need for long-range planning

Planning takes place at several levels, and can cover several different timeframes. Thus an organization might have a ten-year plan and a five-year plan, and will certainly have a twelve-month plan – for example, as shown in a budget. There should be a corporate-wide plan, business unit plans, department plans, and at the operations level the event manager will have medium-term, short-term and daily plans. It can be seen in many event companies that the timescales are different for the larger companies, and their own long-term plans may be only for three years, medium-term plans for between one and two years, and short-term plans taking them to the end of the current year.

The corporate plan is the longer-term plan for the whole organization. It establishes the objectives of the organization, which are made after consideration of external environmental factors and balanced against the internal competencies of the organization. As previously discussed in Chapter 2, in the first stage of the event operations management model the overall thrust of the corporate plan is often articulated in a mission statement. The corporate or business plan, however, requires more than just the few well-chosen words of a mission statement.

Generally the plan will need to be supported by target figures, which will include past trends, broken down into different events and different target markets, and forecasts of future demand. The plan is also likely to include capital equipment budgets, cash flow forecasts, profit and loss forecasts, human resource and training requirements, venue and technology requirements, and so on.

For each twelve-month accounting period, an annual report with financial statements showing actual results should be made available. A budget should be produced for each coming event. The success of the plan and budgets should be compared, and judged against forecasted results.

Many event companies may be working with annual events, or their future events may not be similar to those that they completed in a previous twelve-month period. This provides a challenge to the event manager when predicting the costs and income for a forthcoming event, if these cannot be based on past performance.

Event managers will be concerned with meeting immediate and short-term future demands. However, looking back to what happened last time might well assist in planning for the future. It is therefore important that after each event detailed notes are made about the success, strengths and weaknesses of the event and its planning. Evaluation will be covered in full in Chapter 14.

The cynic would say that each year a great deal of time and effort will go into the business plan, and each year before the plan is issued it will be out of date. Due to the dynamic nature of business, there is a measure of truth in this. Notwithstanding, unless an organization has a long-range plan it will not be possible to develop future goals and appropriate capabilities as conditions change. Changes or additions to the portfolio of activities, location, computer systems, recruitment and training of people etc. cannot happen overnight, but once such decisions have been taken and carried out they cannot be undone in a hurry.

The event manager, pressed with 'real' day-to-day operational problems, may be tempted to avoid involvement in what might be seen as esoteric long-term planning. However, if the event manager is only marginally involved in long-term planning, the business policies with important long-term operational ramifications will be made by strategic planners, accountants and marketing directors. Generally these people will not fully appreciate the time and effort needed to develop a distinctive operational competence for unique events and for a unique client base. Indeed, they might consider that the *real* work has been done in gathering the information and in making the plan, and that implementing the plan is by comparison a straightforward matter. Rather than trying to avoid involvement in long-term planning, the astute event manager will therefore press for inclusion in the planning process. In many of the small event-management companies, the event manager is already a member of the Board. Only by involvement in the long-range planning process can the manager hope to influence future operations and the style of events.

An event management company will need to have established its own goals and objectives, and where it sees itself in over three years time. In many cases the event management company will have other companies as its clients. In order to satisfy those clients, who in many cases will therefore be its customers, it is important that the event management company understands its clients' goals and objectives as clearly as it understands its own.

The following explanations can apply to an event management company or to a department within a larger organization, and to the myriad of clients that it serves.

The detailed six-stage event-planning process

The six-stage event-planning process consists of the following steps:

1. Define goals and the target market
2. Research critical success factors (CSFs)
3. Determine the skills and resources required
4. Link the skills and resources to the CSFs
5. Develop strategies
6. Finalize plans.

The first step in the planning process is to define the organization's goals and objectives, and to set priorities. This step will be built on the vision (the reason for being of the operation), and can be presented as a mission statement. A series of questions is suggested below to aid planners in asking pertinent questions and in thinking strategically about the business and where it wants to be in the future:

- What sort of company are you?
- Where do you want to be in a few years' time?
- What are your main targets?
- Who or what is the main market?
- What is your main style of event?
- What do your customers value?

It may take some time before the answers to these questions can be answered honestly and clearly. The answers, and the analysis which preceded them, will assist in this first step.

The second step occurs when, having decided on your main market, your main customers and your main style of events, you need to ascertain what it is your customers want. Remember, we looked at this in Chapter 5 during the analysis stage of the event operations management model. Questions include:

- What are the critical success factors that your customers demand?
- What will make you better than the competition?
- What opportunities exist?

The third step is to determine the competencies, skills and resources required to deliver your customers' needs. You would do this by critically auditing your internal strengths and weaknesses. In Chapter 5 we considered the elements of an organization and the linkages between each of the functions within the organization. How can these linkages and relationships be strengthened in order to add strength to your organization?

For example, a winning football team is not just eleven fantastic players working well with the ball, attacking their opponent's goal and defending their own goal. It is instead a gigantic team of partnerships working well together, being aware of each other and together being so much more than just eleven players. If each player equals one point, then the sum of a well-integrated team on the field should equal at least twenty. This is the theory of synergy, where $2 + 2 = 5$!

The fourth step is to link competences and resources to external forces and situations. As discussed in Chapter 3, this is done by reviewing external influences under the headings of political factors, economic factors, technology, and competition, and by carrying out an internal audit. The results of these analyses should form part of the summary of the organization's SWOT (strengths, weaknesses, opportunities and threats) analysis.

Opportunities and threats are external to the business, and strengths and weakness are internal aspects. Examples of strengths might be financial stability, good networking opportunities, and a good client base and reputation; weaknesses might be lack of skilled staff and a poor cash flow. An opportunity might be an emerging new market, and a threat will surely be new and emerging competition.

Case study 7.1

The Royal Horticultural Society

An objective as articulated in the mission statement for the Royal Horticultural Society might read:

> *to support our members and protect Britain's gardening heritage and help gardeners everywhere.*

From its foundation in 1804, the Royal Horticultural Society has grown to be the world's leading horticultural organization. In order to achieve their aim, one of the Society's objectives could be:

> *to continue its commitment to gardeners through inspirational flower shows, gardens, and over 1000 lectures and demonstrations, and to make sure these are easy to access throughout the UK.*

In order to support this objective, it can be seen that they have four flagship gardens – Wisley in Surrey, Rosemoor in Devon, Hyde Hall in Essex, and Harlow Carr in North Yorkshire.

Using our internal audit from the theory above, these gardens should be classed as one of the Society's major resources. Not only are they superb gardens, but also their added value is that they provide year-round interest and demonstrate the best gardening practices and new techniques.

When we consider internal competences, it can be seen that the RHS has, through networking and strategic alliances, promoted gardening by joining forces with over eighty gardens in the UK and twenty in Europe.

The Society organizes The Chelsea Flower Show and two other garden shows, at Hampton Court Palace and Tatton Park in Cheshire. It collaborates with botanists, entomologists, plant pathologists, plant physiologists, soil scientists and general horticultural advisors to ensure that the best and most up-to-date advice is available for all.

Note the simplicity of this part of their mission statement. There are no grand statements, such as to be the best, to provide excellent service, or that people are our greatest resource and so on.

Note also the brevity of the strategies, and how each is limited to supporting the mission. It could be said that ideally strategy is specific in the abstract, but not specific on detail. By not attempting to provide the specific details, plenty of scope is left for operational contingencies within the broad framework of the general strategy.

(Further information is available at www.rhs.org.uk.)

It is not sufficient merely to list strengths, weaknesses, opportunities and threats. The real purpose is to determine what actions have to be taken to capitalize on the strengths, eliminate the weaknesses, counter threats and to exploit opportunities. Often a threat, if considered in a positive manner, can be turned into an opportunity.

The fifth step is to develop strategies to enable achievement of the business objectives. In simple terms, objectives/goals are *what* we want to do, and strategies are *how* we will do it – i.e. the necessary actions required to make the objectives happen. Case study 7.1 provides an illustration.

The sixth step is when the strategy is finalized, and action plans can then be made. These concern the specific details about the event – for example, how many people are coming, over what time period, and how much space is required?

Implementation of these plans will be discussed in Chapter 14.

Life cycle of services

Now that we have covered the different stages within the six-stage event-planning process, we can turn to other aspects that are essential to support the planning and of which every event manager should be aware. These can be seen within the second stage of the event operations management model. This chapter investigates the life cycle of services and the Boston Consulting Group Matrix (BCG); the other aspects are covered in subsequent chapters within Section 2 of the book.

Service products have definite life cycles (see Figure 7.1). In some regards this is no different to our own mortality. Human beings have a finite life, and so do products and services.

As illustrated in Figure 7.1, the stages of the life cycle are:

- *Development* of a new idea. This stage requires research and market testing; no income is received and costs (often substantial) are incurred.
- *Launch* of a new service. This stage can include heavy marketing costs and small initial returns. Entry into the market is often risky, and may be accompanied by pilot stages. However, in events it is very difficult to pilot new ideas – ideas are needed in full by the client.
- *Growth*. This is marked by rapid market acceptance and increasing profits. Also, competitors typically will copy or develop new market segments in order to avoid direct competition (Evans *et al.*, 2003). This is an important time to win market share.

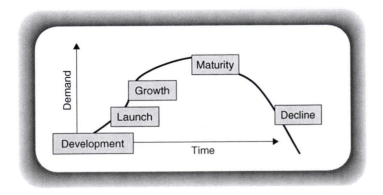

Figure 7.1 Life cycle of events

- *Maturity*. At maturity, income stabilizes as growth levels off. This stage can range from days or weeks to many decades. It is less likely within the event industry that the timescale will be so long. The positive cash flows should be reinvested in new products to replace the mature ones that are leaving the marketplace.
- *Decline*. During decline, sales fall and eventually the service is phased out or updated and the cycle begins again. Organizations should be ready with new products, or have strategies to extend the life cycle if this is felt to be feasible.

Case study 7.2 reports on the progress of the Badminton Horse Trials.

Case study 7.2

The Mitsubishi Motors Badminton Horse Trials, 4–8 May 2005, South Gloucestershire, England

The Mitsubishi Motors Badminton Horse Trials are generally regarded as the World's premier three-day event. Held every year since 1949 in the beautiful parkland of the Duke of Beaufort, the event always attracts the majority of the leading horses and riders in the world.

The number of spectators is close to 200 000, while the tented village contains 275 trade stands.

The first phase of the event, dressage, is split between the first two days, Thursday and Friday. Saturday sees the spectacular cross country test – the horses covering over ten miles before they tackle the four-and-a-half mile course of obstacles around the park. Action is continuous, with a horse starting every three to four minutes. Finally, on Sunday, comes the climax, which is a normal set of show jumps – but after the cross country, clearing them is not easy.

(Information supplied by Langston Scott Ltd; for more information on hospitality at the Mitsubishi Badminton Horse Trials see www.langstonscott.com.)

The following report was written in 2003:

Mitsubishi Motors Badminton Horse Trials to build on last year's new-look success

A revamped Badminton in 2002 drew record crowds, after the year lost to foot and mouth disease in 2001. The course was re-jigged using the traditional pathway, but starting in the main arena. This has encouraged event Director Hugh Thomas to introduce more innovations. 2002 also saw the introduction of the Badminton Club, which is located by the arena and allows members to relax ringside and see the action unfold on all four days of the competition. The stature of the world's premier three-day event is likely to be further enhanced by the recently announced change of the Olympic competition to one-day event status. Badminton will continue to provide a major target for the world's leading riders.

The Box Office opened on 6 January 2003 and, as ever, attracted business immediately. The enhanced on-line booking service from the website is likely to prove popular as the best way of booking. (www. badminton-horse.co.uk).

In an attempt to speed up entry into the park, a new ticketing policy has been introduced for day sales. Forward car parks will now only be available for advanced sales.

Due to popular demand, and a jump in radio earphone technology, Radio Badminton makes a comeback with a new team, and should add another dimension to the enjoyment of all enthusiasts.

(Information supplied by www.badminton-horse.co.uk.)

The final report was written in 2004:

Badminton to stick to present format

The organizers of the Mitsubishi Motors Badminton Horse Trials announced today that the event would not change its format for future events.

Event Director Hugh Thomas commented:

When the International Equestrian Federation decided to drop the Steeplechase and Roads & Tracks from the cross country day for the Olympics on the grounds of cost, we supported the change. We also recognize that the slightly less taxing form of the sport may well be appropriate when it is necessary to generate the widest possible international participation. However, we have always believed that the 'full' sport provides a greater all-round test of horse and rider, and we were very disappointed when the Federation also dropped these phases for its own World Equestrian Games.

We have consulted very widely about the future, and it is clear that the vast majority of participants in the sport want us to continue to offer the ultimate challenge. Badminton was founded to prepare horses and riders for the rigours of the Olympic Games, and since then it has evolved into the world's premier three-day event and we intend to ensure that riding at and eventually winning Badminton remains the great aspiration for all youngsters entering the sport.

To compete for the Mitsubishi Motors Trophy is of course an exclusive privilege that has to be earned by excellent performance; but we know from the number of 'first timers' in recent events that new, young talent can indeed come to the fore at Badminton – if you are good enough, you can compete. Equally, the Roll of Honour includes the very best horses and riders of each generation, acknowledged to be so partly because of their success here.

We are consulting with our colleagues at Lexington and Burghley as to how we might widen and deepen the links between these top 'four-star' events, building on the success of the Rolex Grand Slam, won by Pippa Funnell in 2003. Possibilities such as a 'Masters' or 'Super League' series will be explored, so that the top riders are well rewarded for success at the top events.

Our sport has evolved over many years, and we at Badminton have no desire to stay rooted in the past. We will remain flexible to meet challenges from whatever quarter, including the British weather.

(Information kindly provided by the Press Office; further information about the Mitsubishi Badminton Horse Trials can be found at www.badminton-horse.co.uk.)

Reflective practice 7.1

Consider Case study 7.2.

1. What challenges does Badminton face at this stage in its growth?
2. What would you consider the stage to be?
3. What external influences could have an impact on the life cycle of Badminton Horse Trials?

Management actions

Each stage of the life cycle will require different actions and decisions.

The development stage will require operations to be involved in determining feasibility, acquiring necessary resources, training people and establishing a standard procedure.

The launch stage will need the ability of operations to service fast-growing demand, and to be able to handle novel and unexpected problems. Procedures might have to be modified and people retrained to act in a standard fashion.

In the growth stage, operations will likely be challenged by fluctuating and uncertain demands.

By the time the maturity stage is reached, standard procedures should be in place and people will know instinctively how to react to problems; in short, stability should have been achieved. This is the stage when there should be time to look for improvements to the service and to improve efficiency. Unfortunately, when the pressure is off, sales are good and objectives are being comfortably achieved, the temptation will *be not* to look for changes, and complacency sets in. Nonetheless there will always be room for improvements, and ideally the culture of the organization will be to seek to make incremental improvements.

The decline stage will bring another set of problems; either changes of a decisive nature will have to be made to the service to arrest the decline, or an entirely new service will have to be developed.

Kotler (1991) identified four implications arising from the product life cycle:

1. Products and services have a limited life
2. The different stages pose different challenges to the professional
3. Profits rise and fall at different stages of the life cycle
4. Products and services require different marketing, operations, purchasing and personnel strategies in each stage of the life cycle.

Slack (1998) points out that this last point implies that the operations manager will have to set new objectives as the product or service ages in its market.

Case study 7.3 describes the development of the Notting Hill Carnival.

Case study 7.3

The Notting Hill Carnival, London, England

The Notting Hill Carnival, held annually in August, actually began in St Pancras in 1964 and moved around until it found its home in Notting Hill. The Carnival's roots date back to the Abolition of Slavery Act in 1833, when the first Caribbean carnival was held in Trinidad and black Caribbeans took to the streets for their own carnival party, with song, dance and costumes.

Over the next century, carnival developed into a strong Caribbean tradition, particularly in Trinidad, where the five disciplines of carnival were established.

This great festival in Notting Hill began initially from the energies of black immigrants from the Caribbean, in particular from Trinidad, where the Carnival tradition is very strong, and from people living locally, who dreamed of creating a festival to bring together the people of Notting Hill, most of whom were facing racism, lack of working opportunities and poor housing conditions, resulting in generally low self-esteem.

There had been racial tensions in the late 1950s, and black people were subjected to constant pressures. Dances were organized in halls in North London, where black people could come together freely. At the same time, Trinidadians who had immigrated to this country were playing steel band music each Sunday at the Colherene Pub in Earls Court. From this evolved the idea of inviting the steel band to take part in a street festival in Notting Hill, to encourage people, mainly children, both black and white, to come onto the streets and express themselves socially as well as artistically. This first Carnival took place in 1964 in St Pancras Town Hall, organized by *West Indian Gazette* editor, Claudia Jones. As other West Indian immigrants and white locals joined the festivities year on year, the carnival grew to its current huge proportions.

In recent years the Notting Hill Carnival has grown and grown, reflecting the multicultural nature of our society, with participants from Afghanistan, Kurdistan, Bangladesh, the Philippines, Bulgaria, Russia, Brazil and many other places as well as from all parts of the Caribbean, Africa, Central and South America and the United Kingdom. The Notting Hill Carnival operates an all-inclusive policy, encouraging artists to celebrate their cultural traditions through the art, dance and music media with which they feel most comfortable.

In addition to the procession of costumes, soca and steel bands which wend their way over a route of some three miles, the area plays host to 45 licensed Static Sound Systems, each playing its own selection of soca, reggae, jazz, soul, hip-hop and funk music, house, and garage. This is the aspect of the Carnival that appeals to young people and is evolving at an unpredictable pace with innovative styles and forms of music.

There are hundreds of licensed street stalls selling exotic foods from all corners of the globe, as well as arts and crafts. The Carnival aims to celebrate the cultural heritage of its founders and at the same time be open enough to take on board evolving contemporary culture with its multiracial, multicultural trends.

In addition to the traditional aspects of the Carnival, there are also three live stages within the Carnival area, featuring local bands, top international artistes, and music from all around the world. These stages play from 12 noon to 7 pm on each of the two days. Artistes that have appeared at these stages have included Eddie Grant, the Mighty Sparrow, Arrow, Freddie McGregor, Burning Spear, Jamiroquai, Wyclef Jean, Amaponda and Courtney Pine, amongst others.

For many people, the Notting Hill Carnival has become a celebration and reflection of London's uniquely multicultural make-up. But what of the next 40 years?

Any talk of improving the event usually centres on two things – a change in route, and economics. In 2003, the Carnival suffered the disappointment of a reduced attendance compared to previous years. As a result, it lost its status as Europe's biggest street party to the Zurich Street Parade.

Recent attendance figures are as follows:

2003	600 000
2002	1.4 m
2001	1.25 m
2000	1.5 m
1999	1.4 m
1998	1.15 m
1997	1.3 m
1996	1 m

The 2004 Notting Hill Carnival celebrated its 40th anniversary under the theme 'Freedom and Justice'. Because the safety and enjoyment of everyone at the Carnival was paramount, they decided not to focus on increasing the number of activities; instead a longer programme of events was planned that started in April 2004 and ran through until December. This included the World Steel Band Music Festival in October 2004, which featured steel bands from Europe, the Caribbean, North America, Grenada, Antigua and, of course, Trinidad – the birthplace of the steel band.

The long-term vision for the Carnival has to be its continued development and growth – not in terms of the numbers attending the event but in the development of commercial and professional opportunities for bands, individuals and the company; and the integration of Carnival arts into mainstream education.

The long-term aim of London Notting Hill Carnival Ltd (LNHCL) is:

to attract the level of sponsorship for the Notting Hill Carnival that is commensurate with the income that it generates, and which is in line with the level of sponsorship for other national events, without compromising its integrity.

(Debbie Gardner)

According to a report by the London Development Agency (LDA), the Carnival creates £93 m for London. Figures from the LDA show that the event supports 3000 full-time jobs. Many feel that the best way of maximizing the benefits of the Carnival would be to change the route. The narrow streets of Notting Hill provide a cramped – and according to London's mayor, dangerous – environment for the million or so revellers.

Although the roots of carnival are Trinidadian, the Notting Hill Carnival is a British event. This is something that should be celebrated, as it is what makes the event unique.

(Information supplied from www.mynottinghill.co.uk and from BBC News at bbcnews. co.uk.)

Reflective practice 7.2

Regarding Case study 7.3:

1. How has the Notting Hill Carnival developed over the past forty years?
2. What stage of the life cycle do you think the Carnival has reached?
3. If the Carnival were in decline, what steps could the organizers take to change this?

Criticisms of the product life cycle

Evans *et al.* (2003) point out that it is difficult to forecast the future, and to pinpoint accurately where a product or service will leave one stage of the product life cycle and enter the next. However it could be said that *not* to try to forecast and *not* to anticipate changes in the external environment and actions by your competitors is dangerous practice.

Managers should be careful not to over-anticipate decline and believe that it is happening when the reality may be somewhat different. If management assumes that decline will come, come what may, then decisions may be made to reduce investment, and so decline will come sooner than it might have done.

The Boston Consulting Group matrix

The product life cycle can be clearly linked to the Boston Consulting Group matrix. This offers a way of examining a company's portfolio of products. In the event industry there may be a flourishing company that specializes in student club nights, twenty-first birthday party events, hen parties and club tours. Some of these events may be in different capital cities throughout the UK, and the same company may also have links to different student unions and take bookings direct from them. Each of these different 'products' and different major clients forms part of the company's portfolio.

A broad portfolio signifies that an organization has a wide range of products and market sectors (Evans *et al.*, 2003), and conversely a narrow portfolio implies that a company only operates in a few or even one product or sector. The narrower the portfolio the more emphasis can be put on that product, but it can also be more vulnerable to a turndown in demand, or exploitation by a competitor or supplier.

The Boston Consulting Group (BCG) matrix (Figure 7.2) simplifies the analysis of the range of products or services within a company's portfolio. There are two axes on

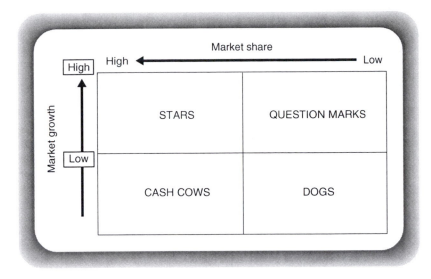

Figure 7.2 The Boston Consulting Group matrix

the matrix; the vertical axis denotes rate of market growth, which indicates the potential and attractiveness of the market, and the horizontal axis is an indicator of the strength of the competitive position of the product – i.e. its market share.

Using the BCG matrix

The BCG matrix divides products into cash cows, dogs, stars and question marks.

Cash cows

'Cash cows' are products with a high market share in a low-growth market. They are normally profitable and generate cash – i.e. they can be milked. Like living cows, however, they should not be neglected. Since the market is low growth, customers are able to change their loyalties, and competitors may be able to move swiftly. The products or services in this part of the matrix should be watched closely. Used wisely, the profits from cash cows can be used to support new ideas and rising stars.

You can see that there is a similarity between cash cows and those products and services, which have reached maturity on the product life cycle.

Dogs

'Dogs' are products that have a low market share in a low-growth market. They are typically not very profitable, but beware – some dogs are essential to your cash cows, so don't throw them away without thinking. It may be expensive to cultivate the market to create market growth, but perhaps a niche market could be found. Generally, dogs are associated with only a small positive cash flow or indeed a negative cash flow.

You can see that there is a similarity between dogs and those products and services that are in decline in the product life cycle.

Stars

'Stars' have a high share in a rapidly growing market. They could be absorbing large amounts of cash, but may be highly profitable. It is often necessary to spend heavily on advertising, but in the end stars may become cash cows. If market share is lost, they may become dogs when the market ultimately stops growing – so they need to be watched.

You can see that there is a similarity between stars and those products and services that are in the growth stage of the product life cycle.

Question marks

Some texts refer to these as problem children. Question marks create a dilemma for the company manager. They have a foothold in the market, but if market share cannot be improved they will become dogs. Resources need to be channelled to them to improve market share. These products, services or a particular event should be questioned.

You can see that there is a similarity between question marks and those products and services that are in the growth or indeed the decline stage of the product life cycle. They use cash, and at this stage do not generate high returns.

Chapter summary and key points

In this chapter the need to plan has been discussed. In simple terms, planning is forward looking and considers what we want to do, how we will do it, and when we will do it. However, planning is both forward looking and backward looking. The wise planner looks back to see what happened, what went right and what went wrong for similar events. The planner then attempts to forecast what will happen and what might happen, based on past experience, knowledge of the current external environment, an understanding of the relative strengths and weaknesses of the organization (internal environment), and taking into account changes that are likely to happen in the external and internal environments. The cynic will say that a plan is out of date as soon as it is made, but without planning, chaos is likely. Plans need to be reasonably detailed, but those carrying out the plans must be allowed a degree of flexibility.

We have shown that planning is linked to the product life cycle and that different stages of the life cycle require different management actions.

Chapter 8
Product development

Learning Objectives

After reading through this chapter you will be able to:

- **Appreciate product development and innovation**
- **Use Ansoff's growth matrix to assist in the creation of new ideas**
- **Understand the simultaneous development of new events**
- **Apply the design process to events and use flow charts.**

Introduction

Chapter 7 introduced the first part of the detailed planning stage. In that chapter we discussed the positioning of different products both on the product life cycle and within a company's portfolio. It is now important to see how event managers can develop products. This aspect is covered within the second stage of the event operations management model.

Changes in society, markets, economies and society have led to a shortening of the product life cycle, and it has intensified the need for organizations to innovate in terms of the products they offer (Evans *et al.*, 2003). Similarly, increasing competition has made innovation a necessity, and event managers must always be aware that they are not able to sit still, believing that they are on the right track and therefore immune from competition and change – you must always be looking over your shoulder, or you will get knocked over by the next passing train!

In today's fast-moving market, event managers have to be able to react quickly to marketplace changes. Time is at a premium in gaining the initiative over the competition with a new service, or in catching up and reacting to a new service offered by a competitor. Customers are fickle, and once lost are hard to regain.

New products and services

New products and services and ideas for different events can be achieved by:

- Repackaging – i.e. promoting in a different manner
- Making minor modifications to existing products and service
- Introducing completely new products/events
- Reaching new markets.

For example, outdoor adventure tours (white-water rafting etc.), once designed for young backpackers, might now be toned down (safer water) and repackaged as 'grey power' adventure experiences for the older market.

Other initiatives might mean the same basic service but with extra benefits, a reduced price, or at a different time. Whenever changes are being contemplated, the events manager needs to be in a position to make suggestions and to be involved in the final decision.

Innovation

Some event organizations will position themselves as market leaders; this can be a high-risk strategy, as time and money will be required to develop and set up the infrastructure needed. On the other hand, being first in the market can reap large benefits.

Other organizations will seek to imitate the innovations of others, and will attempt to join in the initial growth phase of a new service.

Still others will join in with adaptations before the market becomes saturated with suppliers, or will endeavour to find a specialized niche market. Others will add nothing new, but will rely on size and efficiency to enter the market at lower prices.

Ansoff's matrix

Ansoff (1987) developed a matrix which highlights the choices managers can make when designing new products and services. The matrix, shown in Figure 8.1, shows potential areas where a company can extend. There are four broad alternatives:

1. Market penetration – increasing market share in existing markets utilizing the same existing products/services
2. Market development – entering new markets but still using the same existing products/services
3. Product development – developing new products/services to serve existing markets
4. Diversification – developing new products to serve new markets.

There are risks with all new developments. It is a risk as to whether the event that has been planned is going to be well received and successful. The risks are smallest when development is largely based upon existing products and services, and takes place in existing markets (Campbell *et al.*, 2003). The risks are greater the further an event

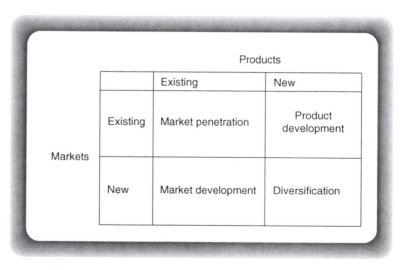

Figure 8.1 Ansoff's Growth Matrix

organization moves away from its existing markets and products, and the more it develops new ideas and events. This entry into new ventures should depend upon the event manager assessing what opportunities present themselves, the likelihood of success, and how well the proposed event matches the core competences and skills of the organization, their past experiences and existing resources.

Simultaneous development

Simultaneous development of a new product, service or event is where the process of development is expedited by integrating each stage of the development using multifunctional teams rather than having each function working individually in sequence stage by stage. Multifunctional project teams can be set up to design and develop a new event. In this manner, strong two-way communication is fostered. Because event operations are reliant on customers as input for the event to happen, the design of a new service will mainly involve the process by which it will be delivered.

It is difficult in event management to produce a prototype 'product', although a new approach can be tested in a small, localized market. As customers must be involved, a flow process chart can be a useful tool for development and comparison of alternatives. The flow process chart will show in detail all the processes through which the customer will pass. However, for many events the customer will never come into contact with the back office activities, such as exist for a horticulture show, a football match or a banquet. Nonetheless, such activities are essential to the provision of the event, and it is crucial that these areas, and the suppliers to the system, are not ignored when considering the feasibility of providing the event. Therefore the flow process chart will need to cover the value chain from supplier to customer, and should consider the time taken for each activity. Examples of flow process charting are provided later in this chapter.

The design process

The design process for a new event, or for the development of a variation to an existing ongoing repeated event (such as weekly football matches), has six distinct phases:

1. The idea – the initial thought
2. The concept – determination of a need and the start of creating a package
3. Systematic and rapid screening of various alternatives
4. Development of the new approach and preliminary design
5. Testing the new approach or offering
6. Launching on a commercial scale.

The idea

Ideas for new products or services, and concepts or new ways of delivering an event, can come from a variety of external and internal sources.

Slack *et al.* (2004) have identified external sources as being customers and competitors, and internal sources as being staff who are in contact with the customers, and the research and development department (see Figure 8.2).

Internal sources

1. *Staff*. People who work within an event organization can be rich in ideas regarding what is possible in the future. Similarly, those who are in contact with customers glean a lot of information, both informally in conversations and formally in focus groups, or

through letters of complaint and thanks. Sometimes your staff may have worked for one of your suppliers in the past, or indeed have worked for one of your competitors. Staff have both a very good general and specific idea of what customers like and dislike. They may have gathered ideas from other people, or they may make suggestions based on their own observations. All the time you need to find out what your customer rates as being the key success factors and then create ideas as to how you can close the gap between what you do provide and what the customer wants. Use your staff for ideas and do not just rely on your own intuition.

2. *Research and development*. Research is a function that might be formally set up within the event organization, or just assigned to certain people for short periods of time. Research involves discovering and developing new knowledge in order to solve a problem. Development is the means of putting that new knowledge into practice. Research may centre on different forms of creating and delivering the event to see if, by harnessing different ideas, new opportunities may present themselves. This may involve different technologies, or just carrying out activities in a slightly different way – perhaps by being open to ideas and trying them out. For example, using on-line

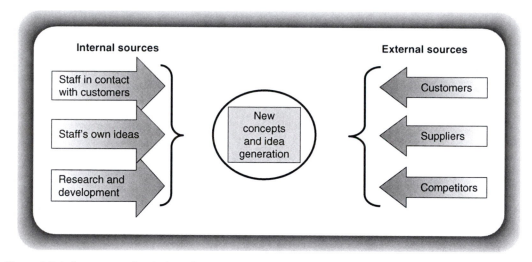

Figure 8.2 Influences on the design of an event

Case study 8.1

Royal Ascot, 15–19 June 2004, Ascot Racecourse, Berkshire, England

Wi-Fi facilities were introduced at Royal Ascot in 2004.

Although Ascot Racecourse was being demolished in 2004 to be replaced by a new state-of-the-art racing venue, new Wi-Fi facilities were installed for the media in the two pressrooms. This enabled the photographers and reporters to download pictures and copy instantly to their editors from anywhere within these areas, and was seen by the media as an important improvement. It was especially useful because of the huge national and international interest from the public and the media who attend Royal Ascot Week.

(Information printed by courtesy of Royal Ascot; for more information see www.ascot.co.uk.)

Reflective practice 8.1

Regarding Case study 8.1:

1. What benefits, apart from the obvious increased transmission speeds, do Wi-Fi offer the media?
2. How does the use of technology enhance the competitive edge of Royal Ascot?

booking rather than selling tickets at a box office led to a Rod Stewart concert in New Zealand being sold out in half an hour. Case study 8.1 provides another example. Ideas may come from different industries, and those concepts transferred to the problem under investigation.

External sources

1. *Customers.* Marketing is responsible for keeping an ear to the ground in order to identify new opportunities and possible services that would be appropriate. However, event managers should not just rely on this source. There are many ways to gather intelligence, some formal and some informal – for example, newspaper reports, journal articles, popular TV shows, information commercials, chat in the clubhouse after golf etc. The message is that all event managers should listen to ideas, hold focus groups, use systematic analysis and discussion, and look carefully at both complaints and suggestions. Above all, they should be aware of what the competition is doing, or successes other organizations have had in related areas and sometimes not closely related areas. For example, Henry Ford developed the conveyor belt approach to assembling cars after visiting an abattoir and seeing animals being disassembled on a moving production line.
2. *Suppliers.* In the events industry we use many different suppliers and partnerships with other specialists. They may have come across different situations and different remedies, and often their ideas will be helpful to both you and the supplier and, eventually, to your customers.
3. *Competitors.* You may have the choice of following the actions of your competitors or coming up with a similar idea but using some new approaches. You are aiming to take the lead and be innovative, but you may be able to learn from your competitors' mistakes or achievements.

Ideas are not the same as concepts. Ideas get transformed into concepts so that they can be evaluated and put into operation by the organization (Slack *et al.*, 2004).

Concepts

Concepts are different from ideas in that they have clear statements and can state the overall form, function and purpose. The concept should be easy for the event manager to communicate to all of the different stakeholders (see Figure 8.3).

In Figure 8.3, the concept has started to give meaning and shape to the event. In particular it has defined its duration, purpose, facilities available, target market and some perspective of price and costs. Spin-off opportunities could include refreshments and merchandising. A sponsor might be a soft drinks company.

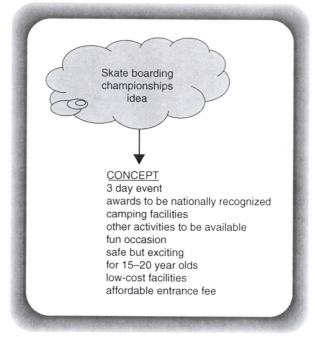

Figure 8.3 Ideas are not the same as concepts

Systematic and rapid screening of various alternatives

Not all the concepts generated will be appropriate or capable of being taken further. The event manager will have to be selective and screen which concept to progress. Slack *et al.* (2004) offer several different screening processes that could be used in order to appraise the suggested concept systematically. There may be other screens more appropriate for different event companies in different situations, but Slack *et al.*'s are offered here.

1. *Marketing screen.* The event manager must ask certain questions and answer them honestly:
   - Will this new approach work in the current market?
   - Is it very similar to other competing products?
   - Is it too different from other competing products?
   - Is there sufficient demand to make it worthwhile?
   - Does it fit with existing marketing policy?
2. *Operations screen.* The operations manager, or the event manager, should judge whether the new concept is feasible and whether it can be achieved:
   - Are sufficient quantities of the right resources available?
   - Is there sufficient space capacity?
   - Are the skills in the staff currently employed relevant and appropriate?
   - What technology is necessary?
   - What is the expected cost?
3. *Finance screen.* The finance department needs to calculate the financial implications of the new ideas. If there is no finance department the event manager will probably have to work out the associated costs, such as:
   - Capital costs
   - Operating costs

– Profit margins
– Likely payback rate.

This set of questions, offered by Slack *et al.* (2004), is very useful for the event manager, but it may also be necessary to consider more pertinent issues that should be added to the above lists. Each company is different, and each situation has its own issues, limitations and opportunities.

Development of the new approach and preliminary design

Having generated an event that is acceptable to the various functions within the company, it is now necessary to specify all the components parts and service required, and to define how the event will be created and delivered.

Take, for example, for a two-day outdoor teambuilding weekend. Each activity will require certain materials. One activity could be eight people making a square from a long rope whilst blindfolded. The materials needed would be:

- A bag containing eight blindfolds
- 60 metres of rope
- Instructions for the exercise
- A stopwatch.

Other activities will require their own lists of equipment, materials and skilled personnel. Gradually all the materials required for the whole of the two-day event, including all food and accommodation, will be listed. This is sometimes called the Bill of Materials (BOM).

Once the BOM has defined all that is required for the event, the next stage is to specify how the days will run. How will all the processes be put together to create the final event?

Different flow charts showing all the people and information 'flowing through' the event can be used. All the activities that take place can be listed and how they fit together shown. Imagine doing this for the Olympics!

All the flow charts are useful for event managers. They show, in a diagrammatic form, the shape of the event and the sequence of activities that will take place. This is useful in three respects:

1. It makes the operations manager think through all that is intended to happen
2. It acts as a communication tool for all the other personnel and suppliers who are involved
3. It identifies any bottlenecks or possible problems.

Slack *et al.* (2004) have identified several different flow charts: We will discuss the following as being relevant to the event industry:

- Simple flow charts
- Flow process charts
- Customer processing charts.

Simple flow charts

Simple flow charts identify the main elements of the event. They may also show the key decisions that need to be taken, and the implications of these decisions. They can be used for a set-up procedure for all the shell stands at an exhibition, or they can be used to track a data inputting system for registration at a Charity Gala Dinner where clients may sponsor whole or part tables.

Flow process charts

This type of chart not only shows the flow of work and activities undertaken, but also uses symbols to identify the different types of activities (Figure 8.4). They can therefore be more detailed. You can see the use of the symbols in flow process chart in Figure 8.5.

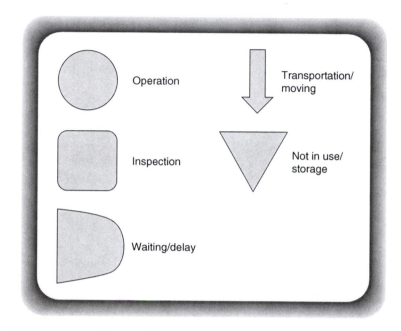

Figure 8.4 Flow process chart symbols

Case study 8.2

Thomas the Tank Engine Education Week, Embsay and Bolton Abbey Steam Railway, North Yorkshire, England

Figure 8.5 shows the flow process chart of the visit of one school group to the Embsay and Bolton Abbey Steam Railway Thomas the Tank Engine Education Week, starting at Embsay Station. There can be up to ten different schools attending between 10:30 and 14:30; all have to travel on a steam engine and a diesel, have lunch, see the entertainer, play the games, go to the shop, stand on Thomas's footplate and go to the toilet. The groups range in number from ten to fifty, an age range from toddler to 6 years. There are two starting and finishing stations, Bolton Abbey and Embsay, which both have large car parks and take buses. The shops and toilets are located on the platform, picnic areas are behind the stations, and entertainment and games are at the side of the stations. There are trains leaving from each station at thirty-minute intervals, alternating between steam and diesel (there is only one steam train and one diesel train).

Figure 8.5 shows the flow process each school will need to go through to visit and take part in all the activities scheduled for the day. Therefore there can be up to ten versions of this process each day during Education Week. More than one group can watch the Punch and Judy and have lunch, but all other activities are for one group at a time only.

(For more information on Embsay and Bolton Abbey Steam Railway see their website at www.pogo.org.uk/railway.)

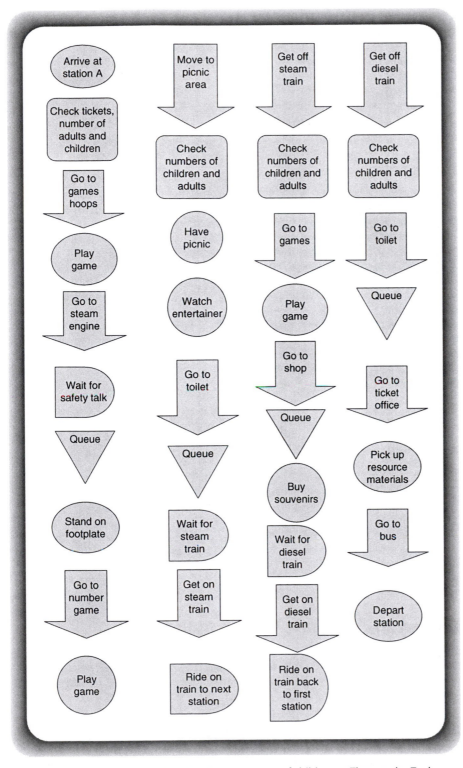

Figure 8.5 Flow process chart showing the movement of children at Thomas the Tank Engine Education Week

Customer processing charts

These charts are of great value to an event manager. They anticipate the choices customers will make as they enter an operation, for example an exhibition. Which way will they turn? What is the shortest route around the exhibition whilst still seeing all of the stands? Where is the information desk, and where are the toilets and the refreshments? Where is the meeting place for friends?

Further questions to be considered include:

- Where is the point of entry into the event?
- What is the first point of contact with a member of the operations team?
- When does the transformation process start?
- When does the customer leave?

An event manager needs to 'walk the event', using the eyes of the customer, and put it down on paper. The customer flow chart can be discussed with other staff to see if they can consider any alternatives and solutions where necessary.

The chart will show the complexity of the event and how many activities will be running in parallel with each other (see Case study 8.2, Figure 8.5).

Figure 8.5 uses the traditional flow process chart symbols to represent the flow, but instead of using the conventional format, information has been incorporated inside each symbol. This, in the opinion of the authors, allows the event manager to have a clearer view of the process.

The process is followed from the top of the first column to the bottom, back to the top of the second column and to the bottom, etc. It charts all the activities required for each group of schoolchildren from beginning to end. By using the symbols, it is possible to see where congestion may occur and in which areas the most movement is taking place.

Reflective practice 8.2

Consider Case study 8.2, and Figure 8.5.

1. If this is the flow process, what impact will it have on customer flow?
2. Look at the chart and identify where blockages may occur.
3. How would you schedule the ten schools? For this exercise, the total number of schoolchildren is 220.
4. At what point is the first point of contact with the operations team?
5. When does the transformation process start, and what is the point of delivery?
6. What other information would you require in order to schedule this event?
7. As a new event, what changes could be made to improve the flow for the customers?

Testing the new approach or offering

The purpose of this stage is to analyse the event and see if it can be improved before being tested in the market. Can the event be designed in a better way, more cheaply or more easily, or so that it matches the customers' expectations and exceeds what the competitors can achieve?

Launching on a commercial scale

Once all the other stages have been completed and systems have been tested, the processes developed can be used to launch other events in different areas. For instance, a successful Christmas Concert in the south of England could be repeated, but with the addition of a second concert in the north of the country. The following year this could be repeated with the addition of other venues in other parts of England. Each venue and concert will potentially present differences, but if the generic model is there it should be easy to translate to the situations. Remember, all the time information is being gathered which will be used to develop and improve the original product.

Chapter summary and key points

This chapter, as part of the second stage of the event operations management model, has considered new product development and shows the advantage of using multifunctional project teams in the design stage.

The spark for new ideas and concepts, apart from the event manager, can come from staff, especially those close to the customer. It can also come from formal research and development teams, opportunities from changing technology, customers, suppliers, and an understanding of what the competition might be up to. Not all concepts will be practical, and systematic screening of concepts will be necessary.

In short, does the market want the event that is being proposed, is it feasible, do we have the resources (including reliable suppliers), do we have the know-how, what will it cost, and is it financially viable?

Once the concept has been screened and accepted, then detailed design is necessary.

The chapter has shown how flow process charting can be used to show the flow of work and activities, and also to show the flow of customers through the event. Once all the above stages have been systematically worked through, the launch can be considered and planned.

Chapter 9
Supply chain management

Learning Objectives

After reading through this chapter you will be able to:

- Understand the importance of supply chain management
- Apply the basic objectives of purchasing and understand the importance of developing relationships with suppliers
- Observe and comment upon the trends in the style of supply networks
- Be aware of the decision points in purchasing.

Introduction

The previous chapters, within the first stage of the event operations management model, illustrated the diversity of the event industry. In Section 2 we look closely at the need to plan carefully and manage the event as a project. The resources and specialisms that are used for each event are diverse, and can be sourced from many different suppliers. Some of the resources may be under the events manager's direct control, and others may be subcontracted or outsourced to agreed specialists – for example, lighting and sound contractors, caterers, musicians and pyrotechnic companies.

This chapter examines the relationships that are essential along the chain of suppliers, and the contribution that this network offers in creating competitive advantage and reliability of each event.

The supply chain is the complete flow of products and services into, through and from the organization (Wild, 2002; Figure 9.1). Managing this chain will normally involve dealing directly with purchasing and supply and inventory management. The feedback that flows backwards is essential because it allows the event manager to see how well received the products, supplies and services were, and whether there should be any changes in the future.

Managing the supply chain

Supply chain management is concerned with managing the flow of materials and information. This flow of resources should be managed from its very origins right up to the point where the customer consumes it – i.e. when the event is put on and being consumed. For example, it is in the event manager's

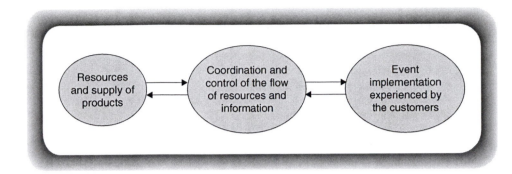

Figure 9.1 The supply chain, showing resources moving forward and feedback flowing backwards

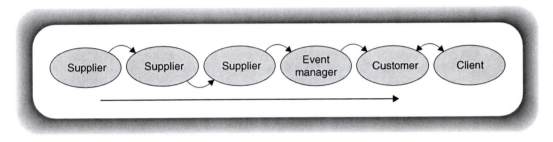

Figure 9.2 The supply chain, showing resources moving forward

interest to know the dance routine and the health and safety procedures of a visiting Spanish dance group using pyrotechnics as part of their show at an outdoor International Festival booked though an agent. Although the agent will have covered many of the details, the event manager will still need to be assured about the suitability of the performance, how it will match the needs of the audience, and how it can be coordinated with all the other activities into a whole event.

In an event there can be many different supply chains through which the varied resources flow. They all have to be managed and coordinated into one event, which is delivered at the moment it is consumed.

Supply chain management is a holistic approach that stretches forward across the event manager's own organization to the client and customers (see Figure 9.2), and backwards through the many different suppliers and to *their* suppliers. By having this holistic approach and integration across company boundaries there can be substantial benefits for all stakeholders. It should be viewed as a chain, and any break in that chain will have an adverse affect on the customer.

The aim is to develop an integrated supply chain to achieve those critical success factors demanded by the customers, the organization and other stakeholders. Unlike most other industries, the project that the event manager is responsible for cannot fail. It must happen on time, and there is no chance of a repeat. For example, a wedding cannot be repeated if the photographer was not booked correctly; Nelson Mandela's speeches, when touring, cannot be repeated if the sound system fails to work as predicted; the Olympic 100-metres final cannot be rerun if the speed recording mechanism fails. If the resources delivered are not of the right standard, the event manager rarely has enough time to look for another supplier. Good project management should leave time for a legal review of all contracts.

Basic objectives of purchasing

Event managers are responsible for providing events at the right cost, the right time, to the right specification and quality, and for the right duration. As discussed previously, the event should achieve a wide range of objectives set by the varied stakeholders, and in order to fulfil those aims the event manager has to purchase and procure all of the resources that make up the event. Slack *et al.* (2004) discuss the traditional objectives of purchasing as being the five 'rights of purchasing'.

1. At the right price
2. For delivery at the right time
3. Of goods and services to the right quality
4. In the right quantity
5. From the right source.

Wild (2002) similarly sees the operations manager as being responsible for providing goods and services of the right specification and quality, at the right time, in the right quantity and at the right price.

These requirements are made even more challenging when many of the resources are purchased through third and fourth parties.

Equally important, as Wild points out, is the need to obtain efficiently, by any ethical means, the best value for every unit of expenditure, and to maintain good relationships with other departments, both within and outside the organization, to ensure an effective operation as a whole.

In Chapter 12, we will also consider how we can develop staff and procedures to ensure the achievement of the event manager's objectives.

Purchasing activities and developing relationships with suppliers

Often within an event company there is not a specific purchasing officer, and many of the staff may create buyer/supply relationships with different companies. Some products may be bought outright and owned by the organization, and others will be used for only one event. In the case of some of the purchase agreements, for example the caterers or pyrotechnic suppliers, it is the whole service and system that is purchased and the contracted company will bring their own products and staff.

To be successful, these relationships and the method of purchasing or leasing must be managed effectively since they all provide vital supply chains throughout the operation.

As discussed in Chapter 5, it is very important to see the companies from whom products and services are purchased not just as suppliers but also as customers. They are customers in the way we ask them for quotations and in respect of whether we pay their invoices on time and accurately. All businesses are both customers for some other businesses products and services, and suppliers of products and services to their own customers (Slack and Lewis, 2002). Every operation and part of an operation should be seen as a network, linking together customers' customers and suppliers' suppliers. Within each company there are many different supply chains that are taking place internally, within the organization and between departments. In the event industry many of the suppliers are specialists and have their own marketplace and rules and regulations to which they must conform. The whole marketplace includes health and safety, government agencies, international companies and international customers, and many other organizations. This can be termed the 'total business environment'.

The event manager should be able to stand back and see the myriad of operations and contracts, working together to deliver the event, as a whole and integrated network of supply chains.

Reflective practice 9.1

On a large piece of paper, draw an integrated diagram of all the different types of suppliers and customers working for an international charity organizing a walk along the Great Wall of China. You should consider all the products and services that are required, from the initial concept until the final review of the event after its completion.

Drawing the supply and customer network has only revealed part of the event manager's work. Slack and Lewis (2002) point out that there are qualitative issues to understand:

1. How does an operation relate to other players in its network?
2. What knowledge of its supply network does it have? Is it close and intimate?
3. Does its supply network have an intimate and close understanding of its own operations, and ultimately its customers' needs and objectives?

Single sourcing or multi-sourcing of suppliers?

To assist in answering these questions, the event manager should be questioning the number of suppliers with whom the organization is involved. Does one supplier provide a 'one-stop shop' where many of the resources required can be purchased, or are there a great many suppliers providing a range of different services for the same event? If the latter is the case, then there are consequently more supply chains to manage, and to manage effectively. It is likely in this case that many brief relationships will be made, since there is not enough time to develop loyalty, trust, and understanding of each other's needs. In reality, depending upon the type of event, a combination of the two policies would be used.

For instance, if you produced classical concerts nationwide you could use a UK-wide sound and lighting company that produces bespoke requirements for each event, including design and set-building, but you would most likely use a local caterer and security company. If it is the former option, i.e. using a 'one-stop shop', the relationship with that supplier can be built upon and this will provide loyalty and understanding of each other's needs. Silver (2004) says that many event professionals recommend that all projects or purchases should be put out to three bids every time to ensure competitive pricing.

On the other hand, we could argue that a company that can be assured of continued business with an organization will provide competitive prices. It avoids quotation and administrative costs, and knows that staff and resources necessary for the provision of the service will be required over a long period of time. This close relationship might be jeopardized if frequent competitive tendering is undertaken. However, complacency within this special relationship must not be allowed to propagate and lead to decreased customer satisfaction or value for money.

Wild (2002) considers the effect of single or multiple company sourcing under four headings:

1. *Effect on price*. Where there is single-supplier sourcing, the price may be reduced due to the increased quantity needed. The price may also be reduced, since the supplier will feel that there is security of sales of the required products and services. However, the price may also be kept lower where there is multi-sourcing, due to increased competition.
2. *Effect on supply security*. Whilst the supply of service will be made simpler by using one supplier, the organization is at risk if something happens to that supplier – for example, strike action, fire or liquidation.
3. *Effect on supplier motivation*. Whilst using one supplier may increase motivation, since the supplier feels valued and may improve the service supplied accordingly, the service may lack competition and therefore there is a risk that poorer service might occur.
4. *Effect on market structure*. If the event organization grows and continues to single-source, it may develop into a monopolistic situation, with the eventual elimination of supply – and hence bring about lack of choice for the customer.

Those services and products that are purchased externally can be outsourced or sub-contracted, and tend to be non-core activities – i.e. those activities that are not central to the company. The difference between outsourcing and subcontracting is dependent upon the transfer of control.

For example, the manager of a gymkhana contracts a catering firm and a local cleaning company and stipulates exactly what he expects them to do as part of the contract – provide a sit-down meal for twenty VIPs, and ensure all rubbish is cleared from the site during and after the event. This is an example of subcontracting – the manager has control over what is done.

In our second example, the management of a racecourse outsource all their catering requirements for the next five years to an outside catering company. The racecourse management want the racegoers to have hospitality available on race days, and to enjoy other functions in keeping with the type and variety of clientele expected to attend the course. How this is achieved and resourced is totally up to the catering company; they have the control. This is outsourcing.

Outsourcing takes place when an organization transfers the ownership of a business process to a supplier. The key to this definition is the aspect of transfer of control. This definition differentiates outsourcing from subcontracting, in which the buyer retains control of the process, or in other words tells the supplier how to do the work. It is the transfer of ownership that defines outsourcing and often makes it such a challenging, painful process. In outsourcing, the buyer does not instruct the supplier how to perform a task, but instead focuses on communicating what services it wants to buy. It then leaves the process of accomplishing those results to the supplier.

Some companies prefer to complete everything in-house – both important and non-important activities. This style of company is known as being vertically integrated; that is, it creates and supplies all the necessary resources and services from within its own boundary.

An example of a vertically integrated company is a circus owner who owns the circus animals; has the artists on payroll; owns the big top, other tents, caravans and transporters; employs his own costume-makers, scene designers and constructors; has a supply of memorabilia for sale; runs a refreshment booth; and does his own promotion.

Case study 9.1 describes the Star Events Group, which is a vertically integrated company.

Case study 9.1

Star Events Group, Bedford, England

The Star Events Group provides staging and rigging products and services for indoor and out-door events. This is achieved through its five divisions, Mobile, VerTech, Design, Orbit and Rigging, all based at Thurleigh, Bedford. The company designs, builds and maintains its own equipment, and its site provides workshop facilities, office accommodation and storage for this purpose. It is an innovative organization that use research and design to promote and develop new safe ways of working while providing the best solutions for their customers. This is a ver-tically integrated organization that can provide all the structures and services required for indoor or outdoor staging, from planning to execution.

Star Mobile provides mobile staging, such as an articulated trailer as a portable version of a permanent structure, some with a solid roof to allow hanging of lights, others with built in electrics and generators.

Star VerTech offers a modular system for staging and structures with in-house structural engineering CAD design and support, plus ground support, screens and special structures.

Star Design provides feasibility, planning, layout, structures, high-level access, rigging, legal requirements, legislation, and safety procedures and checks.

Star Orbit offers classic dome-shaped and arched staging structures.

Star Rigging provides a team experienced in supplying creative rigging solutions, including permanent installations and one-off productions.

(Printed by kind permission of the Star Group; for further information see www.star-hire.com.)

Reflective practice 9.2

Consider Case study 9.1.

1. What other services might Star Events Group consider adding to its portfolio?
2. Would the company need to look for forward or backward integration?
3. If the company were to outsource part of its organization, what would you consider to be an area that is not core?

There are companies that choose to do nothing in-house and to buy in all of their require-ments. This style of company is referred to as being virtual. The merits and disadvan-tages of these approaches are discussed in Chapter 6. Slack and Lewis (2002) describe the networks in virtual organizations as providing information and contacts with other suppliers who can supply the organization with all it wants and needs to supply its customers.

An example of a virtual company is a promoter who arranges the tour of an over-seas ballet troupe, hires the theatres, arranges accommodation for the artists, hires the orchestra, etc., and uses an advertising agency for promotion. In essence, the promoter owns nothing and works from a rented office.

Vertically integrated organizations

As discussed above, vertical integration is the extent to which an organization owns the companies that supply the products and services that it uses.

Making a choice to buy out a supplier, or to make/provide those products and services in-house, would be known as *backwards integration*. In the event industry that might entail buying out a lighting specialist or a catering company, or making all the props for themed evenings in-house rather than using an external company. This may be worthwhile if that specialism is being used a great deal within all events, and if the cost of acquisition and integration into the company would create savings and increase a better provision of what is needed. Other advantages include preventing competitors from gaining control of key suppliers.

Forward integration, as its name suggests, is when an organization buys out or actively completes the work done by a customer. In the event industry, an example might be a lighting or catering company which, instead of always waiting for an event company coming to them to ask for a quotation to supply certain goods and services for an event, proactively seeks out customers and puts on the event itself.

Trends in the style of supply networks

Slack and Lewis (2002) identify three trends in the provision of goods and services and the way that these are sourced. These trends can be seen very clearly in the event industry, possibly because it is a relatively new industry, and possibly due to the diversity of suppliers that are needed and which are not always a part of a small entrepreneurial organization. The trends are:

1. An increase in the proportion of goods outsourced. This enables the organization to concentrate on a few important activities and outsource the rest. This could offer greater competitiveness and efficiency. In the area of technology, in particular, outsourcing enables the company to use up-to-date equipment and specialisms rather than outdated resources. Outsourcing also reduces the amount of capital tied up in assets that might seldom be used.
2. Organizations are reducing the number of suppliers. When you consider the decision points outlined in Figure 9.3, later in this chapter, you will see that there are many activities involved in buying goods and services. If these can be reduced, money and time will be saved. An additional benefit includes building relationships with suppliers that you can trust. Trust develops through past experience and working together. Generally, organizations are developing partnerships with suppliers and customers. In the event industry this may take the form of long-term contracts and an openness of costs and prices between the supplier and the event organization. The suppliers should feel that they are contributing to the success of the event. With this in mind, actively listening to the other party's expectations and needs is a skill. Hearing and giving subtle indicators to each other during negotiations and discussions is an experienced art, and the lowest cost need not always be the driving force (O'Toole and Mikolaitis, 2002).
3. Partnering methods can be taken from other industries, such as construction, which rely on organizations developing a process of mutual trust and understanding within their supply chain. This then opens up the possibility for suppliers to work together in a non-adversarial way and to cooperate on areas such as strategy, benchmarking, process, equity and feedback to develop an integrated supply chain within which all parties can agree to be members (Bennet and Jayes, 1998).

A fourth trend is that of e-commerce and Internet usage. Use of the Internet can provide organizations with up-to-date pricing and availability using on-line ordering. It

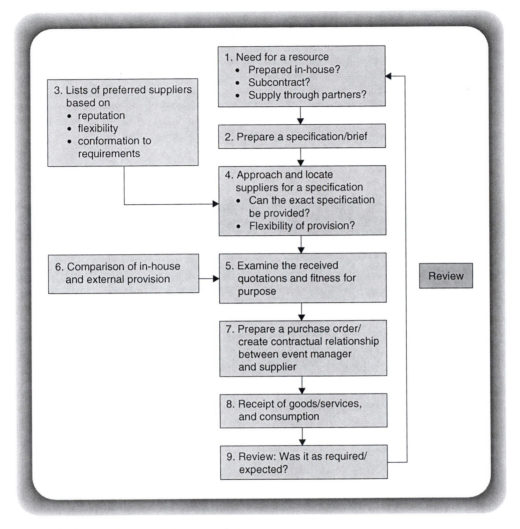

Figure 9.3 Chain of decisions and decision points

eliminates paperwork and can speed up the many processes that would previously have relied on telephone calls, postage systems and person-to-person communications. The Internet also opens up a greater choice of providers.

It can be seen that there are different styles of companies – those that fully own all the parts of the supply chain, and those that regularly outsource and subcontract parts of their services to other specialists.

The major concern is that all parts of the service delivered to the final customer should be managed and integrated. Wild (2002) believes that the strategic objectives of the company will influence how the organization is managed, and that often the integrated flow of materials and services through and from the operation is a prerequisite for achieving high-quality, rapid and low-cost provision for customers. Therefore managing the supply chain is a major concern and of major importance for event organizations, where a high proportion of their products and services often come from different suppliers or different parts of the organization.

In delivering this well-managed supply chain, the aim of the event company should be to diminish obstacles between functions and departments within the organization, minimize activities undertaken, and improve the links between the departments so that there is no unnecessary repetition. External to the organization, the event manager should look to improve communication and relationships with suppliers.

O'Toole and Mikolaitis (2002) see the contract as central to the correct procedure for project planning and implementation. Much is written about contracts in engineering, building and software industries, and event managers can take advantage of lessons learned from successes and failures in these other industries in their use of project management. Each contract specifies who will do what, when and how. It can contain many details, or be a simple letter of agreement or a purchase order.

Case study 9.2 provides an example.

Case study 9.2

Reed MIDEM, Paris, France

Reed Exhibitions (part of the Reed Elsevier Group) is the world's leading organizer of trade and consumer exhibitions, with a portfolio of over 430 events in 32 countries. The company creates high-profile, highly-targeted business and consumer exhibitions, where buyers and suppliers from around the world meet together to do business.

Reed has developed many partnerships with organizations, and through this has provided partners with access to Reed's resources, networks and contacts. Reed has built strategic alliances with a wide range of interested parties, from trade associations and government departments to exhibition venues and organizers. Reed MIDEM is a Paris-based subsidiary of Reed Exhibitions, specializing in B-to-B tradeshows for the television and new technology industries (MIPTV and MIPCOM), the international property industry (MIPIM), the retail real estate sector (MAPIC), and international urban management (GLOBAL CITY). These shows take place in Cannes, France.

A recent example is shown below.

Cannes, 5 October 2004

Reed MIDEM, the organizer of professional, international tradeshows, has signed a ten-year agreement with the City of Cannes, maintaining its international tradeshows on the Cote d'Azur until at least 2014.

'Reed MIDEM has been holding trade shows in Cannes for the past 38 years,'notes Reed MIDEM Chief Executive Officer Paul Zilk. 'I'm delighted that this "marriage" will continue for at least another decade. This agreement allows the City of Cannes and the Palais des Festivals and ourselves, to adopt a long-term strategy. Together, we will continue to work on improving services to our international clients.'

Bernard Brochand, member of France's National Assembly and Mayor of Cannes, says, 'this agreement cements the good relations that have been built up over the years between Reed MIDEM and Cannes. Reed MIDEM is an historic partner with the city and with the Palais des Festivals, which has hosted many of its new exhibitions over the years. Each partner knows what the other brings to the table. Over the last three years, Cannes has significantly improved security, cleanliness and logistical services in order to meet the demands and expectations of exhibition attendees and of the local population.'

David Lisnard, Deputy Mayor of Cannes and Chairman of the Palais des Festivals et des Congrès, comments, 'this deal is the fruit of the considerable hard work from local hoteliers, taxi professionals, restaurant owners and service providers. It recognizes the quality of the services provided by the Palais des Festivals staff and represents economic security for the Cannes region. This is a win–win agreement. It means greater capacity to grow the exhibition business, safeguards the prosperity of Cannes and guarantees jobs. Now we all need to continue to work to further to improve Cannes' ability to compete in this vibrant sector.'

(Printed by courtesy of Reed MIDEM; for more information see www.reedmidem.com.)

Reflective practice 9.3

Consider Case study 9.2.

1. What benefits are there for each party to the ten-year agreement?
2. Chief Executive Paul Zilk says this agreement will allow adoption of a long-term strategy. What might this be?
3. Who are the stakeholders?

Decision points in purchasing for an event organization

The flow diagram in Figure 9.3 outlines the procedures that should be followed leading up to the contract.

Purchasing follows a chain of decisions and points 1–9 are identified below.

1. When it is initially considered that an event should go ahead, there is a need for a range of products and services. There should be detailed discussion regarding how these might best be procured – in-house or from an external company.
2. The next stage is to create a clear specification of what is required.
3. Some organizations may have a list of preferred suppliers. This provides useful contacts regarding reliable companies who are known to deliver as per specification of quality and who also respect and value working with the event manager's organization.
4. Suppliers should be approached for a price and an overview of what they could provide – Can the exact specification be provided? Is there flexibility of provision?
5. When the quotations are returned it is important that they are examined fairly and checked to see that what is being offered is as per specification.
6. The price and quality and reliability may be compared against in-house provision where that is possible.
7. When the event manager is satisfied that the goods and services are as required in all respects, including competitive price and appropriate provision, then an agreement can be made with the supplier. This may be called a purchase order, but in reality what happens is that a contractual relationship is formed between the event manager and the supplier.
8. The goods and services should be delivered as expected. In many instances within the events industry the actually delivery and consumption will be simultaneous. For example, a rock band delivers its services at the moment it is playing for the audience.
9. The final stage is a review. Did the purchased product or service deliver as expected and as required? The review will inform the next set of decisions about a similar service/product.

Further elaboration of decision points 1–9
1. Recognizing a need for a resource

The event manager should critically examine all that is needed for each event, and what resources and provision the customer really values. Is the item or service to be purchased absolutely essential for the event, either indirectly or directly? What exactly is required, and where can it be sourced from – internally or externally? If it can be prepared in-house, what is the cost of this provision and the effect on other activities within the organization? Is the product or service that is required needed for the smooth running of the organization or for a forthcoming event?

Silver (2004) believes that the event organizer should consider the time, money and human resources available. She gives the examples of having sufficient budget but very little time or few personnel to handle certain aspects of the event; or that there may be plenty of volunteers but very little money. The situation may therefore dictate whether products and services are provided from in-house or sourced externally. Whatever the decision, it must ensure that the appropriate resources are sourced effectively and efficiently.

2. Prepare a specification/brief

O'Toole and Mikolaitis (2002) describe a specification as the written description of the required product or service. The suppliers use the specification document to estimate a price and to bid for the contract. However, many of the services required by an event manager are unique and non-standard products, and are not just bought 'off the shelf'. Thus the specification may only act as a guide. Indeed, it may be written only in terms that the organizer understands rather than those that the supplier is more accustomed to.

O'Toole and Mikolaitis (2002) believe that the specification can be described in three ways:

- By function, i.e. what it is supposed to do – for example, the caterers should provide a choice of dishes, the meal should be themed to the evening's entertainment, and enable the customers to serve themselves.
- By technical description – for example, the caterer will supply sufficient food for 100 guests, all food and hygiene laws should be observed, hot food should be served at a minimum temperature of 72°C and cold food held at a maximum temperature of 5°C.
- By performance – for example, the food should be laid out in a buffet style and cleared within 45 minutes, and during this time staff should be on hand to keep the buffet tidy and replenished.

The technical specifications can be very detailed to prevent any misunderstanding. It is very difficult to compare bids from different companies where they are quoting against seemingly different specifications. Diagrams, floor plans and site maps are essential.

The invitation to bid must ensure that the quotation will contain all costs associated with the delivery and implementation of the service (Silver, 2004).

Other useful information for the potential suppliers could include the context and details of the event, the budget limitations, the selection criteria that will be used to select the supplier, and whether references are required (Silver, 2004).

Getz (1997) lists desirable items to be included:

- Specification liability clauses – i.e. who is responsible, and insurance requirements
- Future options for renewal
- Termination and amendment procedures
- Subcontracting rights
- Compliance with appropriate laws
- Penalties for non-fulfilment
- What is NOT covered.

3. Lists of preferred suppliers

The selection of possible suppliers can be very time consuming, and it is therefore useful to have a list ready. Where the event management is part of a larger company, as in British Waterways, it may be beneficial to have agreed lists of suppliers or to share experiences with other organizations. O'Toole and Mikolaitis (2002) list some of the attributes that should be looked for:

- Reliability
- Suppliers' experience with events of a similar size and scope
- The ability to focus on your event, and assurance that you are of the same importance as other customers
- Guaranteed quality of the product or service
- History in the event industry
- Discounting for large orders.

4. Approaching and locating suppliers for a specification

As well as using the lists of preferred suppliers, event managers can use the Internet, membership directories, trade magazines and industry publications for recommended suppliers. Networking with other colleagues can guide the event manager to different and reliable sources. Prior to sending out the specifications to different suppliers, it is important to ascertain that they will be able to achieve your objectives. You must also make certain that the supplier is legally and ethically able to supply what you need. By providing an evaluation instrument at this stage you could reduce the number of suppliers you contact. This evaluation instrument should include price, number of staff required from the supplier or your own organization, and other critical success factors related to this part of the service.

In Chapter 10 we present an evaluation instrument. In the example shown there, it is used for selecting an ideal venue for your event. However, exactly the same principles can be used for any supplier. The main essence is that the criteria used to evaluate a service, location or product cannot just be measured by using equally weighted criteria. Price would be just one criteria; reputation, proximity, speed of delivery and creativity might be others. Each criterion should be weighted in its importance for that particular product or service, and consequently the event manager will be able to select suppliers and their services more appropriately.

Approaching specialists must be done carefully, and some specialists may need booking a long time in advance, and require a deposit and arrangements in the case of cancellation by either party (Shone and Parry, 2004).

5. Examination of the received quotations and fitness for purpose

In some situations, all the quotations received should be opened at an agreed time and place. This avoids any criticisms or charges of unfairness. All 'quotes' should be opened and considered as presented without having prior knowledge of their contents, and without giving one company a potentially unfair advantage over another. When the quotations are received, it should be ascertained that the companies are capable of fulfilling all the requirements of the activity for which they were asked to quote.

6. Comparison of in-house and external provision

The evaluation instrument described above and in Chapter 15 will serve to differentiate between the different tenders received. The purpose of this stage is to assess the capabilities of the supplier and the in-house provision, and to compare the strengths and weaknesses of the different quotations. You should be able to demonstrate that your choice of supplier is devoid of personal preference and prejudice. Your objective is to select reputable, dependable and competitive suppliers for a particular product or service – in short, the best that fits your purpose (Silver, 2004).

7. Prepare a purchase order/create contractual relationship between event manager and supplier

This is the stage where there is formal agreement between the supplier and the receiver.

A contract is a legal covenant representing the agreement and responsibilities between the supplier and the event organizer. It defines the performance and other obligations of both parties (Sonder, 2004). Contracts may also be useful for defining and specifying other details, such as how logos and company names can be used and the types of merchandise permitted (Getz, 1997). A contract is said to exist when something is offered and accepted in writing or verbally with witnesses. Its purpose and provisions must be legal, and the different parties should be capable of entering into the agreement. The standard contract elements, according to Catherwood and Van Kirk (1992), are:

- Specification of the agreeing parties
- Purpose of the contract
- Duration of the contract
- Terms
- Signatures
- Witnesses and date signed.

8. Receipt of goods/services and consumption

In a factory situation, quality begins with checking that materials received meet specification (fit for purpose). This is known as input control. The same applies for events management; it is important to control the input of materials as received, and that equipment etc. is properly installed and tested before the event begins. There is nothing worse than a sound system that fails.

9. Review: was it as required/expected?

Review after the event, when successes and problems are still fresh in the mind, is essential. What went right, what went wrong, what would we do differently next time? It is advisable to keep notes, including contact names and addresses, on file for future reference. Each event should be better managed than the last one. There is always room for improvement.

The Japanese word for continuous improvement is *Kaizen*. Event managers should ask staff and subcontractors what they think could be done better, and their opinions should be taken seriously.

Customer relationship management

Customer Relationship Management (CRM) software now exists to capture data to improve overall supply chain performance. The objective of CRM is to develop a customer-centred organization that ensures every opportunity is taken to delight the customers, foster customer loyalty, and build long-term relationships that are mutually beneficial. The ultimate gain is to ensure that each customer's current and future wants and needs are satisfied. This involves recording details of each time we work with a customer, and developing a picture from this information of what the customer liked and didn't like in our past dealings. Although software exists to capture these data, for smaller operations such information can easily be recorded as notes on the customer's file.

Chapter summary and key points

This chapter has examined the relationships along the chain of various levels of suppliers, through the operation of the event out to the direct customer and on to the end user.

As many of the previous chapters have been spent in considering what customers want and how to satisfy them, this chapter has concentrated on the other end of the supply chain – the suppliers.

The first step is to recognize that a resource is needed. The next step is to determine the various sources for the resource (in-house, subcontract or purchase). Depending on the complexity of the required resource, a specification will be needed. In events management, due to the unique nature of some events, often the specification will be more of a guide than a precise technical description.

The chapter has also explained the advantages of developing preferred suppliers, where reliability (meeting specification and delivery on time) might be more important than price. If you buy on price alone, you will get what you pay for. Cheap can be expensive in the long run. With events management it is important that materials are checked and tested on receipt, or certainly before the event begins. After the event it is wise to review its success or otherwise, and to keep file notes on the reliability of suppliers and other issues.

Chapter 10

Location management and choice

Learning Objectives

After reading through this chapter you will be able to:

- Make location decisions and develop selection criteria
- Design the layout of activities and fixed arrangements at an event
- Be creative and accommodate special needs, and be aware of all crowd control issues
- Create and display clear and unambiguous event signage
- Be aware of occupational health and safety issues and ergonomics.

Introduction

We have set events and their day-to-day operational issues, problems and decisions within the broader framework of the total organization and its external environment. Much of this has been analysed in the first stage of the event operations management model. It has been shown that business policy determines the services offered and the level and quality of service that will be provided at an event. We have seen that business policy may limit the resources available to an event, and also how business policy will establish the operating structure.

Event objectives include customer satisfaction and, at the same time, efficient use of resources. These often conflicting objectives have to be balanced by the events manager within constraints of price, quality and overall feasibility, as limited in the short to medium term by existing resources. A challenge for the event manager is, therefore, first how to make the best use of *existing* resources, and then how best to purchase or 'contract in' new resources. Much of this has been discussed in Chapters 6 and 9.

This chapter addresses in detail the resource of space, its best available use, and business location. When staging an event, space will often be limited and an efficient layout will be important.

Location of the business premises

There are several factors to be considered when deciding on the location of the business premises for an event organization:

1. A business policy that requires speed of service to customers, or ease of access by customers, will lead to the requirement for a location near to where the customers are. Therefore it will be important

to locate near to major tube lines, motorways or airports, dependent upon the location and diversity of the client base.

2. A policy that stresses efficient use of resources will lead to the question 'can we make do with less?', Do you need permanent business premises, or can you hire hotel rooms/office space as and when needed?
3. A business policy that takes the supply chain approach, where the suppliers are dedicated and regarded as an extension of the whole organization, might well consider proximity to suppliers, rather than customers, to be a criterion when determining location.

With electronic means of data transfer, proximity may of course be defined very differently today from twenty years ago. For example, for sound and acoustic suppliers you may use a range of different suppliers across the country, dependent upon where your event is to be held. However, printing and stationery suppliers can be reached easily via today's electronic environment, and actual location in this respect may not be as important. In not-for-profit organizations, revenue may not be as relevant an issue as cost and customer service.

Operational concerns are either resource-related (so access to suppliers is important) or market-related (so proximity to and ease of access for customers is more significant).

Wild (2002) says that the choice of location is vital for any new business, and that a poor choice of location may be responsible for many new businesses having brief and troubled lives. Poor location decisions are expensive and may have long-lasting effects on the events that can be delivered. A wrong initial location decision will lead to further expense and disruption if a subsequent move to a new location has to be made. If the decision is made to stay with the existing unsuitable location, ongoing costs will continue and frustration is likely to escalate. Often the ongoing effects of a poor location decision are hidden, as the costs will be in the form of lost opportunities, lost sales and lost business. If the location is wrong, it can have a significant impact on profits (Slack *et al.*, 2004).

Opportunity costs of a wrong location, such as lost sales and extra operating expense, cannot be separately accounted for, since often they will not be known. Thus they are not shown in annual financial reports. This lack of exposure and consequent scrutiny and comment regarding the costs generally means that only the event manager will be truly aware of the extra effort required, the extra costs of transport, the cost of double handling and so on due to poor location.

Location decisions

Basic location questions that should be asked include:

1. Why move?
2. Where to?
3. How much space is required?
4. Lease or buy?
5. What are the differences between cost and the benefits to be made?
6. Have alternatives been evaluated?
7. Again, 'WHY?'

Why move?

'So why move?' The answer is not always obvious. Perhaps the question should be rephrased to ask: 'How will the move to new premises improve the business operation, or improve customer service?' If a satisfactory answer can't be given, then why move?

Sometimes the reason for moving is due to a change in competition or local costs (rent, taxes etc.).

Wild (2002) suggests that if the reason for moving is due to an increase in demand, then this in itself creates more questions:

- Should the present capacity and facilities be expanded?
- Should other locations for additional facilities be sought?
- Should existing facilities be closed down in favour of larger premises elsewhere?

If the reason for moving is to meet increased demand, the question must be: 'Is it possible to expand the existing premises rather than relocate?' It might be possible to rearrange the layout of the existing premises so as to make better use of what space already exists. On the other hand, if a move is really necessary, then piecemeal additions or *ad hoc* solutions can result in facilities that will *always* be inefficient. Money thrown at an inadequate facility will be money wasted.

Many organizations, with enthusiasm fuelled by rapid initial growth or in periods of national economic growth, have committed themselves to costly new premises only to find that growth has not continued at the same initial meteoric rate. It has to be recognized that the economy is cyclical, and when there is an economic downturn expensive premises are hard to unload. Before committing to expensive premises it is important to be reasonably certain that the increase in demand is ongoing and not short term.

Slack *et al.* (2004) ask the following four questions when considering expansion or for choice of initial locations, and these have been slightly amended for the event industry:

1. Where should the facilities be located?
2. How should the operations network be managed across national boundaries?
3. Should events held in different countries be allowed to develop their own way of doing business or maintain a corporate approach?
4. Can an event which has been successful in one part of the world be transferred to another part?

Many decisions to move to new premises are made for prestige purposes rather than to improve the efficiency of the operation or to give a better service to the customer. Sometimes the reason given for a planned move is nebulous, and it cannot clearly be demonstrated that the move to new premises will improve operations or add to customer satisfaction. In this scenario the event manager must investigate what is required to safeguard existing levels of operating effectiveness.

As explained earlier, it is not necessarily the event organization that feels the need to move to a new location; the event itself may move location (see Case study 10.1).

Case study 10.1

32nd America's Cup, Valencia, Spain

(23 June 2007 onwards; pre regattas held in 2004/2005/2006; Louis Vuitton cup selection of challenger April to June 2007.)

Brief history of the America's Cup®

The America's Cup® challenge has been the premier yachting event in the world since its first sailing around the Isle of Wight in 1851.

For the 32nd America's Cup, a new venue has been sought and a management company employed to run the event.

This is a revolutionary step in the context of modern America's Cup history. Previously, the America's Cup Match would be organized by the defending yacht club, while the Challenger of Record would set up a selection series, the Louis Vuitton Cup, with the other challengers to determine who would race the Defender in the Match. The two events were usually completely independent, resulting in duplicated effort and, at times, frustration or confusion for partners, participants and spectators alike.

(Information supplied by AC Management Valencia; for further information see www.americascup.com.)

The news releases below detail the process undertaken to select the location for the 32nd America's Cup.

Geneva, 12 June 2003:

AC management publishes the venues shortlisted for the next America's cup

With the objective of choosing the venue and host city for the 32nd America's Cup, AC Management (Event Organizers) retained eight European venues in March this year. At the time the eight were each requested to supply in-depth technical information to facilitate AC Management's task in making the best choice of venue for the next event of the world's oldest sporting trophy, the America's Cup. In particular, the eight cities were asked questions concerning specific weather patterns, outline plans for the hosting arrangements, as well as details of their initial thoughts on the likely infrastructure and logistical facilities.

'I have followed the process carefully', says Pierre-Yves Firmenich, Commodore of the Societé Nautique de Geneve (Trustees of 32nd America's Cup and winning yacht club of the 31st America's Cup), 'and each of the eight candidates presented outstanding bids. It has obviously been extremely difficult to make the choice. However, ultimately, only one venue can be chosen and so it is now time to publish a short list.'

'The remaining venues are Lisbon (POR), Marseille (FAR), Naples (ITA), Palma de Mallorca (ESP), Valencia (ESP).'

Michel Bonnefous, CEO of AC Management, commented: 'With this shortlist we have refined our goals considerably and will now work closely with each of the remaining venues thorough the next crucial steps in the process. Over the coming months, we will be concentrating on the more precise details for hosting the America's Cup. We need to understand clearly the minutiae of every positive and negative element associated with each venue. It is probable that the next announcement in this process will be the identity of the final choice.'

2 November 2003:

Two major announcements were made in Geneva this morning. The first, and by far the most eagerly awaited, was that Valencia has been chosen as the host venue for the next America's Cup. In winning the bid the Spanish team had beaten off stiff competition from Naples, Lisbon and Marseille.

'The sailing and sporting conditions were always our main criteria', said Michel Bonnefous, AC management's chief executive. 'One of the aspects was to consider the worst-case scenario for the weather. In Auckland (31st Cup held in Auckland) we were looking at a possible 15 days lost to the weather, in Valencia the worst case scenario suggests just 1 day. This means that in Valencia we can more or less guarantee to sail, which is obviously good for the racing and the television coverage.'

Another change to the new look America's Cup is that the length of the races will be determined by time and not distance, a detail that should help avoid some of the frustrating delays that dogged the last event.

According to Bonnefous, another advantage of Valencia is that the nature of the location means that the public and spectators can get very close to the racing and that the America's Cup village is next door to where the sailing will take place.

(*Yachting World*, 26 November 2003)

(Content supplied by *Yachting World*; for further information see www.yachtingworld.com.)

Where to?

Having determined that new premises are genuinely needed and demand will continue, then the next question is, where should the event organization move to?

Slack *et al.* (2004) discuss the different resources used by organizations, and it can be seen that these should be borne in mind when choosing a location for an event organization. They include:

- Labour costs. Although within a country labour costs might vary from location to location, such variations will be considerably more pronounced from country to country. It is not just the cost of wages that should be taken into account, but also non-wage costs such as employment and social security costs, safety and health requirements, holiday payment, exchange rates and other welfare provisions.
- Land costs. Land and rental costs vary between countries, and between city and out-of-city locations.
- Transportation costs. In the event industry these may involve the cost of bringing in resources to the premises, although often in the event industry the resources are taken directly to the event. Other transport costs include movement of goods from the office or warehouse to the event.

When choosing a site, it should be considered whether that particular location is appropriate for that event company and the style of company and events it represents. This depends on the image that is wanted and the convenience of location for clients or suppliers.

International locations

Some event organizations cannot limit themselves to within their own national boundaries. Many of the organizations buy their supplies from abroad and deliver their services abroad. The horizon for event managers is increasingly a global one. If overseas locations are being investigated, it is most important that the broader issues such as political and economic stability, local customs and culture, tax structures and incentives, reliable communications and energy supplies etc. are considered. Suffice to say an overseas venture for an organization will require very detailed considerations. Often local problems do not emerge until the project is well under way. It is most sensible to solicit local assistance and knowledge from the outset when contemplating an overseas venture (see Case study 10.2).

For UK companies, Business Link (www.businesslink.gov.uk) and UK Trade and Investment (www.uktradeinvest.gov.uk) websites provide a good starting point to find out information for overseas markets and contacts. UK Trade and Investment lists general information regarding the state of the economy, currency, public holidays, religion etc., plus more specific information remarketing and contacts.

For American companies, the website www.buyusa.gov provides commercial information for importers and exporters along the same lines as UK Trade and Investment.

Case study 10.2

Setting up an overseas event

Imagine you want to set up an event in Denmark. If you need staff, these can be sourced through local government employment agencies (*Arbejdsformidlingen*) or through commercial firms such as Manpower Rekruttering or Kelly Rekruttering.

The UK Trade and Investment website lists information regarding taxes, legislation, and all government departments embassies, associations etc. It is very important when working overseas to understand culture, and the website offers these guidelines on business etiquette:

Most Danes read and speak English very well. Correspondence and telephone calls can usually be conducted in English without difficulty.

British companies soliciting business or introducing products should note that, in the initial stages, letters should be addressed to the company and not to named individuals. Some Danish companies specify this on their letterhead. Once a business connection has been established, correspondence can then be addressed to named individuals.

Arrive punctually for meetings. Notify by telephone or fax in advance if you are going to be late or if you have to cancel.

State times using the 24-hour clock rather than using a casual 'half-five', which a Dane would understand to be an hour earlier.

Give a firm handshake on arrival and departure.

Don't be embarrassed to talk about price and payment. Danes are normally straightforward and easy to communicate with, even on money-related matters.

(Information provided by the UK Trade and Investment website, www.uktradeinvest.gov.uk. Crown copyright material is reproduced with the permission of the Controller of HMSO and the Queen's Printer for Scotland.)

How much space is required?

The amount of space is dependent on two issues; the first is demand and potential growth, and the second is how efficiently space is used. It is a truism that the more space is available, the more wasteful of space we will be – i.e. space requirements expand to use up the space available. It is also true that in a growing organization there never seems to be enough space. It could be argued that an organization can never have too much space, but space costs money – particularly in an expensive area of the world or country or part of a city.

Lease or buy?

Once land has been purchased and buildings erected, large amounts of money will have been spent. If subsequently it transpires that the location or the buildings themselves are not suitable, it is often the case that a substantial loss will be made if the decision is made to sell. Large capital expenditure in land and buildings equates to large amounts of funds being tied up in real estate, which reduces the amount of funds available for working capital for the business. Reduced working capital may result in the business being forced to raise a series of short-term loans. If short-term borrowing cannot be serviced out of cash flow, or short-term loans cannot be repaid on due date, then although the business has large amounts of fixed assets on the balance sheet it will face insolvency. Generally, in a forced sale situation buildings will not realize their Balance Sheet value.

Although leasing is less final than building or buying, nonetheless the location decision must still be made just as carefully. If it later transpires that a leased property is in the wrong location, there will be disruption internally to the smooth running of the operation and externally to the customer, and effort and money expended in finding new premises and moving, that could have been avoided had the correct decision had been made initially.

What are the differences between cost and the benefits to be made?

Break-even analysis can be a useful tool to determine location. Break-even analysis is a technique that shows the amount of sales revenue required in a given situation to cover the costs of the operation. For break-even purposes, costs are divided into fixed costs (i.e. those costs that don't change no matter how many sales are made) and variable costs (those costs, that increase or decrease in proportion to sales activity).

Have alternatives been evaluated?

Given a choice of locations, perhaps the easiest method of evaluation is by a checklist of relevant requirements. In the checklist shown in Table 10.1 a point rating system has been

Table 10.1 Evaluating weighted criteria using a fictitious event management company, which organizes university award ceremonies throughout the UK. Rated from 1–5 where 5 is superior.

Criteria (a)	Weighting 1–5 (b)	Location A meeting criteria 1–5 (c)	Total points (d) (i.e. b × c)	Location B meeting criteria 1–5 (e)	Total points (f) (i.e. b × e)	Location C meeting criteria 1–5 (g)	Total points (h) (i.e. b × g)
Proximity to local customers	1	1	1	1	1	1	1
Proximity to local suppliers	1	1	1	1	1	1	1
Access to good road links	4	2	8	5	20	5	20
Low cost of property	5	1	5	1	5	5	25
Land opportunity to expand	1	5	5	5	5	1	1
Attractive location	1	5	5	3	3	3	3
Availability of using local staff	1	5	5	5	5	1	1
Total			30		40		52

incorporated. This is using a fictitious company that organizes university graduation ceremonies throughout England. The importance of each criterion is given a weighting, and then in the second column a further rating is given as to how well the criteria are met by the first organization. These figures are then multiplied to give the weighted criteria. For example, access to good road links weighted 4 × location B meeting criteria 5 gives an overall weighted criteria of 20.

It can be seen that the company cited above does not weight heavily the need for a close proximity to their suppliers or customers. It does, however, rate highly the need to be close to a good road network. This would be typical of a small virtual company that uses suppliers from across the UK and meets its customers on their own properties, or uses short-term hired premises close to the event where they can meet their clients. Similarly, in the example given, the need to use local staff is rated low, so those venues that are close to a useful labour supply do not rate highly in the final analysis. The need to have property that is capable of further expansion is not of high importance.

It can be seen from this example that if you as the event manager identify the criteria that are of importance to you, and weight them carefully, you can use the above technique to assist in location selection. This technique can also be used in venue selection for an event (see Table 10.2, which illustrates the example of choosing a wedding venue).

However, over time the weighted criteria may change in some way. The logical location that appears to be the best at one point in time may seem inferior at a later date. This is due to a change in one or more of the many factors that influenced the original choice. This can prove costly. The event manager should therefore aim to anticipate changes in needs in order to make the best and well-informed decision.

Table 10.2 Evaluation of weighted criteria identified by the bride and groom for a wedding planning company

Criteria (a)	Weighting 1–5 (b)	Venue A meeting criteria 1–5 (c)	Total points (d) (i.e. b × c)	Venue B meeting criteria 1–5 (e)	Total points (f) (i.e. b × e)	Venue C meeting criteria 1–5 (g)	Total points (h) (i.e. b × g)
Proximity to church for guests to travel	2	5	10	4	8	3	6
Capable of sitting required numbers	5	1	5	5	25	1	5
Choice of menu	4	5	20	5	20	3	12
Sole use of venue	5	1	5	5	25	1	5
Cost	3	5	15	3	9	3	9
Overnight facilities	4	4	16	5	20	4	16
Photograph opportunities	4	3	12	5	20	3	12
Facility to store opened wedding gifts	3	5	15	5	15	5	15
Total			98		142		80

Choice of location for an event

Every event is held somewhere. It could be in purpose-built facilities or heritage sites, on the fells for a marathon, on purpose-built waterways for the rowing championships at the Olympics, at unique one-off sites, or in a conference venue. Large public events can be held outside in public parks, in the streets or shopping malls, or in the middle of the desert (Silver, 2004). Some events are held annually in the same venue, while others seek new and unusual sites for subsequent events.

Silver (2004) says that numerous studies have shown that an essential criterion in selecting a destination for events is safety. Site evaluation should include safety and security. Political unrest, crime-ridden areas, extensive roadway construction and other hazardous situations should be evaluated carefully.

Developing selection criteria

Although the list below is not likely to be comprehensive, it does give an idea of what an event manager should consider when choosing a location for an event. The event manager should compile a list that takes all the likely issues into account.

The points below are set out in no particular order; the event manager would have to return to the objectives and critical success factors in order to establish an order of priority:

- Availability
- Accessibility of location for customers, suppliers and emergency agencies and all staff members
- Suitability for a safe flow of consumers within the site, customer services, participants and visitors
- Cost – of hire and supplementary costs of making the site appropriate for the event
- Appropriateness, atmosphere, attractiveness and image of the venue for the event and for the client
- Capacity of the location, spatial considerations and likely obstructions, and versatility
- Safety and security issues
- Parking facilities
- On-site services available, or the cost of bringing those to the site
- Facilities available
- Personnel on the site and professionalism of the venue management
- Impacts on the environment – such impacts would include noise pollution, turf replacement, and the cost of returning the site to its previous condition
- Storage considerations
- Suitability for those with special needs
- Hygiene and cleanliness standards
- Legal considerations and possible constraints on the event
- High visibility to attract customers, if necessary
- Crowd management and control issues
- Technical facilities.

Having developed the selection criteria, the event manager will need to consider the choices that are available. The Internet provides many useful websites for venue finding and networking opportunities, and contacts can help narrow a list of options down to a few. It may be that there is no choice; the venue is already decided upon, and the event manager has to adapt the location in the best ways possible to meet the objectives of the event.

Where it is possible to have a choice of venue, then a site visit is essential. Photographs can be taken of the site in order to record important data and to enable consideration to take place at a later date and with the clients and suppliers. It is useful for the event manager to walk through the premises as if a customer in order to evaluate distances, sight lines and any unforeseen issues. The weighted criteria analysis approach is very useful, since it takes into account those aspects that are most and least important.

The same style of analysis that was used to evaluate the choice of venue for the office premises can be used to evaluate weighted criteria for the choice of location for an event. In the example shown in Table 10.2, we have used the choice of venue as preferred by a bride and groom. The wedding planner has identified with the bride and groom those aspects that they consider to be important criteria for choice of venue, and has then asked them to rate these criteria.

It can be seen from Table 10.2 that the bride and groom do not weight the cost of the event as highly as some of the other criteria. The criterion that they do weight highly, but is not met by venues A and C, is that on the day of the wedding they have sole use of the venue. Perhaps there is nothing worse than having more than one wedding celebration taking place at the same time, and two brides meeting, or the photographer going to the wrong wedding. The final decision may be that venue B matches the weighted criteria the most closely.

This technique can be employed for many other resources that the event manager will use. It enables the critical areas to be weighted and yet all criteria to be acknowledged. If the event organizer is working on behalf of a client, this style of analysis can be shown to the client so that he or she can see how the choice of resource (e.g. venue) has been made. The criteria have arisen from the client in discussion, together with their weightings for each criterion. The table can be used to identify the event manager's research and decision-making process.

Reflective practice 10.2

1. Identify the criteria that should be considered when choosing a venue for a pharmaceutical product launch and conference in Spain. There will be over 500 delegates, and partners are invited. The delegates represent different sectors of professional people. There will be entertainment provided on two nights, and there should be opportunities for the partners to be entertained during the three days.
2. Weight the criteria using the evaluation of weighted criteria table.

Case study 10.3 discusses the factors affecting the choice of location for the British Grand Prix in July 2005.

Case study 10.3

British Grand Prix, July 2005, Silverstone, England

Negotiations between Bernie Ecclestone and BRDC (British Racing Drivers Club) were only concluded at the end of 2004 re. the 2005 British Grand Prix. It was possible that the British Grand Prix would not be part of the 2005 Formula 1 season.

In the middle of October, Bernie Ecclestone and Jackie Stewart (chairman of the BRDC) broke off negotiations regarding the British Grand Prix at Silverstone being part of the 2005 season. The BRDC chairman admitted that the length of contract and not the fees due to Ecclestone was the main stumbling block in negotiations. He said:

> *The only way forward for us is a two-year contract, which would give us time to plan and secure the long-term future of the British Grand Prix.*
>
> *We need a British Grand Prix to sustain the long-term stability of the valuable British motor sport industry and for the sake of Silverstone.*

However, new circuits are vying for the opportunity to be part of the Grand Prix circuit, which has repercussions for the teams that are taking part.

The Concorde agreement, which governs the running of the Grand Prix, allows for seventeen races to be run; dispensation was given to competitors in 2004 to allow eighteen races because of the addition of the new state-of-the-art racing circuit at Bahrain. In 2005 there is the addition of Turkey, which increases the number of races to nineteen. Fortunately for the British Grand Prix, all ten Formula 1 teams have agreed a formula whereby they will shoulder the costs for the two extra Grand Prix but will decrease their number of test days, thus giving a reprieve for the French and British Grand Prix.

The full provisional season, as at November 2004, was as follows:

March 6	Australia
March 20	Malaysia
April 3	Bahrain
April 17	France (contract under discussion)
April 24	San Marino (subject to compliance with contract)
May 8	Spain
May 22	Monaco
TBC	Europe
June 12	Canada
TBC	United States
July 3	Britain (contract under discussion)
July 17	Germany
July 31	Hungary
August 21	Turkey
September 4	Italy
September 11	Belgium
September 25	Brazil
October 9	Japan
TBC	China

On 9 December 2004, it was announced that the 2005 British Grand Prix was confirmed as part of the 2005 season. A deal is now in place between Bernie Ecclestone and the BRDC which guarantees that the event will take place at Silverstone until 2009, with promotion the responsibility of the BRDC.

(Information reproduced and supplied by courtesy of Brynn Williams MD, at www.crash.net.)

Reflective practice 10.3

Regarding Case study 10.3:

1. What factors have contributed to the locations of the 2005 Grand Prix?
2. If 2006 saw the introduction of Grand Prix in Mexico and India, what might the repercussions be for the other Grand Prix?
3. What are the benefits of holding a Grand Prix in Mexico or India?

(Research Bernie Ecclestone and FOM at http://en.wikipedia.org/wiki/Formula_One_Management and at www.formula1.com)

Layout of activities and fixed arrangements at an event

Having determined where the event organization will be located, the next issue is to consider the layout of the event with the overall objectives of facilitating efficient operations and first-class customer service. As in most area of operations, the first principle is to establish the relative importance of customer satisfaction *vis-à-vis* efficient use of resources.

At an event, there may be a physical flow of people or materials around the site, as at an exhibition or an agricultural fair. Alternatively, customers may be seated once having entered the venue, as at a conference or a concert. Layout planning aims to:

1. *Optimize movement*. In an office or a backroom area, the aim will be to reduce movement. However, at an exhibition the aim might be for a layout that will increase the distance to be travelled by the visitor. For example, visitors may be channelled up and down aisles, and the actual distance travelled maximized rather than minimized so that the customers are obliged to pass by each stand. In this way exhibitors would not feel that their stand is disadvantaged.
2. *Reduce congestion*. One of the objectives of the event manager is to add value and eliminate non-value adding activities. Seldom is value added by having customers waiting in queues. There is a limit to how long people will queue, no matter how good the service or product at the end of the queue. However, in some cases queues are unavoidable, and here the event manager should use them to advantage – for example providing extra advertising or selling extra products. At outdoor events there are many different forms of diversions that can be used, such as street entertainment, catering spots and live demonstrations. The entertainment may help to build up anticipation and the feeling that the event has already begun. Providing entertainment during the time people may be waiting reduces frustration and consequent problems.
3. *Maximize the use of space*. As we have seen, space costs money. Thus it is important to make the best use of space. For example, if there is spare space it can always be used for display purposes. Likewise, with the customers' interests at heart, it follows that where possible more space per person should be allocated to customer areas and less space to backroom facilities and supporting functions.

Putting on an event is similar to a project; there are two aspects which are finite – time, since the event has to be implemented by a certain day and time, and also space.

Computer-aided event planning

Layout planning of a large complex event, such as an exhibition or outdoor event where many different activities are occurring around fixed positions of marquees, stalls and sub-events, is a time-consuming process. The industry is now using computer-based approaches transferred from other industries, such as building and construction, to assist in this process. The benefits of these approaches are as follows:

1. Alternative layouts can be quickly generated for comparisons and evaluation
2. Interactive processes between the positioning of equipment/stands and the flow of customers can assist in visualizing the reality of movement of customers in the finished design
3. The computer software can be linked with other software packages to quantify resource needs and to develop site maps showing full details and part details for different groups of people
4. Costs can be predicted for different configurations.

Types of layouts for events

Much of the operational management literature explores the different types of layouts that are available to any service manager. These include:

- Process, where all operations of a similar nature are grouped together
- Product, where groups of facilities are arranged according to the needs of the event, and ideally the process should be continuous with the customer moving from facility to facility
- Fixed position, where neither the customer nor the service provider moves
- Hybrid, which is a mixed form of layout – for example, an exhibition may contain catering facilities with self service (product layout), table service may be also be offered (process layout), and seminar facilities (fixed position).

However, these structured definitions do little to help the event manager, who must contend with an enormous variety of different events in an enormous variety of different locations. What is of supreme importance is that the event is well set out with maximum use of space and minimum congestion. We will consider capacity management in Chapter 13, as this also has to be taken into account in when planning and designing an event.

Creating the site plan

A site inspection is essential, and photographs are also useful. For large events, an accurate, scaled plan will enable a visual understanding of space, both on the ground and by elevation. Elevation is often overlooked and only considered when tall structures are actually being brought into position. Similarly, space should not just include the actual dimensions of structures but also customer movement. The plan acts as a communication tool indicating the proposed use of space for all the different stakeholders. It is essential for some suppliers, who may need to know distances between fixed positions and electrical supplies, or the dimensions of entrances for ease of access. Suppliers will also look on the plan for the storage areas and drop-off points for their goods, and what facilities are set aside for maintenance.

Although many revisions may take place, the final draft should be sent to all interested parties. However, it may be possible to create several versions of the plan, one for suppliers, one showing the provision of power services and water facilities for the event, and others for particular groups of people with different information needs. The entertainers and speakers will want to know the location of the green room and where they can wait and relax during the event. Similarly, if the event is attracting media interest the media area should be specified and/or the site for any related press conferences.

These plans may be required by other agencies, such as the Health and Safety Executive (HSE) and fire chiefs. The HSE will need to ensure that all their regulations have been taken into account and that the event will be able to function safely.

Silver (2004) states that the site plans should include all the features and constraints of the site, such as doors, windows, electrical connections and the amount of power available, cleaning and drinking water, waste outlets, posts and pillars, and access roads etc. The plan should indicate where everything connected to the event will be placed, and how the customers will circulate.

The need for detail and accuracy in site plans increases in direct relationship to the size and complexity of an event.

As stated earlier, the plan can be created by computer or drafted by hand. The event manager should use an accurate, scaled plan, and the northerly direction should always be indicated. Having a universally accepted direction on the plan is a sound risk strategy, so that when suppliers or other groups come onto site, there can be no misunderstandings.

Any symbols that are used on the plan should be explained. There is now a common visual symbol language, and this must be used at all times so that people from different countries can 'read' the plans. All entrances and exits and parking facilities must be clearly marked. First aid and emergency access must also be clearly shown, so that these areas are kept free of obstructions, and emergency vehicles should be able to access all areas. Not all items need to be on one single map, since it can then appear too complex and again lead to misunderstandings.

O'Toole and Mikolaitis (2002), whilst agreeing with the elegance and precision of computer-generated plans, state that a hand-drawn, well-illustrated plan may be better for communication with the target audience, and may also set the right mood for the event. Consideration should be taken of those who will be reading the plans. Often the customers are not 'plan literate', or may not have the inclination to spend time trying to sort out the various intricacies of a complex plan. Plans can be designed to be displayed on the Internet, and they should be appropriately simple and yet offer good communication. By indicating lost-children points, information and telephone points, cash withdrawal facilities and mobile recharge facilities on the plans, the event manager is demonstrating that the event and the management are child and people friendly. An aerial orientation may be suitable for this purpose.

Visual aids are an important element of layout planning. These comprise representations, including drawings, templates, three-dimensional models, movement patterns and cartoon maps.

The site plan may also be used for a seating chart at a concert, or within a festival programme to show where the different entertainments and facilities are sited.

Crowd-related issues

Virtually all events will require space from the arrival to the departure of the guests, participants and performers, suppliers and volunteers. The varying requirements of each of these groups must be considered, as they pass through the event, creating potential bottlenecks, overcrowding and reduced customer satisfaction. Getz (1997) suggests an excellent checklist for event managers to consider to enhance customer experience and help prevent crowd-related problems:

- Provide ample space at access and egress points
- Avoid dead ends and bottlenecks that will lead to congestion or movement against the flow

- Provide adequate and appropriately orientated signage
- Disperse toilet facilities and cloakrooms throughout the site
- Ensure that all staff, including security staff, are customer-focused and able to help with directions
- Screen and block off no-go areas where risks may be high
- Separate vehicle and pedestrian movements where possible
- Use public announcements and signs to advise customers about problems and opportunities
- Trial run the event site if possible
- Provide on-site security facilities and services
- Install security devices and CCTV
- Use lighting to avoid hazards and maximize security
- Segregate potentially aggressive groups
- Maximize staff communications
- Provide, test and adequately sign emergency exits and procedures
- Avoid potential crowd stressors, e.g. excessive waiting, overcrowding, overwhelming security, and barriers which would restrict escape.

Certain elements of the event should be next to each other, and others should be considered carefully – for example, the closeness of catering and sanitary facilities. The entrance to an event should be large, spacious and well signed. Research has shown that movement as customers enter an event slows down as people look around and orientate themselves, hence it is essential that this be taken into account in the design.

Accommodating special needs

In many countries there are legal requirements to provide certain facilities for people with various disabilities. However, the professional event manager should not only be striving to comply with these laws but also seeking other new ways to be more sensitive to disability issues and needs. It could be that the event has attracted customers, suppliers or staff who are very tall, very short or very large. Their requests should be accommodated in a non-judgmental manner. With regard to the content of the event, the speakers should be kept informed of the various needs of their 'audience' so that extra handouts can be supplied, and they should be aware if a person is 'signing' to those members of the audience who are hard of hearing. The audiovisual team should also be aware that the interpreter must be well lit and visible.

For those with difficulties with movement, all entrances and routes should be kept free of obstructions, and ramps, stair lifts and curb lifts provided.

Equally important as the actual provision of physical amenities is that all staff should be sensitive to the needs of all of their customers, and that their tone of voice and manner should be the same as to any other individual.

A useful *aide memoire* for an event manager when considering special needs includes the following:

- Provide information about the services provided
- Use large-print signage and/or Braille, and site signs at the right height for wheelchair users
- Consider different type of fire alarm systems for those who are hard of hearing
- Provide special communication devices for use during the event
- Where possible, remove physical barriers to ensure access to all buildings and elements of the event
- Consider the width of the aisles, the gradients to be covered, the dimensions of gates and doors to be passed through, and their ease of opening
- Install accessible toilets and washing facilities

- Add handicapped parking places with easy access to the site
- Discuss with a range of people with difficulties what they feel would be useful to make their visit to the event more comfortable and enjoyable.

Event signage

Very little seems to have been written on temporary signage. Where it is thought through in advance and installed correctly, it generates very little comment. At other times it is just grumbled about as being unsuitable, inadequate and illegible, not useful, and looking hurried and temporary. It might be thought that some events which are held annually at the same venue may not need a great deal of signage, but when a new customer attends and has not learnt all the unspoken and unwritten language which comes from familiarity there will be problems.

There are six types of signage used at an event:

1. External to the venue, giving directions and parking areas for different sorts of vehicles and purposes
2. Internal directional signs, e.g. registration this way, 'you are here' boards
3. Statutory, e.g. fire exits, slippery floor, 'wash your hands now' notices, first aid facilities
4. Room and space identification signs, e.g. for toilets, restaurant, children play area
5. Sponsorship signs
6. General signs, e.g. 'thank you for coming and have a safe journey home.'

One of the elements to be included on the site plan should be where all the signs are going to be located. On the schedule of work for the event it should be noted when signs are going to be put up and when they are going to be taken down.

It is essential that the signs have a corporate feel about them, and are all made to look similar and professional. Uniformity in their design enables the customers to recognize at a glance what is being said. The signs could reflect the theme of the event by colour, shape, and the words used. With regard to their design, thought should be given to their size and legibility from a distance, and where they should be sited, bearing in mind that once the customers have arrived they may obscure them.

Different colours could be used to denote different types of signs – for example, a certain colour could be used for directional signs and another colour to denote room and space identification. Care should be taken with certain colours, because of colour blindness.

There may be some restrictions regarding where signs can be located and fixed, and this should be investigated as part of the original planning procedures. It is useful if the height and sites for placing can be consistent so that the customer becomes used to looking at a particular height and in a particular direction for information. Care should be taken with regard to their durability, in case of rain, and because they may in fact disappear with souvenir collectors.

The signage is another of the resources that the event must obtain either through an in-house team or from an external supplier.

'You are here' boards

John Nightingale, of the UK Centre for Events Management at Leeds Metropolitan University, has undertaken research into 'You are here' maps and their usefulness in directing people to alternative parts of a venue. He cites many examples where the 'You are here' map is badly orientated and may serve to confuse rather than assist in directing customers to alternative parts of the venue.

Some events take place in venues that are very familiar to most attendees. For example, season ticket holders in a football ground can probably find the way to their place with very little help after having attended for a few matches.

However, very many events take place in venues that are unfamiliar to their customers, and often in a strange town. Indeed, one of the attractions of events such as the Olympic Games is going to a brand-new stadium in a far-away country. It is these customers who need to be able to find their way around the site. Nightingale says that they do this by using a variety of techniques, including:

- Following the crowd
- Asking directions (from other customers or staff)
- Navigating using sign posts
- Navigating using a site plan (often provided in a brochure or programme)
- Navigating using fixed maps mounted on boards provided by the venue.

This section concentrates on the last of these – the 'You are here' board. It is important to locate boards appropriately and to orientate them correctly. Similarly, it is important to avoid vandalism to the boards or their becoming obliterated by graffiti, and to check them regularly to ensure that excessive fingering is not eroding popular destinations.

Maps are commonly used for navigation, whether driving, walking or cycling. Different scales of maps are used in different circumstances. It is therefore important for maps to include details of the scale, so that customers can estimate how far away their destination is. Nightingale notes that it is surprising, in practice, how few fixed maps at events contain this information.

The importance of having a map that is correctly orientated to features on the ground is borne out by the plaques commonly found in prominent viewing locations, such as at the tops of mountains. These have been in use since the mid-nineteenth century, and indicate other prominent landmarks, such as neighbouring mountain peaks. These are always precisely orientated so that other landmarks can be easily identified. They are usually set horizontally or nearly horizontally, and are frequently made of engraved metal to give a durable surface in a location that is normally unsupervised.

At events, fixed maps are usually mounted on a metal frame or attached to a wall. In practice the map is usually vertical and orientated for architectural convenience, perhaps on a wall or in a prominent position along the edge of a road or pavement. For reasons of health and safety, planners are often keen to avoid the board being a potential barrier to people walking along the pavement – they do not want people, especially those with poor vision, to be bumping into signposts which are supposed to be there to help.

However, a vertical map can be located so that buildings on the left of the map are to the left on the ground, and buildings on the right of the map are to the right on the ground. Things at the top of the map will then be behind the map board, and things at the bottom of the map will be in front of the board. Nightingale believes that this is the most readily understood orientation, and should be used whenever possible. Any other orientations require the user to revolve the map in their head, causing difficulty in recognizing the correct direction.

Nightingale's research cites many instances of 'You are here' boards that are badly sited and that often lead the observer to go in the wrong direction. In many of these cases it is possible to orientate the map more closely to the ground, for instance by placing it on an adjacent wall at a different angle. Within event venues, this problem can be more easily solved.

It is interesting to compare the orientation of map boards with the signs used on main roads. When you approach a road roundabout, there is usually a sign indicating the exits from the roundabout. This always shows the driver entering from the bottom of the map, so that points straight ahead are at the top of the sign, while the left of the sign indicates a left turn and the right of the sign indicates a right turn. You never see a roundabout sign where you are entering from the right, the left or the top.

Presenting too much information can be as dangerous as presenting too little (O'Toole and Mikolaitis, 2002). Signs are meant to communicate, and if too much information is given and causes confusion then it has failed in its purpose. Acronyms and symbols should only be used when it is expected that all attendees will understand them. Providing key information in the primary languages of the attendees can eliminate confusion and aid in the success of an event. How often have we been to different cities or event venues and started off on a well-signed route only to find that after a short time the signs disappear or give different information?

How often have we seen a badly worded sign, or one where apostrophes are put in the wrong place? Do not rely on an external supplier to spot grammatical errors; there are far too many examples where stupid mistakes are made – e.g. 'Hot dog's stand', 'Icecream's', 'Stationery vehicles cannot be parked here.'

Occupational health and safety

Occupational health and safety and ergonomics might be considered to be a moral issue, but even the Romans realized that well-maintained slaves were more efficient and more valuable. The average fully employed adult will spend 25 per cent or more of his or her life at the workplace, with additional time in travelling to and from work. It could well be argued that employers have a moral obligation in addition to various legal obligations to provide a safe working environment, and that the workers who 'sell' their time have a right to a safe and healthy workplace. Sadly, history shows that voluntary safety arrangements do not provide adequate standards, and thus legislation has been necessary. The fault has not always been with employers, as employees are often found to take shortcuts. Statistics show that the home is still the most dangerous place for most people.

It is a fact that most health and safety requirements of workers are only common sense. It is common sense to have adequate light, correct temperatures, proper ventilation, noise controls, and so on.

Ergonomics

Ergonomics is the science that seeks to improve the physical and mental well being of workers by optimizing the function of human–machine environments. In today's office, workers are surrounded by machines, mostly electronic, and spend long hours hunched over keyboards and in front of VDU screens. In particular, ergonomics concentrates on:

- Fitting the work demands to the efficiency of people, so as to reduce physical and mental stress
- Providing information for the design of machines, key boards etc., so that they can be operated efficiently
- The development of adjustable workstations and chairs etc., so that individuals can self-adjust the workstation to meet their needs
- Provision of information on correct body posture to reduce fatigue and to minimize OOS (occupational overuse syndrome – formerly known as RSI or repetitive stress injury)
- Give guidelines for lighting, air conditioning, noise limits and so on.

Most governments throughout the world have a department or agency that will happily provide, free of charge, ergonomic advice and information geared to local needs.

Reflective practice 10.4

What are the criteria that you would use in determining the optimum location for:

1. An event management company that has students as its main market and specializes in student nights in a university town?
2. A teambuilding company that mainly has large businesses in the North of England?
3. A promoter for a jazz band touring Europe?
4. The organizer of the Tour de France?

Chapter summary and key points

This chapter has covered the practical aspects of location, layout and signage, and has considered occupational health and safety issues and ergonomics. All of these areas are intertwined. It is obvious that ergonomics could likely recommend changes to a layout, and in itself layout will be limited by the size and shape of the space available.

These topics are very much operational issues, and yet exist in the broader strategic context of the organization.

Location decisions are essentially to do with where a service operation is best placed to serve the market. The alternatives are speed to customer, or ease of access by customer. Although a location decision will not ignore the extended supply chain, nonetheless generally the supplier will be of lesser importance in the determination of service locations. Business policy will, to a large extent, determine location.

The chapter has identified that there are many influences on the location of premises and the location of individual events and their layout. It has focused on asking questions that must be answered in order to optimize the location, efficiency and effectiveness of the event.

The chapter has considered the use of computer-aided event planning models and how these might be harnessed to model crowds arriving and leaving an event, and within it. Other extremely important issues to the event planner are how to accommodate special needs, healthy and safety issues, and ergonomics, and these have been analysed in relation to events. A useful section within the chapter has been devoted to event signage, since without adequate and thoughtful signage visitors to an event will become dissatisfied and leave with the perception of an inefficient event and event manager.

Chapter 11

Risk management for event managers

Learning Objectives

After reading through this chapter you will be able to:

- Appreciate different definitions of risk and their application in the event industry
- Identify different ranges and categories of risks
- Be aware of the causes of accidents
- Be able to use a range of techniques to identify and manage risks.

Introduction

A risk is some thing that might happen in the future that will result in an adverse effect. Risk management is the art of being aware of all the things that could go wrong and having plans and contingencies to prevent this, not to remedy the situation as best as possible if things do go wrong. Harrison and McDonald (2004) say that the process of risk management involves identifying the risks, specifying their nature, assessing the degree to which the risks could impact upon the event, and developing contingency plans designed to avoid or minimize the potential impacts. It is this structured approach that will be used throughout this chapter. In the operations management literature there are many techniques that have been designed to reduce and manage risk, and we have chosen a few of these to illustrate how event managers can take advantage of previously proven techniques which can be transferred to the event industry.

We are now at the end of the detailed planning stage of the event operations management model. However, from the previous discussion you will agree that in fact the issue of risk management could have been covered in any one of the stages of the model. Since it is usual for the risk and the problem to show itself during the event, it could have been placed in the implementation stage of the event operations management model. It could also have been considered throughout the analysis and even in the evaluation stage. If we were to consider risks in the last stage of performance evaluation, it would be to review any 'near misses' and how well the event manager organized and coped with the aftermath of the risk actually occurring.

However, before we progress we can also put forward the view that risk offers many opportunities. Goldblatt (1997) defines each special event as a unique moment in time, celebrated with ceremony and ritual to satisfy specific needs. Although we accept that all events are special, they do not always have to include a celebratory aspect. By accepting Shone and Parry's (2004) definition, where they emphasize that events are non-routine occasions set apart from the normal activity of daily life, we can see that event managers should indeed take risks. Laybourn (2004) advocates that one reason why events are special is because of risk – the event has not been done before. Allen (2000) says that without risk there can be no competitive advantage. We would add that taking well-defined risks and being a lateral and creative thinker would enhance the event manager's approach to events, and their consequent outcome. Indeed, staying the same would constitute a risk.

What is risk management?

Risk management is an ongoing, integrated and iterative process (Silver, 2004) – as resources are allocated and plans set, so must the event manager be able to be responsive to needs for change.

In simplistic terms, risk management is the art of:

1. Anticipating what can go wrong (i.e. the risk)
2. Risk identification
3. Calculating the probability that the risk will occur
4. Estimating the impact if the risk does occur
5. Determining in advance what can be done to avoid things going wrong, so as to prevent the risk happening, or planning actions that can be taken to correct or ease the situation if the risk does happen
6. Communicating the risks and actions that can and should be taken if necessary.

Laybourn (2004) supports this view and says that risks have to be identified, problems pre-empted and ways to manage them fully integrated into the planning of the event. This will involve having contingency plans ready and fully understood by all the different suppliers and personnel working on the event. Laybourn (2004) also identifies that risk management involves the estimation and use of probabilities.

Anticipating what could go wrong

Even for a straightforward event, there will be many things that can go wrong. Sometimes, because we are used to running similar events we might become complacent, sometimes we might rely on good luck (it can't happen to me), and sometimes we will just be plain ignorant of what might go wrong.

Murphy's law says that if anything can go wrong, it will. Nevan's corollary is 'and at the worst possible time'.

It is a fact that on average a risk will have bad outcomes rather than good ones. For example, bad weather not only stops work proceeding but can also even destroy previous work, whereas good weather does not mean that double the normal work can be done.

However, risks do not always have to have a safety aspect to them, for within our detailed planning stage there are many activities that could go wrong without any threat to safety. For example, although the appointment of a caterer who is providing a complex fresh hot food menu for an event may pose risks in respect of food hygiene and potential food poisoning, there is also the risk that the caterer will not turn up, or that the menu choice will have to be reduced, or indeed that the caterer will go bankrupt just before the event. The consequences of this may be as equally devastating as the safety risks, and perhaps more probable. Other possible risks could be that the artist you have booked for an event is not granted an entry visa by the country where you are running the event.

The risk may have positive consequences, and it could be that an outdoor event is even more successful than expected and the event manager needs to implement a contingency plan of locating and installing more portable toilets (Silver, 2004). The techniques that we propose in this chapter allow for the event manager to consider all types of risks, and not just those with a safety or negative aspect.

Different authors and texts site a range of different risks, and these can change depending upon the event that is being planned and its complexity. We have adapted a list provided by Shone and Parry (2004) which cites seven different categories. This list was originally adapted from that proposed by Berlonghi in McDonnell *et al.* (1999). The seven categories are:

1. Risks to staff and others, due to confused organization and poor health and safety practice
2. Risks arising from overenthusiastic marketing of an event, raising expectations that will not be met
3. Risks in health and safety, particularly with outside complex events which may include an inherently risky activity (e.g. pyrotechnics, dangerous sports)
4. Risks in catering provision
5. Risks with crowd management, depending on density and profile mix, crush points and emergency exits
6. Risks in security where large numbers, VIPs and media coverage present terrorist opportunities
7. Risk in transport of resources to the site.

You could augment this list so it is many times longer and more complex, and it is that act of planning and analysing activities that will assist the event manager during the preparation for an event.

Shone and Parry (2004) consider the range of risks in terms of low-, medium- and high-risk activities:

- Low-risk events are regular, routine events, often indoors and with no unusual activities. Similar events have been organized before, and considerable expertise exists amongst the staff, managers and suppliers.
- Medium-risk events might be large indoor events, possibly in more unusual locations, but where the activities are more complicated than usual. Conversely, the event may take place outdoors, but involve less complex activities.
- High-risk events are these events that involve large numbers of people who come with little experience of the event, and where the managers also have little experience of the activities. Similarly, the activities themselves may constitute a danger – e.g. high-speed motor racing, challenging outdoor corporate teambuilding events, and events where there is a greater interaction with the customers, possibly including young children.

This range of risks can alter drastically given various scenarios. An outdoor event might be considered a low to medium risk when there are not very large numbers and the activities being undertaken are manageable. However, should the weather change suddenly for the worse so everyone crowds into the refreshment marquee, the outcome could be very different.

Silver (2004) identifies the categories of risk as safety, security, capability, internal and external. The safety risks that are referred to include physical harm, sanitation and health issues. The security risks include physical or intellectual property loss, theft and fire. The capability risks include processes, use of technology and unrealistic goals.

The internal risks include resource allocation and changing specifications. The external risks include the legal environment, the weather and staffing issues.

O'Toole and Mikolaitis (2002), on the other hand, discuss two categories of risks: those that create change and may jeopardize the success of the event, and those that relate to a physical risk which could place the event manager in a situation discussing legalities.

The nature of events themselves adds to the importance of having a good risk management strategy. O'Toole and Mikolaitis (2002) site various attributes from a range of different events which predispose the need for a carefully thought-out risk management plan. Their list includes:

- Large number of attendees
- Use of volunteers and inadequately trained staff
- Untried venues
- Inadequate time spent planning, and quick decisions
- Risky activities
- A range of uncoordinated suppliers and lack of incentives to do a good job.

It can be seen that the degree of complexity, the venue, the expertise of the staff and the experiences and profiles of the customers all affect the risky nature of different events. Since an event, by its own definition, is out of the ordinary (O'Toole and Mikolaitis, 2002), it demands an out of the ordinary response during its planning and implementation. Customers are often unused to responding to an out of the ordinary situation, and the risks taken will therefore become that much greater. Silver (2004) clearly believes that in any event there will always be a certain amount of risk, and that the only thing that is constant in our lives is change. However, accepting that a failure will occur is not the same as ignoring it (Slack *et al.*, 2004).

To identify the risks associated with a particular event, the event manager should meet with the different stakeholders to review what has occurred in the past, how the new event has changed, and whether there are new industry standards that should be taken into account. The risk management techniques that are proposed later in this chapter will draw on these brainstorming and information-seeking sessions.

Hygiene risks

In food preparation it is common as standard practice to exercise Hazard Analysis Critical Control Points (HACCP). The approach is to analyse all potential hazards associated with food, to identify critical control points where hazards can be eliminated, and to establish procedures to monitor control points and verify systems. HACCP gained prominence when adopted by the American National Aeronautical and Space Administration (NASA) for space flight.

The seven steps of HACCP are as follows:

1. Analyse potential hazards with food and find measures to control the identified hazards
2. Identify critical control points in foods production from the raw state through processing and delivery to the end user (examples are cooking, cooling and packaging)
3. Establish critical limits (standards) for each control point – for example, one standard might be the minimum cooking temperature to eliminate microbes
4. Establish procedures to monitor the critical control points, such as length of time and temperature to cook, or time for cooling before packaging
5. Establish corrective actions, such as disposing of food if standards are not achieved
6. Establish procedures to ensure the system is being maintained – this might mean checking the equipment, e.g. with temperature probes

7. Establish an effective record-keeping system, more than just 'ticking the boxes', to ensure that the standards and procedures are being kept to.

At NASA level, HACCP principles and standards are backed by sound scientific knowledge and have been universally adopted around the world. At a lower level, this approach means having set procedures relating to hygiene for food workers (rubber gloves, bright-coloured band aids, hats and hairnets), temperature control for food storage (hot and cold), proper cooking of food, and clean protective food covers (if micro-organisms are present in a product, their fast propagation rate will spoil the quality of the product. Some micro-organisms may produce toxic substances, while others might be harmless to health but can have an adverse effect on taste or appearance).

Insurable risks

Since the days of the Industrial Revolution, safety standards at the workplace have steadily and significantly improved. However, processes and equipment have now attained a high degree of complexity. Swarbrooke and Horner (2001) recommend that insurance be taken out wherever possible, and that the event manager should have contingency plans in place and be ready to implement them if problems do arise. However, insurance will not prevent something from happening (Silver, 2004); it will only lessen the financial impact should it occur (see Case study 11.1).

Insurable risks fall into four areas:

1. Direct damage
2. Consequential loss
3. Legal liability
4. Personal loss.

Direct damage can be to the venue or to the equipment being used for the event, and may be caused by fire, flood, bad weather or damage during movement or erection. *Consequential loss* can be lost time arising from the venue being unavailable due to direct property damage, or the loss of a future contract as a direct result of the damage. *Legal liability* may arise from damage to a third party's property or equipment, or an incident leading to injury or illness to a patron or other person. Legal liability also includes failure to perform. *Personal loss* could include a claim for stress by an employee or patron. Personal loss also includes a direct financial loss by the event organizer.

Causes of accidents

An accident is usually the result of contact with a substance or a source of energy above the threshold limit of the body or structure. The accident may result in injury to visitors, staff and suppliers, and to property. The cause of the accident may be substandard working practices and unsafe conditions. Substandard working practices could include personal factors, such as lack of skill, stress, laziness, taking shortcuts, and stupidity. Unsafe conditions in the work environment may include poor or inappropriate equipment, no safety guards, poor training, and lack of maintenance of equipment. It is important to understand that the same factors that are causing accidents may also be creating losses in reputation and profit.

Accidents at an event can, in serious cases, lead to closure plus inspections by government officials and legal costs. At best, there will be the cost of correcting the situation

Case study 11.1

Insurex, Los Angeles, California, USA
When Lightning Strikes

Lightning poses an enormous threat for those participating in outdoor sports and recreation events.

Lightning is the second largest killer due to storms, the first being floods. Each year hundreds of people are killed or injured in lightning mishaps.

The number of lightning casualties in recreational and sports settings has risen alarmingly. One reason is that both thunderstorms and outdoor events coincide at the same time – from 10 am to 7 pm between late spring and early fall.

Here is Insurex's suggested lightning risk management strategy for outdoor events:

- Monitor local weather forecasts and warnings.
- Establish a chain of command that identifies who is actively to look for signs of threatening weather and make the call to remove individuals from the area.
- A lightning safety announcement should be made over the public address system, with information on what to do and where to find a safe location.
- Designate a shelter. The best way to avoid lightning is to take shelter. The primary choice for a safe location is any substantial, occupied building. The secondary choice is a vehicle with a metal roof and closed windows. Avoid small structures (such as picnic shelters or athletic storage sheds), trees, poles, and the highest point in the open.

Thunder always accompanies lightning. The 'flash-to-bang' method should be used to estimate how far away the lightning is actually occurring. This method involves counting the seconds from the point at which lightning is sighted to the point at which thunder is heard. The number should then be divided by five to obtain the distance (in miles) at which the lightning is actually occurring. Experts say if the count is 30 or less, all should be evacuated. It does not have to be raining for lightning to strike. Lightning can strike from as far as 10 miles away from the rain band.

Postpone or suspend activities if a thunderstorm appears imminent – darkening clouds, high winds, thunder or lightning – until the storm has passed, then wait 30 minutes before returning outdoors.

Individuals caught in a lightning storm who feel their hair stand on end, skin tingle or hear crackling noises (signs of an imminent lightning strike) should assume the 'lightning position' (also known as the lightning-safe position, although it still may not prevent a lightning strike); crouch on the ground, weight on the balls of the feet, feet together, head lowered, eyes closed and ears covered. This position lowers the person's height and minimizes the area in contact with the surface of the ground. If there are any insulated objects handy, like a foam pad or soft pack of clothes, stand on them. Never lie flat on the ground.

(Extract from website. Further details available at www.insurevents.com.)

Reflective practice 11.1

You are a UK event organizer arranging an outdoor concert in Los Angeles, and you have been made aware of the risks of lightning strikes.

1. What information would you use to develop your risk assessment?
2. What would your team need, and what would you tell the general public and when?

so that the accident will not occur again. As stated at the beginning of this chapter, if an accident can happen then it will – and usually at the worst possible time. Apart from humanitarian reasons for preventing an accident, prevention will usually be cheaper than putting something right after it has happened. The cost of having systems in place to prevent poor quality situations is discussed in Chapter 16, where we explore the cost of having a good system in place and compare those costs with those that will have to be met if problems occur.

Case study 11.2 describes those risks associated with rock concerts.

Case study 11.2

Rock concerts

Extract from *Casual Rock Concert Events*, by Mick Upton

With the benefit of hindsight it is now possible to assess the level of risk presented by major casual concert events. The following table is the result of research for the period 1974–2002. It is not intended as a definitive list of fatal incidents that have occurred at concert events. It merely illustrates the level and type of incidents that have occurred in similar circumstances in countries thousands of miles apart. The list includes both indoor and outdoor venue types, the common link being that none of these fatal incidents have been fully explained. Consequently they have all been regarded as being caused by the crowd itself due to panic or irrational behaviour.

Incidents such as fire, where it is known that fire exits were locked, and public disorder are not included here on the grounds that the root cause of the incident was established therefore preventative measures can be taken during planning for future events.

Table of fatalities 1974 to 2002:

Date	Place	Killed	Activity
1974	White City	1	F.O.S. crush
1976	Cincinnati	11	Ingress crush
1986	Long Beach	3	Fell from balcony
1986	Seattle	1	F.O.S. crush
1987	Nashville	2	Ingress crush
1989	Donington	2	F.O.S. crush
1991	Salt Lake City	3	F.O.S. crush
1992	Costa Rica	1	Ingress crush
1992	South Korea	1	F.O.S. crush
1993	Hong Kong	1	F.O.S. crush
1994	London	1	Stage diving
1995	Israel	3	Ingress crush
1996	Columbia	3	Ingress crush
1996	Ireland	2	F.O.S. crush
1996	South Korea	2	F.O.S. crush
1997	Michigan	1	Fell from balcony
1997	Düsseldorf	1	F.O.S. crush
1997	Brazil	7	Fell from balcony
1999	Belarus	53	Egress crush*

(Continued)

Date	Place	Killed	Activity
1999	Austria	5	Egress crush
1999	Sweden	1	F.O.S. crush
2000	Denmark	9	F.O.S. crush
2000	Baltimore	1	Fell from balcony
2001	Indonesia	4	P. A. egress crush
2001	Belgium	1	Fell from balcony
2001	Australia	1	F.O.S. crush
2002	Venezuela	11	Ingress crush

Total = 132 victims
F.O.S. indicates front of stage.
*Indicates egress-related
P.A. crush indicates an egress from a public appearance by an artiste at a shopping mall.

In order to gain a better understanding of the causes of these unexplained incidents, this research then focused on rock concert events from the emergence of the subculture termed '*Nu metal*'. Nu metal emerged in the late 1980s as a subculture of punk rock. By the mid-1990s it had established itself as a fusion of black culture (Rap and Hip Hop) and new wave rock. Possibly the first indication that the culture brought with it serious crowd control problems was at the 1994 Woodstock (USA) festival. The press at the time reported that there were 4000 people treated by first aid, of whom 250 required treatment by the on site hospital. Many of these injuries were bruises, bloody noses or broken bones thought to have been caused by cultural behaviour.

Nu metal rock culture has its own language for cultural activity – for example *moshing*, *skanking*, *crowd surfing* and *stage diving*. Any of these activities can create localized, high-density, dynamic or lateral surging or a crowd collapse, yet the crowd regard these conditions as being perfectly normal.

The above table shows fatal incidences at concerts that have occurred worldwide over a 28-year period.

(Printed by kind permission of Mick Upton, Head of the Centre for Crowd Management Studies, Buckinghamshire Chilterns University College, England.)

Reflective practice 11.2

1. As part of your risk management strategy, what would you do to manage the risk of moshing, skanking, crowd surfing and stage diving without affecting the enjoyment of the crowd?
2. Bearing in mind the cultural significance of these actions, who should be responsible for putting this strategy into operation?

Risk identification

The first lesson is to expect risks where they are not expected, since risks can occur at any stage of an event. A gap analysis approach (Silver, 2004) can be used for this, which

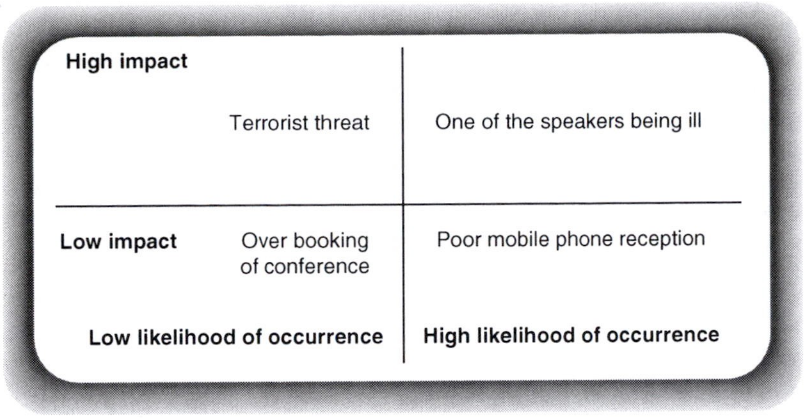

High impact		
	Terrorist threat	One of the speakers being ill
Low impact	Over booking of conference	Poor mobile phone reception
	Low likelihood of occurrence	**High likelihood of occurrence**

Figure 11.1 Impact and likelihood of risk occurring at a conference

would identify gaps in the planning process to expose any disparities between what can be expected to happen and what might happen.

As stated previously, there are many opportunities to gather information from a variety of stakeholders in order to try and identify risks both obvious and far fetched. As event manager, you should use expert judgement, and don't ignore your intuition. Ask the questions, What if? Then what? If you and your staff think of things that can go wrong and have a counter plan, you will be able to react quickly. You should involve the advice of specialists and other professionals, such as the fire service, police, and health and safety executives.

O'Toole and Mikolaitis (2002) recommend discussions with suppliers and subcontractors, since they have a great deal of experience. They also list other groups of experienced people, including risk management experts and the staff and volunteers working on an event, who may bring their experiences from similar events in the past.

To assist in the brainstorm, a quadrant could be used to plot the likelihood of a risk occurring and the degree of impact that could be expected from it (see Figure 11.1).

Figure 11.1 shows a few scenarios that could occur when organizing a conference. This approach could be useful, with a group of people, in identifying the range of risks that could occur. It enables risks to be plotted according to their likelihood of occurrence and the level of impact that would arise if the risk occurred. However, this technique does not propose any solutions to the risks. Once risks have been identified, the event manager should also assess the impact of the risks should more than one occur at the same time (O'Toole and Mikolaitis, 2002).

Techniques for managing risks

Fault tree

One method proposed by O'Toole and Mikolaitis (2002) and Slack *et al.* (2004) is to construct a 'fault tree', which starts by deciding on a bad outcome (such as the event losing money) and then working through the various areas and functions to identify the possible causes. This principle can be seen within Chapter 14, where the use of the Ishkawa fishbone diagram is used for solving problems occurring at an event.

Risk assessment sheet

A more typical risk assessment sheet, often used by event managers, lists the possible risks on a table (see Table 11.1). The possible risk is listed onto the first column, and then subsequent columns require the event manager to assess who would be affected, the worst-case outcome as a rating from 1–5 (5 being highest), the likelihood of occurrence rated 1–5, and the numerical consequence of these scales being multiplied together. Further columns then allow the event manager to state what precautions are already in place, and what further action is required to reduce the likelihood of the occurrence or its impact. This leads to another column, listing the assessed new level of risk. Some sheets would then indicate who is responsible for this action, and the date it was taken. It can be seen that this is a working document; ideally one that is set up electronically and can be continually updated.

Oakland (2000) and Slack *et al.* (2004) propose a technique called a failure mode effect analysis (FMEA). This analysis identifies the circumstances where failures are likely to occur. By identifying these before they happen, a checklist can be produced which asks three questions:

1. What is the likelihood that failure will occur?
2. What would the consequence of the failure be?
3. How likely is such a failure to be detected before it affects the customer?

Not dissimilar to the risk assessment sheet in Table 11.1, a quantitative evaluation is then calculated for each potential cause of failure. Corrective action should then be applied. The main difference from the typical risk assessment is that this approach looks at all elements of the event – not only at safety issues and the points where there

Table 11.1 Extract from an event risk analysis sheet for a conference

Risk	To whom	A = worst-case outcome	B = likelihood	Level of risk (i.e. A × B)	Existing precautions	Further action to be taken	New level of risk	Who is responsible
Fire	All people attending	5	1	5	Fire extinguishers, alarms, briefings	Briefings with delegates at start of event	5	Duty manager
Access and egress crushing	Delegates	3	1	3	Clear route, wide aisles	Clear signposting	3	Front of house staff
Trips and falls over carpets	All people attending	4	3	12	All carpets and rugs to be secured	All trailing wires to be taped and put at high level	4	Maintenance
Poor communication	All people attending	3	3	9	Good audio equipment	Pre conference checks	3	Audio manager
Food poisoning	All people attending	5	3	15	Reputable supplier	Temperature probes in use and time controls	5	Resource manager and supplier

are negative impacts. It can be applied in a much more thorough way, and is essentially a seven-step process:

1. Identify all the component parts of the event
2. List all the ways that the service could fail
3. Identify the effects of the failures – down time, safety, repair, effects on customers etc.
4. Identify the possible causes of failure
5. Assess the probability of failure, the severity of failure and likelihood of detection
6. Calculate the risk number by multiplying all three ratings together
7. Instigate corrective action to minimize failure on those points that have a high rating.

Oakland (2000) extends the concept of FMEA by ranking the results in an order of seriousness (i.e. their criticality). This then becomes a failure modes effects criticality chart (FMECA). The FMECA determines the features of the design of the event that are likely to cause failure. It should use the experience of all the different stakeholders, marketing, design, technology and purchasing etc. The potential failures should be studied to determine their probable effects on the event as a whole. The criticality enables an examination of the severity of each failure in terms of lowering the performance of the event and its eventual success.

FMECA may be applied at any stage of the event operations management model, and in this instance it is shown in the third stage – that of implementation. However, it can also be applied during the design stage in order to identify possible causes of failure and prevent their occurrence.

The eight steps of the FMECA are as follows:

1. Identify the components of the service
2. List all the possible failure modes for each component
3. Set down the effects that each mode of failure would have on the event
4. List all the possible causes of each failure mode
5. Assess numerically the failure modes on a scale of 1–10 (p = probability of the failure mode occurring, s = seriousness or criticality of the failure, d = the difficulty of detecting the failure before its effect reaches the customer)
6. Calculate the product of the ratings, i.e. $C = p \times s \times d$; this is the criticality index
7. Indicate briefly the corrective action required, who is responsible, and the expected completion date
8. Rank the failures accordingly.

Risk assessment is discussed in Case study 11.3.

Reflective practice 11.3 (This relates to Case study 11.3.)

Risk assessments have to be considered as a living document, so while in the planning stage all possibilities have to be considered. In reality, during the event unforeseen circumstances can and will happen. Therefore the process used has to be able to be updated, changed and adapted as the situations occur. This chapter has highlighted the needs and requirements for managing risk.
Put together a process for managing risk effectively during an event.

Moment of truth

A final technique that we will present in this section is that of moments of truth (MoT). This is the moment in time when a customer first comes into contact with the event and the point at which that customer makes a judgement about the quality of the

Case study 11.3

National Outdoor Events Association (NOEA), Wallington, Surrey, UK

Letter from the Chairman, Richard Limb, re. risk assessment, 2004:

Risk assessments

Risk assessments, a term often used, a term often misunderstood, and believed by some to be yet another bureaucratic, paper-producing exercise. Let's examine the concept in more detail in relation to events.

We need to have appropriate site design, appropriate safety measures and standards and competent contractors, tailored to suit the event. Under- or over-provision can cost time, money and, of course, lives. The combination of venue, event and audience profile is totally unique. Specific standards are required that are practical and pragmatic and workable. A risk assessment approach is essential (as well as a legal requirement). The approach is simple, but should be carried out by competent persons. All hazards (potential to cause harm) should be identified for each work activity and the event as a whole. (This will require skills to superimpose the event on the venue). Those persons affected by the hazards should be identified and the risk (likelihood and severity) evaluated. The most important step is then to determine the most appropriate safety measures and then to re-evaluate the risk to determine if acceptable. Safety measures should first consider removal of the hazard before considering other control measures. The results of this process should then be communicated to all relevant personnel.

Risk assessment matrices are available to help evaluate the risk, but should be used with caution. Proper thought should be given to the problems associated with each hazard and the most practical, pragmatic method in exercising control. Otherwise it does become just a paper exercise. Used properly the Entertainment world can achieve good safety standards and also analyse and achieve more exciting, challenging performances. New diverse, unorthodox 'performances' can be fully appraised and often made to work – essential if the Industry is to move forward in a dynamic way and continue stimulating future audiences. Working Naval bases, quarries etc. can be used as venues, fall-out zones from pyrotechnics can include petrol stations. Health and Safety legislation demands full analysis of work activities and the establishment of appropriate safety precautions to protect the health, safety and welfare of all persons affected by the activities. Risk assessments are the way forward. Master them, do them properly and remember it's what happens on site that matters, a mass of papers back at base is a waste of time.

Richard Limb MIOA DMS DipAPC FRSH FIOSH MCIEH, President of NOEA
Director of Leisure Safety
For Capita-Symonds Group Limited

(For further details about NOEA see www.noea.org.uk/)

organization's services and products (Oakland, 2000). In MoT analysis, the points of potential dissatisfaction are identified within the flow chart diagrams covered in Chapter 8. Every step that the customer takes within the event should be considered and recorded. It may be difficult (Oakland, 2000) to identify all the MoTs, but this systematic approach should lead to a minimization of the number and severity of unexpected failures.

Contingency plans

An outcome of whatever risk assessment process is used should be an integrated plan of action to minimize risks in the future. These contingency plans should be communicated to all concerned and put into action if the risk becomes a reality. The plans must be understood by more than just the event manager, both in case he or she is already dealing with another incident and also to give responsibility to others who can carry out the alternative causes of action, knowing that they have been well thought through and approved. O'Toole and Mikolaitis (2002) advise that contingency plans should contain responsibilities, chain of command, and procedures to minimize or contain the impact.

Post-event risk report

A final stage of any event is the debriefing of the staff, collection of any accident reports and evaluation of how the event progressed. These procedures are covered in detail in Chapter 14. However, it is important to conclude this chapter by reiterating the need to report back on the effectiveness of the risk management process. This review will enable learning to take place from any of the activities undertaken to minimize or prevent risks occurring. An outcome would be improved information with regard to failure modes and their effects. The data can be used to produce guidelines for the future and to improve the analysis undertaken for the risk assessments, and of course to minimize uncalled for problems and discomforts to our customers.

Chapter summary and key points

Even for a straightforward event there will be many things that can go wrong. Risk management involves identifying what can go wrong and taking steps for prevention, or organizing a plan of action to correct or ease the situation if the risk should occur. Some risks can be insured against, but often insurance will not cover the total costs. If human life is involved, the results of an accident cannot be measured in monetary terms. The old adage that prevention is better than cure should not be forgotten.

This chapter has provided techniques for:

- Identifying possible risks
- Calculating the probability of a risk occurring
- Estimation of cost should a risk occur
- Planning avoidance of risks, and
- Formation of contingency plans if the risk cannot be avoided.

An important aspect of risk management is communication with staff, suppliers and contractors regarding what the risks are, and prevention measures that must be followed. The advice of specialists such as the fire service, police and health and safety inspectors should be sought.

In summary:

- Know what the risks are
- Know the cost of each risk
- Know the chance of each risk happening
- Minimize the chance of risks occurring
- Have a contingency plan.

Event Operations Management Model: Tum, Norton and Wright 2005

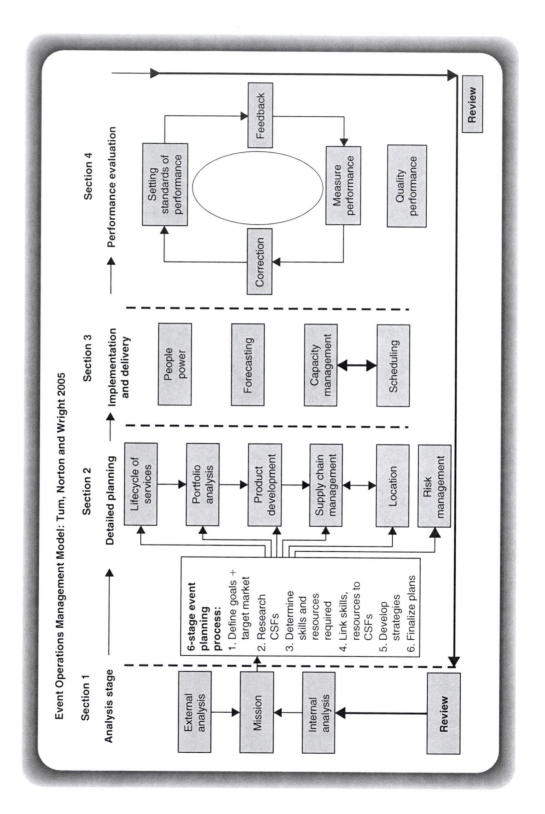

Section Three

Implementation and delivery

Introduction

We have now moved into the third stage of the event operations management model. This is where the detailed operational planning and the execution of planning take place. This follows the analysis and detailed planning covered in stages one and two. Section 3 comprises Chapters 12–14, and considers the four key operational issues of managing people, forecasting, capacity management and scheduling. Chapter 14 concludes with some advice on personal time management.

Chapter 12 considers the importance of people to all events, and how the manager can make best use of this resource. Within the event industry this resource may be one of the most costly. We have already considered in previous chapters, particularly Chapter 9, how to manage resources, locate the optimum source and use the most appropriate and relevant type for each individual event. All of these concepts are valid when we consider the management of people. An event manager has to manage this valuable and expensive resource just as carefully as all other resources.

However, people are not inanimate; they can make choices, be motivated and have different reactions in different circumstances. This chapter covers the basic theories of motivation, and explains how to get the best from all those working towards and within an event, and the importance of a strong organizational culture. The chapter recognizes that some staff may be unpaid volunteers. Volunteer staff are often used within the event industry.

Chapter 13 links the two concepts of forecasting and capacity management, as discussed in Chapter 5. Forecasting is a critical area for an event manager. The marketing function estimates the numbers likely to arrive at a particular event, and this forecast determines the amount of resources required to satisfy the expected numbers of customers. The more accurate the forecast, then, the more accurate can be the provision of resources. The actual resources needed and the ways they are presented are based on our knowledge of the customers' critical success factors.

The business policy might well state that there should be full utilization of resources and accept that on some occasions customers will queue and that some customers may be lost to the system.

Part of the responsibility of the event manager will be to determine what resources are needed overall, what can be achieved with existing resources, and how best to allocate resources on a day-to-day basis so as to achieve a successful event.

In short, Chapter 13 establishes the importance of calculating the demand and then matching resources to meet the expected demand. We have selected various techniques from the operational management literature and applied these to typical events. The chapter ends with a very useful section on queuing theory.

Chapter 14 considers scheduling, which is the critical aspect of planning and timing of activities. What is feasible and what is desirable influences how activities are scheduled. The chapter is concerned with arranging resources and setting timeframes so as to achieve the objectives of the event as efficiently as possible. Many of the techniques covered in traditional operational and project management literature are explored to consider their usefulness to event management, and how these can assist with scheduling both complex and simple events.

The chapter ends with some tips on how to manage your own time and how to recognize, and excel in, those aspects of our work that are the most important. Time is a precious commodity, and whether you are doing time, marking time or spending time, time is running out. Your only hope is to do it *now* – procrastination is the thief of time.

Chapter 12

People power – the most valuable resource?

Learning Objectives

After reading through this chapter you will be able to:

■ Appreciate the importance of motivated people, and identify and describe key motivational theories
■ Understand more about volunteers in the event industry
■ Critically discuss aspects of organizational culture
■ Use motivational theory and organizational cultural awareness to achieve the critical success factors demanded by customers
■ Appreciate the purpose of Investors in People.

Introduction

This chapter is the first regarding the third stage of the event operations management model. It covers those moments when the event is no longer at a planning stage, but is happening and being consumed by those who are attending the event. In this chapter the importance of people, 'the human resource', is considered, along with how the events manager can make the best use of this resource.

As most of us will have read (or heard) in a Managing Director's or Chairman's annual address, an organization's most 'valuable' resource is its people. The Chairman could also probably have added 'and the most expensive'.

In the event industry, the level of service provided to customers and the internal efficiency of the organization depend heavily on people – the human resource – and their consistent performance. The event manager has to manage this valuable and expensive resource just as carefully as any other resource. Many of the same strategies included in the procurement process (i.e. planning, sourcing, selecting and evaluating performance – see Chapter 9) are used when staffing an event with paid and volunteer human resources (Silver, 2004).

However, the difference between managing non-human resources and managing human resources is that actions taken with inventory, equipment and machines will lead to predictable results, whereas people are not predictable. Sometimes in a given set of circumstances people will react one way, and sometimes in similar circumstances, for no apparent reason, they will react differently.

Understanding this chapter is crucial for every event manager. People are one of the resources that the manager will have to direct and employ. They are possibly the most important resource and thus, as Lashley and Lee-Ross (2003) state, managers must be able to align an individual's needs with the objectives of the organization for the benefit of their employer, for themselves, for the client and for the outcomes of the event.

Basic requirements leading to self-motivation

As Bowdin *et al.* (2001) say, the ability to motivate other staff members is a fundamental component of the event manager's skills. Without this motivation, paid employees and volunteers can lack enthusiasm for achieving the organization's goals and delivering quality customer service. Without motivation, they may also show a lack of concern for their co-workers and customers (Bowdin *et al.*, 2001).

Getting the best out of people will be achieved by a combination of:

- Making sure that the people of the organization have all the necessary materials and equipment to do the job
- Making sure that staff know what to do and how to do it (this is often set out and explained in a job description)
- Encouraging self motivation and development.

These points are supported by Griffin (2000), who proposes that individual performance is generally determined by three factors:

1. Motivation to do the job
2. Ability to do the job
3. The resources to do the job.

If an employee lacks the ability we can train that person, if other resources are a problem we can supply them as necessary; however, if motivation is missing then the task for the event manager is much more challenging.

In Chapter 10 we looked at the physical aspects of working conditions with a view to increasing efficiency. These physical aspects included location and layout, health and safety issues, and methods of simplifying work. If the physical aspects are not right, if the layout does not make it easy to be efficient, if conditions are uncomfortable and if the work includes unnecessary steps, then it is not likely that staff will be motivated to extend themselves. Indeed, much of their energy will be absorbed in combating or adapting to the difficult conditions in which they are expected to work.

In this chapter it is assumed that the physical aspects are appropriate, and the non-physical (or intangible) aspects that will encourage self-motivation of people will be considered.

People power

Event organizations utilize volunteers to fill some jobs that might otherwise be staffed with temporary employees. It might well be more economic to hire temporary staff to cover certain menial tasks (e.g. litter picking) and to use volunteer resources for more meaningful tasks. Motivated people will provide high levels of service for the customer at no extra cost to the organization, and at the same time they will constantly be looking for the most efficient way of using other resources. Much has been written about motivation, and many theories have been developed, and still many organizations do not have high-performing, self-motivated people.

The importance of motivated people

The importance of motivated staff can perhaps best be shown by example.

In Chapter 2 we discussed what customers expect from a courtesy bus shuttle service at an outdoor sculpture event, taking passengers to different parts of the park.

We said that achieving specification, cost and timing would meet customers' basic needs – that is, a safe journey from 'A' to 'B' at the right time and at a reasonable price. We also said that meeting basic expectations would not in itself be considered to be a 'quality' service, but that on top of basic requirements customers would appreciate punctuality, a clean bus, a friendly well-presented driver, and consistency of service. We agreed that cleaning the bus, issuing the driver with a smart uniform and training the driver to be courteous and well groomed would incur some minimal costs, but that the overall perception to the customer would be an improved, or perhaps even a 'quality' service achieved.

If drivers can be sufficiently motivated to think of the bus as being 'their' bus, then it is possible that much of what management would like – a clean bus, adherence to the timetable, friendly and helpful service to customers and so on – can be gained at no extra ongoing cost to the organization. The only cost will be the investment in the time to change the *culture* of the organization. Once the culture is right, the drivers will not think of their job as just a means to get a weekly pay packet; instead they will be proud of what they are doing, believe that their actions can make a difference, and constantly surprise management with helpful suggestions.

For instance, at Disneyland staff are regarded as actors. They are not sweeping the grounds and picking up rubbish; they are members of the cast, acting a part.

Motivated event staff

Many staff in the event industry enjoy customer contact, and generally prefer to be cheerful and helpful. They do their best to give good service. This attitude may exist even if they receive poor pay, indifferent working conditions and bad management. They have a desire to serve and offer good service despite, in some cases, poor organization and the lack of resources. The reason for this is that they are gaining personal satisfaction from meeting the needs of the customer.

Restaurant workers might provide good service irrespective of poor pay and conditions, in the expectation that the customer will leave a tip – the expectation of a reward may encourage the serving staff to provide a higher level of service. However, in some countries (such as Australia and New Zealand) tipping is not common, and it is noticeable that restaurant service is every bit as good, if slightly less formal than in countries where tipping is expected.

This suggests that people who are drawn to being close to the customer genuinely like working with people and, given the opportunity or encouragement, prefer to give good friendly service, even without an extra reward to motivate. However, where a tip or other reward has become the custom it is not likely that people will remain motivated for long if tips suddenly stop coming, and indeed the tip is regarded as part of their remuneration.

There is no history of tipping in the events industry. You would never find security personnel or bar staff at a beer tent at a Robbie Williams concert being tipped. Our challenge is to encourage all staff, whether in our employ, in the employ of our suppliers or voluntary workers, to provide a high level of service.

Out-of-sight staff

Out-of-sight staff, such as administration support people, marquee erectors, lighting personnel etc., seldom come face to face with external customers and thus to a large extent lack the incentive of seeing or interacting with satisfied 'end user' customers, or conversely of having to field the complaints of dissatisfied customers. They are therefore less likely to be motivated by management pleas that customer satisfaction is important.

However, to a large extent it is the efforts of these out-of-sight people on which overall efficiency and eventual customer satisfaction rest. For example, at a large pop concert if the sound system fails or if temporary toilets are smelly and insufficient in numbers, no matter how fantastic the artist is, the event may be rated poorly.

Thus frontline staff might provide reasonable service to customers, despite poor conditions and poor management, simply because they are people-oriented and like positive relations with the people that they are serving. These people do not need management to tell them that the customer is important. On the other hand, those staff who have less direct customer contact are less likely to be motivated by a plea to provide customer satisfaction, even when management tries to promote the concept of internal customers.

The internal customer theory is that within an organization, the next person in the process is the customer. For example, an event organizer providing information for a brochure to an administrative staff member should consider that member as being the internal customer. As such, the information given should be clear and unambiguous, and given in time for a reasonable chance of completing the task by the time set. However, human nature being what it is, although the organizer might even buy into this concept (that the administrative staff member is the customer), in practice he or she will be irritated if the brochure is not completed on time and error-free.

Investors in People

Investors in People is a National Standard which sets out a level of good practice for training and development of people to achieve business goals. The Standard was developed during 1990 by the National Training Task Force in partnership with leading national businesses and personnel, professional and employee organizations, such as the Confederation of British Industry (CBI), the Trades Union Congress (TUC) and the Institute of Personnel and Development (IPD). The work was supported by the Employment Department.

The Standard provides a national framework for improving business performance and competitiveness through a planned approach to setting and communicating business objectives, and developing people to meet these objectives. The result is that what people can and are motivated to do matches what the organization needs them to do. Investors in People is cyclical, and should engender the culture of continuous improvement.

The Investors in People standard operates in 24 countries.

Case study 12.1 provides an example of the Investors in People Standard in a small business, while Case studies 12.2 and 12.3 illustrate its use in a large organization.

Case study 12.1

Prestbury House Hotel, Cheltenham, UK

(Organization size, 23; sector, Hotels and Leisure; organization location, South West.)

The organization

Until 1990 the Prestbury House Hotel in Cheltenham had been run as a 'restaurant with rooms'. When Stephen and Jacqueline Whitbourne took over the ownership in the early part of 1990, they quickly began to transform the 9-bedroomed property into a 17-bedroomed country house hotel and conference centre.

During the first year they developed the conference facilities and introduced a management training centre. Today, the hotel employs 23 staff (14 full time) and has an annual turnover of £650 000.

The result

Prestbury House achieved IiP recognition in April 1994, and was the first hotel in Gloucestershire to receive the award. Since then, turnover and profit has increased year on year, while the organization's reputation as a first-class hotel – for both staff and visitors – continues to go from strength to strength.

Repeat business (for business and leisure guests) has also increased, as has the number of recommendations – especially for weddings – and in 2001 the organization won a British Hospitality Association Hotel In Excellence Award.

Proprietor Stephen Whitbourne believes that much of the hotel's continued success is down to their commitment to staff training and development. As he says: 'The training programmes which we offer our staff are unmatched in the region. Not only does this make us attractive in terms of recruiting staff – and especially college leavers – but it also makes our employees more motivated and dedicated.'

The challenge

Stephen and Jacqueline Whitbourne had always encouraged staff development and offered on-site training to all their employees. However, as the business continued to expand, and employees had to cater for larger functions, they felt that the time had come to formalize standards and procedures so that all staff reflected the service culture.

The strategy

With the help of Business Link Gloucestershire, Stephen and Jacqueline Whitbourne used their current staff working methods as the basis for a more formal, tailored system that would meet the IiP requirements. They were awarded IiP recognition in January 1994, and are convinced that the process has played a major part in the continued success of their business. As Stephen Whitbourne points out: 'Because staff are such a crucial aspect to our business, it's vital that they are happy and satisfied in their work. By ensuring that sound staff systems are in place and that our training is exemplary, we hope to achieve our aim – providing all our customers with a rewarding service and pleasurable stay every time, no matter what the occasion.'

Case study 12.2

Torquay Leisure Hotels (1), Torquay, Devon, UK

(Organization size, 250; sector, Hotels and Leisure; organization location, South West.)

The organization

Torquay Leisure Hotels is a family-owned business that started in 1948 as a 28-bedroom guest-house. It is now a group of four hotels providing over 400 bedrooms and apartments with extensive leisure and conference facilities. All four hotels are situated on one seven-acre site close to the centre of Torquay. The goal is to have a 'full house 365 days of the year'.

The company has been able to generate revenue and offer employment throughout the year – 250 people are employed on a permanent basis. Each hotel operates as a separate unit with its own general manager. The general managers work closely together and report to a group general manager, who in turn reports to the managing director. In addition, there are small, central, specialist departments to support the management team.

The result

The company has moved to a collective approach to running the business. Improving communications and developing learning opportunities for all employees has had a major impact on performance.

Specific benefits include:

- Turnover increased by 17 per cent
- Profitability increased by 25 per cent
- Room occupancy rates improved (20 per cent above the national average, and growing)
- A high level of repeat business and personal recommendation
- Staff retention improved by 30 per cent
- Recruitment costs decreased by 60 per cent
- Guest comment cards showing 98.5 per cent customer satisfaction levels
- The purchase of a fourth hotel, reflecting success in a time of recession
- Forty managers now being able to design and deliver training packages
- The award of National Training Award to the group
- The use of the company as a case study of good practice in the 1993 ILAM *Guide to Good Practice* and in a BBC training video on learning organizations.

Torquay Leisure Hotels was recognized as an IiP in 1992, and was re-accredited in March 1996.

Investors in People is a long-term commitment and is a learning process encouraging continuous re-evaluation, change and improvement.

Investors in People develops the strength of a business by encouraging everyone to work as a team towards the same objective.

The challenge

The group enjoyed a period of rapid growth in the decade to 1990, developing facilities and marketing and financial systems, but suffered a substantial drop in profitability. A comprehensive business review was commissioned early in 1990.

Research and staff consultation showed that:

- Gross profitability had steadily fallen by 11 per cent from 1987 to 1990
- Standards had deteriorated, resulting in a fall in customer satisfaction
- The company had developed every aspect of its business except its people.

The underlying reasons were identified as being poor communication, limited teamwork, lack of corporate direction, the company having outgrown its family structure of tight central control with a very restricted role for line managers, an authoritarian and reactive management style, and an increase in competition.

The strategy

The senior management team, working with a consultant, recognized two main business objectives:

1. Improved profitability
2. An improved level of customer service.

Two complementary action plans were developed to run concurrently, ensuring total integration of training and development with business needs. Specific business objectives were:

- To increase sales
- To improve standards and customer service
- To improve health, hygiene and safety procedures in line with new regulations.

Organizational and training objectives were:

- To develop the structure and skill of the management team to meet the future needs of the business
- To install a systematic training and development process for all employees to meet business needs.

Necessary fundamental changes in the culture of the company included:

- Total commitment from senior management
- A review of all roles and areas of responsibilities
- Training for all employees
- Full involvement of all employees.

Steps were taken to improve the vital area of communications. The managing director instituted an annual meeting for all staff, to review the past year and put forward the agenda for the coming year. Regular departmental meetings and the introduction of a staff newsletter supported the annual meeting. The company business plan was developed to provide supporting operational plans at hotel and departmental levels to help and encourage all staff.

The company appraisal scheme was extended to all employees, and encompassed:

- Communicating individual contributions to the company
- Identifying and reviewing individual training and development needs
- Providing individuals with feedback on their performance.

All management, staff and supervisors were helped to acquire training skills, enabling those who have the responsibility for training to design and deliver the programmes themselves, and ensuring that the company's targets were achieved. The comprehensive training programmes are management driven and supported by the personnel and training officer. This systematic approach to training has included the identification of needs, setting of objectives for each training action, and constant evaluation and review against business needs. The MD, Laurence Murrell, has stated: 'Evaluation is probably one of the most essential parts of the strategy that we have put in place. It's pushed the whole development of the company forward, and now it's become a norm in the way we think and plan.'

Other initiatives have included the introduction of personnel procedures and the improvement of conditions of employment.

(Case studies printed by courtesy of Investors in People; more information about Investors in People can be found at www.investorsinpeople.co.uk.)

Case study 12.3

Torquay Leisure Hotels (2), Devon, England

Torquay hotel group wins national employment award and has been named the best in the country when it comes to employing staff

TLH Leisure Resort has won the prestigious title at a glittering awards ceremony in London for the hospitality, leisure, travel and tourism industries.

The privately owned hotel group won the award for the 'Best Employer' in the leisure and hospitality sector, beating some of Britain's best-known major hotel groups.

The award was judged on the business performance of the group, which employs over 330 staff in administration, finance, sales and marketing and in its four hotels, the Derwent, Victoria, Carlton and Toorak.

Four representatives from the TLH were on hand to receive the award from Bob Cotton on behalf of Springboard UK, which promotes careers in hospitality leisure, tourism and travel across the UK.

The accolade recognizes the superb opportunities and facilities available to staff at TLH, including ongoing training, staff uniforms, bonuses, long service awards, a staff restaurant and the use of the group's superb leisure facilities.

Chairman Laurence Murrell said: 'This is tremendous recognition of all the hard work which everyone at TLH puts in. Our business success comes from our people. We put a tremendous amount of planning into the recruitment of staff and are extremely proud that we attract and retain the best workforce possible in what is a very competitive industry.'

It could be a double accolade for TLH, as the group has also reached the final of another national award – the Business Excellence Awards, promoted by the Hospitality and Leisure Manpower, which is supported by the Department of Trade and Industry and the Department of Culture, Media and Sports. TLH has reached the final of the 'People' category, and the winners will be announced at a ceremony in London in three weeks' time.

(More information about the TLH Group can be found at www.tlh.co.uk.)

Reflective practice 12.1

Consider Case studies 12.1–12.3.

1. What factors within the three case studies would you consider to be motivating for the staff?
2. What personal experience do you have of staff motivation within an event or an event organization?

Volunteers in the event industry

There is no research that suggests that event volunteers are any different from other volunteer staff. However, Getz (1997) proposes that there might be some unique event volunteer traits:

- They are usually very enthusiastic about the event itself
- They may lack experience and need training
- Many want to have fun
- Many prefer short-term responsibilities, especially at the event itself
- They may be more artistically creative than technically creative
- They may be full of good intentions but leave things to chance, or expect others to do the work.

Case study 12.4

The Alexandra Blossom Festival, New Zealand

Hall and Rusher (2004) describe the case of the Alexandra Blossom Festival in New Zealand, where there used to be many volunteers from the local economy. The Alexandra Blossom Festival is a relatively simple community event, which opens with a street parade. It is the focal celebration for the rural communities. However, as a result of the economic 'reforms' of the 1980s that restructured the New Zealand economy, the work patterns of the residents changed and they had to work on fruit production rather than volunteer for the Festival.

Reflective practice 12.2

Investigate how changes in economic circumstances have changed the number of volunteers for events in your country.

However, it is recognized that this list contains many generalizations and that there are a great range of events, which attract a wide range of volunteers. Event volunteers offer their services and time free, usually in exchange for attendance at the event, and do not expect remuneration. This presents a greater challenge for the event manager in terms of using different means of motivation. Bowdin *et al.* (2001) propose that by conscientiously getting to know the volunteers and developing an understanding of what motivates each individual, it is possible to build up an appropriate system of reward and recognition procedures which might act as motivators for staff and volunteers.

It is important to read more widely about the research undertaken to identify what makes volunteers volunteer in the event industry and how managers can harness and increase their motivation. Some volunteers will come with a range of skills learnt and developed from their other volunteer work. However, as events move from one country to another the number of volunteers may be increasingly abundant or not. This could be due to differing economic conditions in different countries, and changes in the structure of economies (see Case study 12.4).

Volunteer committees for specific events might be made up of six or so people interested in putting together a particular event. The effectiveness of voluntary bodies is often very high (Shone and Parry, 2004), due to the commitment, work and effort that volunteers are willing to put into the activity. Volunteers also go to extreme lengths to find the necessary resources and help for their event.

On the other hand, there are many complex and growing events that see a lot of cooperation between volunteer groups and their own paid professional staff. The event manager may coordinate these different groups of volunteers to produce an event such as a carnival, or the Commonwealth Games.

Some volunteers want to learn new skills while others, possibly in an older age group, will volunteer for personal enrichment and to help others. These uncertainties argue for more research, and a volunteer system that pays attention to the changing needs and motivations of staff.

Case study 12.5 illustrates the diversity of opportunities for volunteers.

The following section relates to motivation theories and how all staff can be motivated to give their time and experiences to an event, whether they are paid or not.

Case study 12.5

USA Swimming

USA Swimming is a non-profit organization made up of very dedicated volunteers. Interested individuals donate their time, energy and expertise at every level, from the National Board of Directors to the local swimming clubs. There are 50 standing committees. Staff liaisons, along with these committees, create, implement and evaluate USA Swimming Programmes. The House of Delegates meets annually to determine the rules and regulations for the following year. Between yearly meetings of the House of Delegates, an elected USA Swimming Board of Directors is charged with the responsibility of making decisions for USA Swimming.

Volunteer jobs

There are unlimited opportunities to get involved in almost any capacity. USA Swimming is always looking for enthusiastic volunteers. Finding a way you can contribute is the most important thing to remember.

Fund Raiser: Raising funds is a priority of every swimming programme. It could involve anything from a bake sale to landing a sponsor for your club. If you have the gift of gab, this might be your area.

Public Relations Person: Promotions within the club and community are important to every team. Those volunteers skilled at public speaking or writing can be useful in this area.

Data Processor/Clerical: This area may include billing, meeting entries, accounts payable and accounts receivable, team newsletters, meeting results. All of this can be done on the computer. If you possess computer skills, you could be an essential part in the management of your club.

Hospitality or Social Chairman: Social events are a fun part of every team. Pool parties, Halloween costume contests, and Christmas carolling all serve to bond a team together. If you like to organize such functions this may be the job for you.

Snack Bar: The snack bar at any swimming meeting can generate tremendous income, especially if items to be sold are donated by the parents or local businesses. Baked goods, fruit and other goodies tend to be very popular.

Board Member: At the club level, volunteers are needed to serve on club boards of directors, or booster clubs. The most experienced volunteers are needed here.

Team Representative: Serve as the club representative or take on another volunteer role within your LSC (Local Swimming Committee).

Retention of volunteers

Communication is a key factor in retaining volunteers. By keeping everyone well informed, your program will function more efficiently and your volunteers will feel more involved.

Be sure to use volunteers in areas that enhance their interests and skills. This will make the job more interesting for the volunteer, and in turn they will be more effective. Before jumping into any activity, identify what tasks need to be done, and what the requirements are. Will the task require technical knowledge, a certain kind of personality or the use of a car? How much time will be required?

Someone who knows how to delegate responsibilities usually leads a successful volunteer organization. Work needs to be distributed evenly so no one person feels overburdened or ill-used. This will prevent burnout later on. Encourage active volunteers to recruit 'new blood' to work with them.

Motivation

Why are people motivated to volunteer? Many parents get involved to help their children. Once these volunteers feel a sense of accomplishment, they realize their contributions are worthwhile and necessary for successful programs.

Ways to motivate volunteers

- *Recognize and reward volunteers for their contributions*
- *Train volunteers to be effective and encourage them with positive reinforcement*

- *Be positive and enthusiastic*
- *Make projects a 'team effort'*
- *Respect volunteers and show appreciation of their efforts.*

The success of a group is determined by how well the people involved see their responsibilities affecting the program in a positive way. The volunteer who feels appreciated will continue to work and be productive. Praise is the easiest and quickest way to encourage someone. Saying 'Thank you' can be the same as a Gold Medal.

(Extract from website; further information can be found at www.usaswimming.org.)

Reflective practice 12.3

1. Consider the theories on motivation – how have these been used to help retention of volunteers in Case study 12.5?
2. What makes a good volunteer?

Motivation theories

Almost all motivation theory rests on the belief that humans have basic needs that motivate their behaviour (Getz, 1997). As stated in the introduction to this chapter, an event manager needs to have at least an understanding of the various motivational theories. However, it has to be remembered that theories are just that – theories – and what will work for one person will not necessarily work for another. Silver (2004) believes that an event manager should establish a motivational environment using rewards and incentives, both tangible and intangible. Tangible rewards may be financial incentives, but intangible rewards could include being appreciated, having interesting work, and being given loyalty and support.

Sometimes management does not understand that motivation is up to the individual. People motivate themselves; all management can do is to provide the environment to encourage self-motivation. However the event manager has additional problems in that the staff may not have worked together at an event before. Remember that an event is a unique occurrence and may not have taken place before, and therefore no habits or loyalties to the event manager can have developed.

The classic approach to teambuilding of forming, norming, storming and performing before reaching optimum productivity may not have time to evolve in an event situation. This approach supposes that there is sufficient time to create teams and to socialize (Shone and Parry, 2004).

Economic man and scientific management

Scottish economist Adam Smith in 1776 (*The Wealth of Nations*) and Frederick Winslow Taylor, late nineteenth to early twentieth century American industrialist, both said that people are primarily motivated by money. This is known as the economic man principle. Both Smith and Taylor also studied the conditions necessary to allow workers to be efficient.

Taylor is known as the father of scientific management. Taylor's approach to motivating people was for him to find by 'scientific' means the best way of doing a job. The best way included finding the right tools and the most efficient process. Once the best way was established it became the standard method. People were trained in the standard method, and supervised to see that the method was kept to. To encourage above-average performance, bonus payments were offered (economic man approach). In one celebrated case, 'the Bethlehem Steel Works', Taylor reported that he was able to reduce the workforce from 600 people to 220, increase profit by 140 per cent, and increase wages for each worker by 65 per cent. He also reported that for each worker:

they were almost all saving money, living better, happier, they are the most contented set of workers seen anywhere.

It should be noted that Taylor's approach was for management to develop the best method with little, if any, input from the workers. Management did the thinking, and workers did what they were told and were rewarded if they performed above a set standard.

Today, over 200 years after Adam Smith, it is evident that productivity will increase if work processes are simplified and people are trained to follow a standard process. To this extent the approaches of Smith and Taylor cannot be disputed, and nor can it be argued that people work for money. What can be questioned is that if people are encouraged to make suggestions and given a measure of autonomy, will they take 'ownership' of a job and become more productive? A second discussion might centre on whether people can be motivated to be more efficient and customer-focused without being paid extra to do so.

Before answering these questions, it is necessary to discuss the importance of money.

Money: a necessity and a means of keeping the score

Our belief is that, depending on their circumstances, some people are motivated by money more than by anything else. People with children and mortgages need money. Money is also a method of keeping the score – it is the one sure way of knowing whether our efforts are appreciated. A pat on the back is nice, and so are kind words, but money is tangible – it is a certain measure of the value given to our efforts. There is also the question of equity. If we are being paid a certain amount for doing a job, even if initially we thought the pay was good, we would be less than human if we didn't get upset on finding out that a colleague is being paid substantially more for completing the same work.

Our belief is that money is important, and it is more important for some people than it is for others. Money is only one factor. But, we believe that if people are being paid a reasonable amount, then it is possible to increase motivation without paying extra amounts. Conversely, simply paying more money cannot ensure increased productivity. Money is important, but money alone is not the answer. All we can be certain of is that the amount paid must be reasonable and equitable.

Motivational theorists

Motivational theorists fall into three broad schools:

1. Content perspectives
2. Process perspectives
3. Reinforcement perspectives.

Content perspectives

Lashley and Lee-Ross (2003) explain that content theories seek to explain motivation by considering individuals' requirements and what must be present in the workplace to satisfy them.

One of the best-known theories of this type is *Maslow's hierarchy of needs*, which is illustrated in many texts. Abraham Maslow (1943), a clinical psychologist, claimed that people have five levels of needs, and that each level has to be covered before the next level will be addressed. The levels of needs are:

1. Physiological – food, water, shelter, and so on
2. Safety – a desire to feel secure and free from threats to existence
3. The need to belong – i.e. to be accepted in a group of people
4. Self esteem – feeling positive about oneself and being recognized by others for achievements
5. Self-actualization – the highest level, roughly translated, means the development of one's capabilities in order to reach one's full potential.

Maslow accepted that each level did not have to be completely fulfilled before people moved on to the next level, but claimed that until a level had been *substantially* covered it was unlikely that people would address a higher level in the hierarchy of needs. In prosaic terms, if you are grubbing around in the gutter for fag ends, wondering when the soup kitchen will open, you are not interested that the ballet company is offering free tickets to the first 20 people who arrive.

It should be noted that Maslow's hierarchy of needs model was developed from a very small sample. He observed fourteen close friends and studied the lives of nine famous people, including Lincoln, Jefferson, Eleanor Roosevelt, Einstein and Sweitzer. His theory has often been questioned because of this lack of depth in his research, but it remains very popular and still reveals many truisms in the workplace today. The hierarchy appears to have an intuitive logic (Griffin, 2000), although it has yet to be fully researched whether people from different cultures have the same need categories and hierarchies.

Herzberg's two-factor theory is another popular content perspective that follows Maslow's line of reasoning (Herzberg, 1966, 1968). Herzberg developed a two-factor theory based on satisfiers and dissatisfiers (or motivation and hygiene factors). Herzberg's theory, like Maslow's, is that until the lower-level needs – the hygiene factors – are covered, the higher-level satisfier factors will not motivate.

Roughly translated, hygiene factors include:

- Adequate wages
- Safe working conditions
- Job security
- Non-threatening supervision and control.

Motivators are the higher-level needs, and include:

- Recognition
- Responsibility
- The importance of the work
- Prospects for growth and advancement.

It can be seen that these different set of factors are associated with satisfaction and dissatisfaction – that is, a person might identify 'low pay' as causing dissatisfaction, but would not necessarily site 'high pay' as a cause of satisfaction. Employees and volunteers are more likely to be motivated and satisfied by achievement, recognition, advancement, responsibility and interesting work (Getz, 1997).

Herzberg's initial study was based on questioning 200 accountants and engineers in the United States. The study was therefore not based on the typical worker, since accountants and engineers would, of course, have been well above the national average for wages and working conditions. Nonetheless, the theory merits consideration. It has played a role over the last century in bringing theories of motivation and the importance of motivation in the workplace to managers' notice. For example, using Herzberg's approach it might be considered that spending money on improving the staff cafeteria in itself will not motivate people to work harder if they have little responsibility. The cafeteria would be considered a hygiene factor, but increased responsibility would be seen as a motivational factor.

On the other hand, responsibility and recognition of achievements might not motivate, if people feel that their pay is inadequate, or if there is the threat of redundancy. Thus being asked to accept extra responsibility without extra benefits might only be seen as an attempt by management to give the recipient extra work – job enlargement rather than job enrichment.

In addition to these theories, research has also focused on human needs. The three most important are achievement, affiliation and power.

Process perspectives

These approaches are concerned with how motivation occurs. Lashley and Lee-Ross (2003) say that this perspective contends that it is essential to understand the process of motivation in addition to knowing why people have different (content) needs at different times.

Rather than attempting to identify motivational stimuli, process perspectives focus on why people choose certain behavioural options to satisfy their needs, and also how they evaluate their satisfaction after they have gained these goals (Griffin 2000).

Expectancy theory is one of the theories offered by Victor Vroom (Vroom *et al.*, 1973, 1988). He argued that people are motivated by expectations, and that performance is linked to the assessment of the probability that increased performance will lead to increased rewards; rewards may be extrinsic (i.e. money and promotion) or intrinsic (i.e. sense of achievement).

Bateman and Zeithaml (1993) added that the assessment of whether the rewards will be sufficient to induce increased performance depends on the self-evaluation of one's own abilities and the availability of necessary resources. In other words, unless the chances of success (and consequent rewards) are reasonable, people will not be motivated to make an extra effort – i.e. it won't be worth their while.

Equity theory contends that people are motivated to seek equity in the rewards they receive for work done, in comparison to the work and the rewards gained by others. The theory suggests that people see their own inputs into the workplace (time, experience and education) as a ratio to the outcomes they receive (pay, recognition, promotions etc.). They are looking for equity between this ratio and the ratios of rewards received by other people.

Reinforcement perspectives

Reinforcement perspectives address why some motivations remain with people over a period of time and why some other behaviours change. One school of thought is that people's behaviour can be conditioned by external stimulus and that it is unnecessary to seek cognitive explanations. Skinner (1971) claimed that if good behaviour is rewarded and poor behaviour punished, people will be conditioned to act in a positive way rather than in a negative manner. For example, if a worker has stayed back to midnight to complete some urgent work and is subsequently given favourable recognition, it is likely that the worker will be encouraged to act in this way again. If, however, the worker is criticized for some minor error, then he or she might feel that the effect of staying back late has resulted in a negative outcome and consequently will be less willing to put in extra effort on a future occasion. Behaviour which is rewarded is likely to be repeated, and work which is criticized is less likely to be repeated.

Skinner's theories were based on tests with rats and pigeons. One experiment included rats in a maze: if the rat took the right option it received a reward in the form of food, if it took the wrong action it received an electric shock. It was found that it did not take long for the rats to learn the correct route, and rewards and shocks were no longer necessary. This approach, reward and punishment, is also known as *reinforcement theory*.

The one common thread that all these theories have is that people's behaviour is goal-directed.

Combined approach

It is probable that most people are torn between many different needs:

- To have a job that pays enough so as to meet personal commitments, family, mortgage, and social activities
- To be in a job they like
- To feel they belong
- To have the opportunity of increasing self esteem with an important job, status and responsibility
- To feel comfortable that they can do the job
- To have job security
- To have sufficient leisure time to enjoy/follow personal interests.

Is work a necessity?

For most people, work is not the be-all and end-all but a necessity. To achieve personal needs people need adequate wages and job security, and it seems obvious that ideally if they have to work people prefer to do something they enjoy and to be given some authority, a sense of belonging and recognition for skill and above average effort – i.e. the esteem factor.

It is reasonable to suppose that people will not be motivated to make an extra effort if they think the job is beyond their scope or if the chances of success are limited. It also seems that people can be conditioned to act in certain ways by reward or punishment. It could be suggested however, that people, rather than acting as robots as a result of conditioning, are aware of the probable outcomes – the rewards and punishments – and consider the likely consequences before they act.

This would seem to cover why people work and what they would like in a job. However, it does not necessarily follow, given the individuality of people, that, even if all the above factors are taken into consideration, people will necessarily be motivated to be more efficient, to make suggestions, or to go out of their way to provide extra service for customers.

We could give plenty of examples of well-rewarded middle managers who have autonomy to make decisions but do not appear to be overly motivated. To achieve a situation where every worker in the organization is excited about what the organization is doing and willingly puts in extra effort requires a special type of organizational culture.

Case study 12.6 describes methods of motivating volunteers at the Olympics in Athens.

Athens 2004

International Sailing Federation
ATHOC Media (as amended by ISAF), Athens, 27 May 2004

In a special event held yesterday in the headquarters of the Athens 2004, the Organizing Committee for the Olympic Games, the volunteers were honoured for their services during the 3rd Sport Events Cluster (February to April 2004).

During the same event, the Organizing Committee President, Gianna Angelopoulos-Daskalaki, presented the uniforms to the volunteers who will be participating in the Olympic Games.

Mrs Angelopoulos extended a warm welcome to the volunteers, stressing that they contributed their time, strength and ideas to the third cluster of Sport Events, and added: 'We thank you because all of you together form now a group of skilled, trained and, most of all, enthusiastic people, who are ready to welcome all humanity in the Games to be held in Athens and help us organize magical Olympic and Paralympic Games in Athens in 2004.'

Mrs Angelopoulos described the volunteers as 'the heart, face and soul of the Games'. Referring to the contribution of volunteers outside Athens, she said: 'We are particularly proud because, through the Football Sport Events held in the Olympic Cities, all Greece made its presence felt in Volunteerism.'

She also made special references to individual cases of volunteers that express the universality of volunteerism as a movement.

One such example is Transport Volunteer Nikolaos Vougioukas, who has taken part in many Sport Events and of whom Mrs Angelopoulos-Daskalaki said 'he has indeed devoted a very important part of himself in our preparations for flawless Games'. She also referred to the offer of volunteer services from people of all ages – from the youngest ball boy (aged 11) to a 73-year-old baseball volunteer, the oldest of all – and to characteristic examples which in this Sport Events Cluster, as in the previous ones, highlight the universality of volunteerism as a movement. 'People from the same families took part in the Events, brothers, parents and their children – united as one, committed to the common effort and the common goal', said Mrs Gianna Angelopoulos-Daskalaki.

The Athens 2004 President also made a special reference to people 'who travelled from places very far in order to be here in Athens, with the most characteristic such example being that of Jure Abraham from Argentina, who came to Greece just so that he could participate in the Artistic and Rhythmic Gymnastics Sport Events and offer to us his specialized knowledge'.

'Jure and many others like him, prove', Mrs Gianna Angelopoulos-Daskalaki added, 'that with determination, zeal and commitment to goals people always find ways to overcome practical obstacles and realize their dreams and hopes – the little, personal ones and the big, grand, collective ones.'

Mrs Gianna Angelopoulos-Daskalaki also made a reference to the 'first Olympic Record', that of individual volunteer applications for the Games exceeding the 160 000 mark at the conclusion of the volunteers' recruitment programme and before the Games – a remarkable improvement on the corresponding figure for Sydney.

Mrs Gianna Angelopoulos-Daskalaki concluded with the following words: 'We always believed that in Greece there is a very active volunteerism movement, which contributes to a great number of areas in social life, without seeking publicity. We consider that all of you here are part of this movement and we hope that you will continue to act in the same way after the Games, becoming in this way what perhaps would be the most important legacy to our society.'

The Athens 2004 President then presented the uniforms for the men and women volunteers of the 2004 Athens Games, worn by actors Apostolos Gletsos and Theofania Papathoma and Olympic medallist Leonidas Kokkas. The uniforms, which were presented for the first time, are part of the sponsorship of Adidas, Official Supporter of the Athens 2004 Olympic Games.

A videotape with shots from the Sport Events and interviews of volunteers, athletes, top officials of International Federations and the Chairman of the IOC Coordination Commission, Denis Oswald, was also shown during the event.

The award of participation diplomas and souvenirs followed the projection to the Sport Events volunteers. In the open area of the Organizing Committee's headquarters where the event was held, a number of stands had been set up, corresponding to the sports of the Sport Events, together with one kiosk for ball persons, to honour junior volunteers.

In the stands, volunteers met the teams of people with whom they worked and received their personal commemorative diplomas, which certify their participation in the 3rd Sport Events Cluster, from the corresponding Venue Managers and volunteers Venue Managers.

(Information supplied by the International Sailing Federation more information can be found at www.sailing.org/.)

Reflective practice 12.4

Consider the motivation theories discussed here and decide which of them would be applicable to the volunteers at the Athens Olympics.

Organizational culture

Organizational culture is the amalgam of beliefs, norms and values of the individuals making up the organization – i.e. 'the way we do things around here'. Griffin (2000) states that the culture of an organization is the set of values that helps its members understand what the organization stands for, how it does things, and what it considers important.

Culture determines the feel of an organization. Organizations are made up of many individuals, each with his or her own set of values. The culture of the organization is how people react or do things when confronted with the need to make a decision. If the organization has a strong culture, then each individual will know instinctively how things are done and what is expected. Conversely, if the culture is weak, people may not react in the manner in which management would hope.

How can managers deal with culture, given its importance and yet its intangible nature? The value of such a culture to an organization that has a dedicated enthusiastic workforce cannot be underestimated. Such a culture begins with everyone in the organization, from the event manager downwards, believing in what the organization is trying to achieve. This means that not only is every person customer-focused, but also each person is determined to eliminate any cost that is not adding value.

For this culture to exist there are several prerequisites, and these prerequisites apply to everyone in the organization:

- Working conditions have to be right (location, layout and process)
- Wages and rewards have to be equitable
- There has to be job security
- Staff must have a chance for self-development (self esteem)
- Staff must feel 'good' about the job – it has to be meaningful.

We could add to this list and bring forward those factors discussed in earlier chapters:

- Everyone in the organization must know who the customer is
- Ideally everyone will know what the customer values (i.e. the critical success factors that make them come to events)

- Everyone must know the level of service that the organization is aiming to provide
- Service must be affordable and sustainable
- Service must be consistent
- Standards must be set and communicated
- Controls have to be in place to ensure that the standards are being met
- People must know how to make corrections
- Finally, but importantly, everyone must feel free to make suggestions, and management must listen and treat suggestions with respect.

Event managers must give more than lip service to the above; they should show by their actions that they believe in the capabilities of their staff.

The event manager still has to make the important decisions and set the policy. Staff will be expected and encouraged to contribute to policy, but once a policy decision has been made, then workers have to conform to the policy. Policy cannot be changed at the whim of individual people – such actions would lead to chaos. Therefore the following must be remembered:

- Objectives must be clearly communicated
- Management sets policy and guidelines
- Staff have the freedom to act within the guidelines
- People should be encouraged to make suggestions to change policy.

In a *bureaucratic culture*, some people (often management) do the thinking and workers do what they are told. In this type of culture the bigger the organization the more rules and procedures will be required, and control will be achieved by supervision and reports. Communication is usually one way, top down. Such a culture may be sterile, and create a nine-to-five attitude – i.e. sign on at nine in the morning and leave promptly at five in the afternoon.

This is probably not the culture desirable in an event organization. Staff will pay lip service to service and customer satisfaction, but will not have the authority, let alone the motivation, to provide above average service, for to do so may result in breaking rules and consequently the possibility of a reprimand.

An *open culture* is where the event manager is highly visible and approachable, there are few rules and procedures, and the staff know instinctively what is right and what has to be done to correct a situation.

The 'way we do things around here' is second nature – not just a slogan or a mission statement. People have authority to act, and are self-motivated.

Using motivational theory and organizational cultural awareness to achieve the critical success factors demanded by customers

Returning to the example in Chapter 5 where we considered a conference venue and the critical success factors that would attract the customers without adding substantially to the cost, we noted that the CSFs were:

- Well-organized coffee and lunch breaks
- Friendly and well-presented reception staff
- Useful and meaningful signage
- Well-organized meal service
- A clean and tidy car park
- A high level of customer care.

As event managers, we want to deliver to a high standard for each of the CSFs. If these were plotted onto a sheet, we could then rate the conference venue (1–5, 5 highest) as to how well it is succeeding in meeting those CSFs. A further column could be added to show how highly motivated staff could advance each of those attributes.

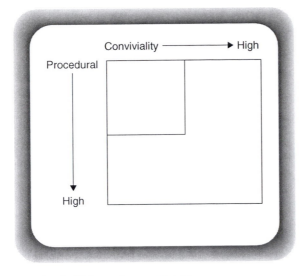

Figure 12.1 Low procedural efficiency, low conviviality

A further approach looks at procedural and convivial outcomes (procedural means carrying out all activities efficiently and correctly, and convivial means carrying out all activities with an interest in the customer).

In order to illustrate this example, let us consider the registration of delegates at an International Book Fair.

Figure 12.1 illustrates a case whereby there is very little procedural efficiency, many mistakes made, and there is poor organization. Similarly, with regard to conviviality there is little interest shown in the delegate, little empathy with the plight of the delegate due to the errors occurring, and a distinct lack of welcome.

Figure 12.2 again illustrates very little procedural efficiency, many mistakes made, and poor organization. However, there is a lot of interest shown in the delegate, lots of empathy with the plight of the delegate due to the errors that are occurring, and a friendly welcome. The conviviality factor is such that procedural problems are almost ignored.

Figure 12.3 illustrates a great deal of procedural efficiency, no mistakes made, and efficient organization. However, with regard to conviviality there is little interest shown in the delegate and a distinct lack of welcome; indeed, the reception is almost arrogant.

Figure 12.4 illustrates a great deal of procedural efficiency, no mistakes made, and efficient organization. With regard to conviviality, there is a great deal of interest shown in the delegate, and an outstandingly warm welcome.

The examples in Figures 12.1–12.4 show the link between having good resources, motivated staff and well-managed events. Only Figure 12.4 demonstrates that the event manager has succeeded in every aspect.

This technique could be used if you felt you were able to complete it honestly – perhaps at a staff debriefing after the event and prior to another event, or in advance of an event, when you could discuss how your organization could achieve both

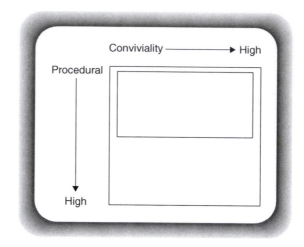

Figure 12.2 Low procedural efficiency, high conviviality

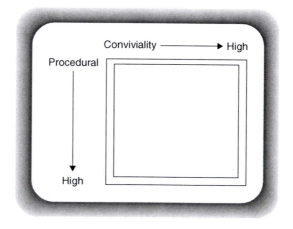

Figure 12.3 High procedural efficiency, low conviviality

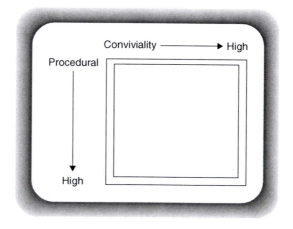

Figure 12.4 High procedural efficiency, high conviviality

conviviality and procedural effectiveness. Staff could be engaged in discussion, enabling them to express how they feel when both conviviality and procedural matters are achieved and what extra support they might need to have a more acceptable outcome.

Reflective practice

Using the motivational theories described in this chapter, go through each of them to see how, as a manager, you could lift the rating of each of these CSFs as portrayed in the table below.

Critical success factor	Current rating 1–5 (5 high)	Suggested method of improving this rating through motivation	Extra resources needed
Well-organized coffee and lunch breaks	3		
Friendly and well-presented reception staff	3		
Useful and meaningful signage	4		
Well-organized meal service	3		
Clean and tidy car park	2		
A high level of customer care	1		

Reflective practice 12.5

1. Why do you think volunteers worked for the Manchester Commonwealth Games, 2002?
2. If you won or inherited a large amount of money, would you still go to work?
3. What do you think encourages your staff to come to work – is it job satisfaction, or is it ONLY for the money?

Chapter summary and key points

This chapter began by saying people are an important resource – indeed often the most valuable resource. However, if not managed correctly people can become a most expensive resource, not only in wages paid but also in the cost of mistakes they make.

The chapter has considered the use of volunteers within the event industry, why people volunteer, and how we can best harness their enthusiasm.

It is crucial that event managers understand what motivates people. It was pointed out that management cannot motivate; people motivate themselves. What management can do is to provide an environment that encourages self-motivation. Such an environment includes health and safety, clear understanding of who the customer is and what the customer needs, an understanding of individual duties and responsibilities, and clear guidelines as to individual authority.

Within this chapter we have discussed several motivational theories and included a section on the importance of money. This indicated that if the money paid is sufficient and equitable, people can be self-motivated if there is an open culture.

An open culture is where management is highly visible and approachable, there are few rules and procedures, and the staff know instinctively what is right and what has to be done to correct a situation. The 'way we do things around here' is second nature – not just a slogan or a mission statement – and people have the authority to act.

The chapter has concluded with a model showing the links between good resources, motivated staff and well-managed events.

Chapter 13

Forecasting and capacity management

Learning Objectives

After reading through this chapter you will be able to:

- Recognize the importance of establishing the demand for an event
- Use and evaluate the different methods available to an event manager for forecasting
- Understand and apply the different theories related to capacity management
- Apply the concepts of queuing theory to a range of different events.

Introduction

Forecasting is an essential element within the event operations management model. This is the implementation stage, although it could be argued that forecasting should form part of the detailed planning. The forecasts that are made are used by various functions within an organization – for example, the marketing function forecast sales and numbers of people who will attend, accountants forecast income and expenditure to create the budget, and the purchasing department forecast the amount of goods to be purchased. Forecasts are needed for almost every management decision. All decisions become effective at some point in the future, so they should be based on circumstances not as they are at present, but as they will be when the decisions become effective (Waters, 1996).

It is difficult for forecasts to be totally accurate because, although expected trends can be factored into the calculations, the basic information used is drawn from what has happened in the past. In considering the past, numbers alone are not sufficient, as the numbers will merely be a reflection of a variety of circumstances that influenced or determined the outcome the last time. Establishing circumstances or events that shaped past demand will not always be easy, as there can be no guarantee that all the circumstances of the past will be remembered or that they will occur in exactly the same way in the future.

The danger for statisticians and researchers is concentrating on the numbers and to ignore the circumstances.

Getz (1997) highlights that trend extrapolation is the easiest way to forecast next year's attendance, but many factors (such as the weather and competition) can intervene. The prevailing conditions of supply and demand must be taken into account.

For some types of demand forecasting, seasonal trends, levels of promotion and perceived competitor activity might well be sufficient to provide a reasonably accurate forecast. In other cases, and especially in the event industry, demand will often depend on a myriad of circumstances and situations.

The importance of establishing demand

Estimating the number of people attending an event is crucial for a number of reasons:

- Forecasts avoid unanticipated overcrowding, which is a health and safety issue – congestion can lead to accidents, stress and even riots (Getz, 1997).
- Uncertainty about numbers can cause bottlenecks and the formation of queues (Yeoman *et al.*, 2004).
- A forecast of attendee numbers helps to determine the level of investment and gives an awareness of the financial consequences if the estimation is wrong. There is a natural tendency to want to plan for the biggest possible crowd, but this strategy has higher costs and risks a substantial loss if forecasts are not met (Getz, 1997).
- Certain decisions have been made, based on the estimate, and it is difficult to change these in the short term.
- The number of attendees is an important consideration in the determination of the price for the event. Break-even analysis, where an admission price is relevant, can be used; however it may be that the price has an influence on the number of people attending. Spreadsheet software can be used to test the cost–revenue relationships in constructing break-even graphs. These allow for a quick evaluation of what can be expected to happen when the price is changed. The break-even point is also sensitive to changes in costs, and the spreadsheet can demonstrate the implications of fluctuations while price is held constant (Getz, 1997). The forecasted numbers affect many parts of the organization, and should be as accurate as possible. For example, should you provide catering for an average attendance or up to peak capacity?
- Forecasts will determine the level of capacity you provide at your event – for example, in terms of size, staffing, equipment and other resources. You will also need to know how attendees will arrive – will they come all at once, or over a period of time? As more people arrive, will others leave? Efforts should be made to disperse attendance in time and/or in space, rather than risk disaster by overcrowding (Getz, 1997).
- Without an estimate of future demand it is not possible to plan effectively for possible situations, only to react to them (Slack *et al.*, 2004).

Forecasting

It should be realized that often at an event the capacity is not static – as some people are entering others may leave – and this is an added dimension for the event manager to be aware of.

Waters (1996) says that forecasts should not be carried out by an isolated group of specialists, but by the entire organization. He believes that forecasting is continuous and actual circumstances can update original forecasts; consequently, plans can be modified and decisions revised.

You might find in your research that there is no useful market information for the type of event that you are planning, but this should not deter you. It could be that historical data may not be available, what is available may not be relevant for the future, there may not be time to make meaningful forecasts, there could be high costs involved, or perhaps the impact of the forecasts would not make the effort worthwhile (Waters, 1996). However, there may be clues that can help, and the literature from general operations management also provides excellent advice. We will now explore some of that literature and apply it to the event industry.

Slack *et al.* (2004) indicate that there are three requirements for a demand forecast:

1. It should be expressed in terms that are useful for capacity planning and control
2. It must be as accurate as possible
3. It gives an indication of relative uncertainty.

Forecasting techniques

There is no one single method of forecasting which is best, and the three that are referred to here cover most timescales:

1. Long-range capacity planning requires forecasts to be made several years ahead. This is typically important for large and complex events that involve a wide range of different groups of people both as participants and as organizers – for example, the Olympics Games, large political events, complex annual events.
2. Short- to medium-term forecasts are usually made between 3 months and 2 years ahead. This timescale is usually due to the need to determine personnel and training needs, renting of premises and equipment, and to establish the details of the event required.
3. Short-term forecasts are needed to plan, order and allocate resources on a monthly, weekly and daily basis. The shorter the timeframe, the more accurate the forecast has to be.

You can see a link here with Figure 2.3, repeated here as Figure 13.1 for convenience. Generally the long-term forecasts are concerned with strategic decisions (i.e. at the top of the triangle of the organization), the medium forecasts are concerned with business decisions and the short-term forecasts are concerned with operational decisions (at the bottom of the triangle).

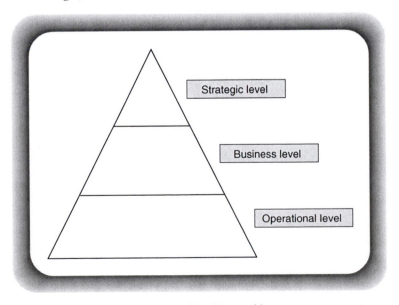

Figure 13.1 The triangle of management and decision-making

Types of forecasts

The three approaches for forecasting are qualitative, quantitative (mathematical or time series approach) and causal. In reality, all three approaches are interlinked and should be taken into account when determining a forecasted demand. The classification of methods does not mean that each can only be used in isolation. Invariably, all forecasts will also have an element of subjectivity associated with them.

Qualitative forecasting

Qualitative forecasting uses judgement, past experience, and existing past and present data (see Case study 13.1). If forecasting on past results and based on current conditions was easy, the bookmakers would soon be out of business.

Case study 13.1

Fleadh Cheoil na hEireann, Ireland

Fleadh Cheoil na hEireann is a festival celebrating Irish music, song, dance and culture, held on and around the last weekend of August annually. Organized by Comhaltas Ceoltoiri Eireann (CCE), the Fleadh is held to coincide with the UK Bank Holiday to facilitate the large numbers of visitors from Britain who attend the Fleadh each year. In any year, over the week, the Fleadh will attract between 130 000 to 150 000 people to the host area.

The First Fleadh was organized by The Pipers' Club from Dublin, and held in Mullingar on Whit Weekend 1951 in conjunction with 'Feis Lar na hEireann'. The stated aim of the event was 'to restore to its rightful place the traditional music of Ireland' by bringing to the midland town 'the cream of traditional musicians from the four corners of Ireland'.

The first Fleadh Cheoil na hEireann attracted only a few hundred hardened but enthusiastic patrons. Within 5 years, this annual gathering had grown to a national festival attracting many tens of thousands of visitors. Nowadays, the Fleadh is a major international festival drawing visitors from all five continents. With the growth in popularity of 'World Music' and the phenomenal interest globally in Irish culture, the amount of visitors from abroad coming to Fleadhanna is increasing exponentially each year.

At the heart of the Fleadh are competitions around which all other events revolve. To advance to these, competitors must first come through County and Provincial series, with qualifying provinces being the four provinces of Ireland plus Britain, North America and other various regions of the world.

In all, there are almost 150 competitions covering soloists and groups, in music, song, dance, and in such varied disciplines as fiddle, slow airs and Pipe Bands. The venues required for the competitions will need to accommodate audiences of 50 up to 1500 indoors and up to 12 000 outdoors for Marching Bands. Considering that in terms of competitions alone the Fleadh attracts over 3000 qualifiers, the scale of the festival can begin to be appreciated. So successful is the event in terms of visitors that it is the policy of CCE's Ard Comhairle not to promote the Fleadh aggressively because if this is done the belief is that there is not a town in Ireland that could host it.

The attendance at the Fleadh in 1999 exceeded the estimates provided beforehand by previous organizers. Going on earlier occasions, the local committee expected the total visitor numbers to be around 160 000/170 000, based on information that they had received from other host towns.

However, most accurate estimates suggest that spectacular numbers of people attended the Fleadh Cheoil. As with all outdoor events it is difficult to quantify the exact numbers of visitors, but estimates from the Gardai would suggest that there were between 80 000 and 100 000 people in the town both Saturday and Sunday. The estimate for Friday is between 40 000 and 60 000 visitors. Certainly, the cumulative figure for the 3 days, the Gardai believe, was easily in excess of 200 000.

Enniscorthy Gardai have considerable expertise in this regard, having been involved in major events over the past few years, such as Le Tour de France en Irlande 1998, 1998 Bi-Centenary Celebrations, and the National Ploughing Championships in 1994 and 1998. The attendance at the Ploughing Championships is easier to quantify, as entry to this event is through 'turnstiles', and the Gardai are confident in their belief that the numbers attending the Fleadh were well in excess of the 150 000 who would regularly attend the 3-day ploughing event.

These figures are confirmed by Comhaltas Árd Comhairle members and Árd Stiúrhtóir Senator Labhrás Ó Murchú.. Regular Fleadh observers, their estimate is that the attendance was up at least 30 per cent on the usual 160 000 expected to attend.

All the empirical data available to the Fleadh Committee would seem to support the above claims:

- Attendance at competitions up by 25 per cent
- Sale of programmes up by 33 per cent
- Attendance at concerts and ceilithe up by 25 per cent
- Overall Fleadh revenue from activities, with no price increases on previous years, up by 36 per cent.

While better organization and financial control could explain some of these increases, the best and most likely explanation for this positive variance has to be a visitor volume increase of at least 30 per cent. With a normal increase of 12–15 per cent for a town hosting the Fleadh for the second time, the organizers have been told to expect an increase closer to 20 per cent for August 2000, bringing the total figures for visitors to the town to nearly a quarter of a million people for the whole week.

Clonmel gearing up for another Fleadh Cheoil 2004

(Eamonn Lacey)

Clonmel is gearing up to host another spectacular Fleadh Cheoil with preparations well advanced for one of Europe's biggest cultural festivals this August when up to a quarter of a million visitors will converge on the town. When Fleadh Fever hits Clonmel this August the town will open its doors and hearts to offer a warm welcome to 10 000 musicians from all over the world. The traditional Fleadh Cheoil weekend will take place from Friday 27th to Sunday 29th August, and will be preceded by Seachtain na hEigse, Scoil Eigse and Seachtain na Gaeilge.

A new Ard Ollamh will be crowned during Seachtain na hEigse, the new dimension introduced to Fleadh Cheoil na hEireann last year by the Clonmel organizing committee. The honour will be bestowed by Comhaltas Ceoltoiri Eireann on Tomas O'Caninn, who succeeds composer Micheal O'Suilleabhain, who became the first Supreme Bard of the Fleadh Cheoil last year in his home town.

The Fleadh Cheoil, now ranked as the biggest cultural festival in Europe, will bring an estimated €15m bonanza to the host town of Clonmel with another €6 million generated in income for accommodation.

A fireworks display will be held on the Saturday night and a Fleadh village will be created in the grounds of the High School with the erection of two domes. This year a huge emphasis is being put on street entertainment. Two gig rigs will be located at Sarsfield Street and the Mick Delahunty Square area, while a number of designated music session areas will be located all over the town. Market Place will host an open-air ceili at 2 pm on the Saturday and Sunday.

Under new Chairman Tom Pollard, the organizing committee is endeavouring to ensure that Fleadh Cheoil na hEireann 2004 is a huge success. 'We are confident that Fleadh Cheoil na hEireann 2004 will be a major success story. We are working with the support of the entire community and no effort is being spared to ensure that Clonmel will host one of the most memorable events in the history of the Fleadh Cheoil', said Chairman Tom Pollard. A massive €400 000 fundraising drive is already well underway and finance committee Chairman Michael Campbell is leading a high-powered team towards that target. 'We have received a fantastic response in the town and throughout South Tipperary. The corporate and business sector are anxious to be associated with the success story that is the Fleadh Cheoil in Clonmel, and business interests in the town want to get on board', said Michael Campbell. Accommodation staff in the Fleadh Cheoil office in Parnell Street are inundated with requests for beds in Clonmel from all over the world. Like every Fleadh Cheoil there will be an international dimension with a big overseas contingent expected to arrive in Clonmel. Bo Junior Fiddlers, a band from Norway, are already booked into accommodation in Carrick on Suir and they will perform over the weekend.

Two domes will be located in the grounds of Clonmel High School. Musicians, singers and dancers will compete for a coveted All-Ireland title in 28 different competitions at 19 venues throughout the town.

Over 800 young musicians will attend Scoil Eigse, the traditional school of music song and language, in the week leading up to the Fleadh Cheoil weekend.

The build-up to the traditional Fleadh Cheoil weekend will be hectic, with the busy Seachtain na hEigse schedule of concerts and high-profile events and Seachtain na Gaeilge activities including an opening concert drama, Trath na Gceist and Ionad na Gaeilge in Clonmel library.

(Extract from website; for more information see www.clonmelfleadh.com and the Fleadh office at County Wexford on www.wexford-online.com.)

Reflective practice 13.1

Regarding Case study 13.1:

1. How could forecasting assist the organizing committee generate the €400 000 required to stage this event?
2. What measures have been used in the past to forecast attendance?
3. What techniques could be used to forecast accommodation requirements?

The best-known methods of qualitative forecasting are:

- Expert opinion (including scenario planning and the Delphi method)
- Market surveys
- Life cycle analysis
- Causal
- Comparisons with other events
- Seasonality of demand
- Common sense.

Expert opinion

Individuals or groups can undertake this method. If we think about it, managers use expert opinion all the time as they plan and make decisions every day.

Scenario planning consists of creating hypothetical circumstances that may happen in the future, and then formulating solutions to each scenario. Trend analysis and understanding causal factors is essential to good scenario planning (Getz, 1997). Imagination is required, as the event manager should then determine the impacts on forecasts using these different scenarios.

Another method of using expert opinion is by using the *Delphi model*. Delphi is named after the city in ancient Greece, which was the site of the most famous and powerful oracle in the temple of Apollo, noted for its ambiguous answers. The approach was if the supplicant asked the right question they got the right answer. A priestess spoke the oracular messages whilst in a frenzied trance, and sitting on a golden tripod. A priest would interpret these sounds to the supplicant (questioner), usually in verse. People seeking help would bring gifts to the oracle, and the shrine became very wealthy.

Nowadays the Delphi method is considered by many to be the most successful of the qualitative methods, although it could hardly be considered useful if it were ambiguous. It is time consuming and costly, and is best used by large organizations. The method uses a set of questions to a group of managers or 'experts' who, working without collusion, give their individual opinions. A coordinator then tabulates the opinions, and if individual results differ significantly then the results are fed back anonymously to the panel with a further set of questions. The process is repeated until consensus is reached. Questions and feedback generally continue for four rounds, with the questions becoming more specific with each round. The benefit of the method is that a group opinion can be achieved without the team meeting. This overcomes one of the weaknesses of a face-to-face group meeting, where it is possible for members to be swayed by a dominant member, or perhaps an 'expert' member may be embarrassed to back down from a publicly-stated opinion.

Market surveys

Although the event manager will be able to give personal insights and experience in order to determine and forecast attendance at an event or for a particular activity, this subjectivity can often be supplemented by useful information collected from potential customers. Market surveys collect data from a sample of customers, analyse their views and make inferences about the population at large (Waters, 1996). Surveys can be carried out by telephone, personal interview, surface mail or email. Market surveys use two approaches; structured and unstructured.

With the structured approach the survey uses a formal list of questions; the unstructured approach lets the interviewer probe and perhaps guide the respondent. The survey enables the event manager to learn why people did not attend, and gives the potential for attracting new segments in the future (Getz, 1997).

Framing of questions is an art, and when the questions are completed they should be piloted to check ambiguity and relevance. The key is to establish from the outset exactly what information is wanted, and then to design questions that will give this information. Questions that are not relevant to the issue are a waste of time and money. Other problems are that sometimes people are unable to answer survey questions because they have never thought about what they do and why. People may be unwilling to answer questions that they consider personal, while others might feel obliged to give an answer rather than to appear uninformed, even when they don't know or even don't understand the question, or they might even try to help the interviewer by giving pleasing answers.

An easy form of market survey includes group interviewing or focus groups. With the focus group approach, six to ten people are invited from a market target group to a meeting. They are sometimes paid a small fee, the conditions are relaxed with refreshments and so on, and after the interviewer has set the scene it is hoped that group dynamics will bring out actual feelings and thoughts. At the same time the interviewer attempts to keep the discussion focused on the subject of the research. The concern with this approach is that too much can be read into the opinions of a small and possibly non-random sample. Holding several focus group meetings on the same subject and then pooling the results can overcome this to some extent.

Getz (1997) believes that market area surveys can be used to make better forecasts of market penetration. Tracking surveys in local, regional and international target markets can measure awareness of the planned event, attitudes towards it, and respondents' assessment of their likelihood to attend. Market surveys are also appropriate to determine the shape or style of a new event, or to find out why an existing event is not attracting people as well as expected.

Life cycle analysis

It is generally accepted that products and services have a time-based life cycle, as discussed in Chapter 7. The launch stage may have fewer people attending an event, the growth stage may show a rapid increase in customers, and at the maturity stage the demand will be relatively stable. For most types of events life cycles are readily predictable and the rate of growth/decline will not be unexpected. Experienced event managers can often, with a high degree of accuracy, forecast how long an event will stay in each stage of the life cycle, prior to a change being recommended. This experience will help them forecast the attendance numbers as the event moves through its life cycle.

Causal

In forecasting, it is easy to get caught up with the method of calculating and to overlook the purpose. The purpose is to get the best possible forecast of what might happen in the future. Therefore forecasts calculated on past events must be carefully considered against all the known facts of what is happening or is likely to happen. The state of the economy and key indicators such as interest rates, inflation rates, currency exchange rates, employment rates, and factors such as the entrance of new competitors, new technology and materials, fashion trends, and planned marketing drives will all have causal effects on future results. Likewise, past results should be examined to determine how they were affected by similar events.

Sometimes rising prices can elevate an event to the status of an exclusive event (Getz, 1997). Knowing the causes for changes in demand is important.

Although the information used has a quantitative source, the application and usage of the data relies on a qualitative interpretation.

Comparisons with other events

Similar past events should be researched, taking into account their geographical position, competitive position and relative attractiveness and reputation of the event (Getz, 1997). Total attendance at festivals and other events may have grown, so a refined estimate of demand should be determined. As the number of events increase, then increased competition should also be taken into account. However, competition may act as a catalyst and customers may become more willing to come to different events, and therefore the total market is increased. These comparisons should be considered alongside quantitative data.

Seasonality of demand

Many events can be affected by weather conditions and the different seasons of the year. However, seasonality does not just mean climatic seasons but also political, sporting, financial, holiday and food seasons, and festivals and rituals. It should be remembered that these vary from country to country, and that you may arrive to set up your event in a different country only to find that all the staff you had considered employing are taking a 1-day break owing to a religious festival. Similarly, seasons or annual holidays in different countries may also affect your attendances.

Common sense

Finally, the commonsense approach with forecasted figures is to test by asking, are these figures sensible, what happened before, and what is likely to happen in the future? This approach shows the link between the use of quantitative data and a qualitative approach, and uses the experience, knowledge and expertise of the event management team. Once the future demand forecast has been agreed, then the event manager must determine the capacity of the organization and what changes might be needed to meet the level of forecasted demand.

Quantitative forecasting

Time series forecasting

Time series forecasting uses mathematical analysis of past demand trends to forecast future demand. However, the accuracy of a forecast will not be known until after the event, and this is usually monitored by the deviation of the actual result from the forecast result. (Standard deviation, total absolute deviation and deviation spread is explained later in this section.)

Short-term forecasting involves taking historical data of demand patterns from a few past periods and projecting these patterns into the future. The simplest method is to take the last period's actual demand and use it for the next period(s) forecast, as shown in the following example regarding attendance at a motor show (see Table 13.1).

The method gives a quick response to a trend; if the trend is upwards, then the forecast will be upwards but may lag behind. If, however, there are marked annual fluctuations, then this method would, following a buoyant year, forecast higher annual attendance. In Table 13.1, for example, the forecast for 2001 is lower than actual, and is higher in 2002 but lower in 2003, but not to such a great extent. However, these poor forecasts would have had a knock-on effect on sponsorship, funding, and all arrangements where numbers of attendees are useful. In every year, the organizers have been wrong about the actual attendance. It could be that their sponsors and suppliers will no longer trust the claims of the organizers, and will right them off as wild exaggerations.

Table 13.1 Forecast from past period's actual

Period	Actual	Forecast	Deviation
2000	600 000	–	–
2001	621 000	600 000	+21 000
2002	500 132	621 000	–120 868
2003	687 981	500 132	+187 849

Forecasting by past average

This method is to average the past results. The accuracy of the method is tested by the deviation from the actual.

The first column could represent anything in the event industry. In Table 13.2, let us assume that it is the number of people who asked for a free back massage whilst going around a leisure exhibition. The knowledge of the take-up is helpful for the company

Table 13.2 Forecasting by past moving average

Hour	Actual demand	Forecast (average of all past actual)	Deviation
1st hour	20	nil	
2nd hour	18	20	+2
3rd hour	22	19	−3
4th hour	23	20	−3
5th hour	21	21	0
6th hour	19	21	+2
7th hour	24	21	−3

Table 13.3 Forecasting by 3 period moving average

Period	Actual	Forecast	Deviation
1	20	–	–
2	18	–	–
3	22	–	–
4	23	20	−3
5	21	21	0
6	19	22	+3
7	24	21	−3
8	25	21	−4
9	22	23	+1
10	23	24	+1
11	25	23	−2
12	26	23	−3
13		25	

that was promoting the experience, so it is able to provide staff for a similar function in the near future.

The total absolute deviation (TAD) is the sum of all the deviations, ignoring plus or minus signs – 13 in this example. The mean absolute deviation (MAD) is the average of the deviations. In this example, although there are seven forecasts there are only six deviations, so MAD = 13/6 = 2.1.

During the third and fourth hours there is a variation of 3 between the forecast and the actual. In the third and fourth hours, if capacity had been arranged to meet the forecasted demand then there would have been an undersupply of labour for back massaging, and clients would have had to queue or would have left the stand.

During the sixth hour there was an oversupply of staff and they would not have had a job to do.

It can be seen that using a past average is not always a reliable method of forecasting.

Forecasting by moving average

This method provides reasonable response to trends, and also dampens fluctuations (see Table 13.3).

In Table 13.3, TAD = 20 and MAD = 2.2.

Calculations for the forecasts in this example were made by taking the previous three periods and then dividing by three. For example, the forecast for period 10 is the sum

Table 13.4 Four-period moving average

Period	Actual	Forecast (Four-period average)	Deviation (Forecast to actual)
1	20	–	–
2	18	–	–
3	22	–	–
4	23	–	–
5	21	21	0
6	19	21	+2
7	24	21	−3
8	25	22	−3
9	22	22	0
10	23	23	0
11	25	24	−1
12	26	24	−2
13		24	

of the three previous periods divided by three, i.e. $24 + 25 + 22 = 71$; $71/3 = 23.7$, which rounds up to 24.

The number of periods used for averaging is a matter of judgement. If there are definite cycles, the number of periods in the cycle can be used to determine the number of periods used for averaging. In the second column of Table 13.4, the last two periods in each group of four have the higher demands (in the first four periods 3 and 4 are the highest; in the next group of four 7 and 8 are the highest; likewise so are 11 and 12 in the final group of four); thus a four-period average might prove to be more accurate. We will test this theory using Table 13.4.

In Table 13.4, TAD = 11 and MAD = 1.4.

You will have noted that we have used the same 'actuals' for each of the last two methods of forecasting (Table 13.3 and Table 13.4). If we compare the MADs, we will see that the last method has given the most accurate forecast.

Statistical seasonal adjustment

Adjusting for seasonality can further refine the forecast.

Let us assume that period 1 is the first quarter of a year and period 2 is the second quarter, etc. We can then recalculate our forecasts as in Table 13.5 (overleaf).

The next step is to average the seasonal factor for each season:

Year	2001
Qtr One	$96.4 + 94.3 + 91.7 = 282.4/3 = 94.1$
Qtr Two	$86.75 + 85.4 + 95.8 = 267.95/3 = 89.3$
Qtr Three	$106.0 + 107.9 + 104.2 = 318.1/3 = 106.0$
Qtr Four	$110.85 + 112.4 + 108.3 = 331.55/3 = \underline{110.5}$

By taking the four-period moving average for the last four actual results, which is 24 ($96/4 = 24$), and applying the seasonal factors, the next four quarters can be forecast as in Table 13.6.

Table 13.5 Seasonal factors

	Actual	Average for year	Seasonal factor (percentage of average)
Year 02			
Qtr One	20		96.4 (20 is 96.4% of 20.75)
Qtr Two	18		86.75
Qtr Three	22		106.0
Qtr Four	23		110.85
	83	83/4 = 20.75	400
Year 03			
Qtr One	21		94.3
Qtr Two	19		85.4
Qtr Three	24		107.9
Qtr Four	25		112.4
	89	89/4 = 22.25	400
Year 04			
Qtr One	22		91.7
Qtr Two	23		95.8
Qtr Three	25		104.2
Qtr Four	26		108.3
	96	96/4 = 24	400

Table 13.6 Forecast for year ahead

Year 2005		Forecast
Qtr One	24 × 94.1%	23
Qtr Two	24 × 89.3%	21
Qtr Three	24 × 106%	25
Qtr Four	24 × 110.5%	27
		96

This gives us the same total (96) for Year 2005 as for Year 2004. As there is an obvious upwards trend, this is not logical. We therefore add a trend factor to our calculations.

The trend factor is obtained by calculating a time lag factor. The formula for the trend factor is (Number of periods of moving average −1)/2 + 1.

In our example, (4 − 1) = 3 and 3/2 = 1.5. The time lag factor will therefore be 1.5 + 1 = 2.5.

We now return to our four-period moving averages, calculate the trend between successive moving averages, and multiply each trend by the time lag factor (Table 13.7).

98.125/4 gives an adjusted average quarter of 24.5.

Using the adjusted average plus the seasonal fluctuations, we can forecast for Year 01 (Table 13.8).

We now have a forecast for the next 12 months (four quarters) which is seasonally adjusted and has allowed for growth based on the past trend. Naturally, as each new 'actual' comes to hand we recalculate our moving forecast.

The main weakness of the moving average method is that equal weight is given to each of the historical figures used, and there is also the need to have (or to build up) a history of information to test against and to forecast from.

Table 13.7 Adjusted average

Actual	Moving average	Successive trend	×2.5	Time lag factor	Adjusted average
20					
18					
22					
23					
21	20.75				
19	21	+0.25			
24	21.25	+0.25			
25	21.75	+0.5			
22	22.25	+0.5			
23	22.5	+0.25	2.5	0.625	23.125
25	23.5	+1	2.5	2.5	26
26	23.75	+0.25	2.5	0.625	24.375
–	24	+0.25	2.5	0.625	24.625
					98.125

Table 13.8 Adjusted forecast

Qtr One	98.125/4 = 24.5 × 94.1%	23
Qtr Two	24.5 × 89.3	22
Qtr Three	24.5 × 106.0	26
Qtr Four	24.5 × 110.5	27
		98

Another disadvantage is the number of calculations involved, although with a computer spreadsheet, once the formula has been entered (and proved), this is not as onerous as it once would have been.

A method known as exponential smoothing overcomes some of these problems without losing any of the accuracy.

Exponential smoothing

Exponential smoothing requires only the previous forecast figure and the latest actual figure. It allows the forecast to respond to fluctuations, but at the same time keeps a level of stability.

We begin by calculating a smoothing constant. The formula for the smoothing constant is $2/(N + 1)$, where N is the number of periods we wish to smooth. For example, if six were the number of periods the smoothing constant would be $2/(6 + 1) = 2/7 = 0.28$.

For our example, Table 13.9, we will use an exponential smoothing constant based on four periods:

$$\frac{2}{(4 + 1)} = \frac{2}{5} = 0.4$$

The actual demand for the last period is multiplied by the factor i.e. 0.4, and the forecast for the last period is multiplied by the sum of (1 − the factor). In our case, using a factor of 0.4, the actual for the last period is multiplied by 0.4 and the last forecast is multiplied by 0.6 (i.e. 1 − 0.4 = 0.6).

Table 13.9 Exponential smoothed average

Period	Actual	Forecast (four-period)	Deviation (forecast to average)	Exponential smoothed average	Deviation
1	20	–	–		
2	18	–	–		
3	22	–	–		
4	23	–	–		
5	21	21	–		
6	19	21	+2	21	+2
7	24	21	−3	20	−4
8	25	22	−3	22	−3
9	22	22	–	23	+1
10	23	23	–	23	–
11	25	24	−1	23	−2
12	26	24	−2	24	−2
13		24		25	

Starting with period 5:	Actual 21 and forecast 21. As there is a nil deviation (for period 6) no smoothing is required, and thus for period 6 the forecast will be 21
For period 7:	The actual was 19 and the forecast was 21. Using exponential smoothing for period 7 the forecast is 0.4(19) + 0.6(21) = 7.6 + 12.6 = 20
For period 8:	0.4(24) + 0.6(20) = 9.6 + 12.0 = 21.6
For period 9:	0.4(25) + 0.6(22) = 10 + 13.2 = 23.2
For period 10:	0.4(22) + 0.6(23) = 8.8 + 13.8 = 22.6
For period 11:	As there is no deviation to actual for period 10, the forecast is 23
For period 12:	0.4(25) + 0.6(23) = 10 + 13.8 = 23.8
For period 13:	0.4(26) + 0.6(24) = 10.4 + 14.4 = 24.8

In Table 13.9, TAD = 14 and MAD = 4.

The example in Table 13.9 demonstrates the mechanics of exponential smoothing. The next steps are to add a trend factor and a seasonal factor to update the exponentially smoothed average. In a four-period seasonal forecast, the factor for period 5 when the actual is known will be upgraded to provide a new seasonal factor for period 9 and so on; it is in effect a closed loop based on the past. The problem is in deciding values for the smoothing constants. Such decisions are often arbitrary, based on past experience, and tested against past information. Computer programs exist which will do this systematically, and are found in cash flow forecasting programs and in inventory control programs.

Finding trends

When looking at a column of figures, it is difficult to visualize if there is an increasing or decreasing trend. A simple method of determining if there is a trend is to calculate a mean and then to calculate the variation from the mean for each period.

In Table 13.10, the first four periods total 20 + 18 + 22 + 23 = 83, and 83/4 = a mean of 21.

We can now clearly see that from Period 8 onwards there is a marked upwards trend. Case study 13.2 illustrates the use of statistics in the events industry.

Table 13.10 Trends

Period	Actual	Cumulative difference from mean	
1	20	−1	$(21 - 20) = -1$
2	18	−4	$(21 - 18) = (-3) + (-1) = -4$
3	22	−3	$(21 - 22) = (+1) + (-4) = -3$
4	23	−1	$(21 - 23) = (+2) + (-3) = -1$
5	21	−1	$(21 - 21) = (0) + (-1) = -1$
6	19	−3	$(21 - 19) = (-2) + (-1) = -3$
7	24	0	$(21 - 24) = (+3) + (-3) = 0$
8	25	+4	$(21 - 25) = (+4) + (0) = +4$
9	22	+5	$(21 - 22) = (+1) + (+4) = 5$
10	23	+7	$(21 - 23) = (+2) + (+5) = 7$
11	25	+11	$(21 - 25) = (+4) + (+7) = 11$
12	26	+15	$(21 - 26) = (+5) + (+11) = 16$
13			

Case study 13.2

Ernst & Young, Australia

How can statistics be usefully used in the events industry? For instance, in the sports sector Ernst and Young has a department in Australia which deals with sports, events and venues. They are quoted on their website as follows:

expectations are higher, productions costs continue to rise and competition for quality events is intense.

Venue managers are expected to create a total entertainment experience within a safe and smoothly operating environment. Venues need to be versatile and capable of hosting a wide variety of events and activities. Sports must be able to maximize key revenue streams that may include media rights, sponsorship and other multimedia opportunities alongside traditional revenue sources such as ticketing, food and beverage, and merchandising. Ernst & Young have the ability to analyse and understand the key issues and priorities that impact upon the participants of this dynamic industry.

A sample of the key services from the Sports, Events & Venues Group include:

- Economic impact assessments of events
- Budgeting and forecasting
- Event selection to ensure it matches target markets
- Stadium and event strategic planning
- Operational reviews
- Process re-engineering to reduce operating costs
- Benchmarking against best practice
- Performance improvement strategies
- Attendance verifications.

(Information supplied by courtesy of Ernst & Young, Australia; for more information see www.ey.com.)

All of the processes described in Case study 13.2 involve forecasting. The techniques and processes used, however, will vary according to the complexity of the event. Ernst & Young has worked with The Australian Olympic Committee and the Australian Sports Commission, as well as Mercedes Australian Fashion Week. However, this does not mean that a local festival, concert or charity ball, for instance, would not benefit from using forecasting. For example, take a student ball; attendance figures and a quantified consumption of alcohol could be used when seeking sponsorship for the next year's event.

Capacity management

We have now spent some time deciding how best to judge and calculate the attendance at an event, or the take-up of specified parts of it. We now have to make sure that we have the capacity in order to meet the needs of our attendees.

Capacity management is a key planning responsibility of event managers. Wild (2002) states that the decisions on how to match the capacity of the organization to the levels of demand will influence many other decisions. The capacity of the event will be determined by the resources available to it – space, time, the number of staff and their various skill levels, the management expertise required and many other resources, dependent upon the scale and style of the event.

Capacity management involves the organization of resources to meet the demand. This will include acquiring those resources, and training where necessary.

Figure 13.2 shows some of the influences that affect the overall capacity of an event.

Can service be stored?

In the event industry, if capacity is not used when available then that capacity is lost for ever; it cannot be reused or saved. For example, seats at a concert or at a conference cannot be stored – once the conference or the concert has started, even though major costs have been incurred in providing for a full capacity, any empty seats cannot be

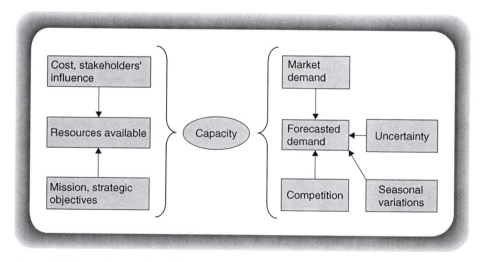

Figure 13.2 Some factors that influence capacity

sold later. In retail services the situation is different; goods not sold today could well be sold tomorrow, and the sale is not necessarily lost.

Measuring capacity

An organization has capacity if it has some of each of the resources required to carry out its function. For example, a conference centre has the capacity to hold a conference and accept delegates if it has accommodation and vacant seats during the proceedings. Wild (2002) states that if insufficient capacity is provided it will be possible to meet only some of the demand, and so some customers will wait or go elsewhere. If too much capacity is provided, there will be under-utilization of resources. Wild (2002) says that another approach is to try to manipulate demand to match the available capacity, by advertising and price promotions. Conversely, if demand is exceeding capacity then demand may be encouraged to fall by, for example, raising prices.

We can see these concepts more clearly diagrammatically. Slack *et al.* (2004) identify three options for coping with demand that does not match the capacity available:

1. Ignore the fluctuations in demand and keep the activities and level of resources constant (i.e. level capacity)
2. Adjust the capacity to match the fluctuations in demand (i.e. chase demand management)
3. Attempt to change the demand to fit the capacity of all the resources you have available (i.e. demand management).

In the *level capacity* approach, the level, the amount, the quantity of your resources available stays constant. For instance, if you employ five staff to run the bar at a busy wedding reception in a marquee, you use this number throughout the proceedings. During the reception there will be times when the bar staff are underemployed and idle, and at other times they will be very busy and guests may have to queue and wait to be served. It can be seen that this is possibly a waste of resources, although at many times when the bar is open the guests will receive excellent service and only on certain occasions will they have to queue.

The time line on Figure 13.3 represents hours. The vertical line represents the number of staff (capacity). The darker, straight line represents the staffing resources provided by the event manager to run a busy bar in a marquee at a large wedding reception, while the lighter, wavy line represents the numbers of guests going to the bar to collect drinks.

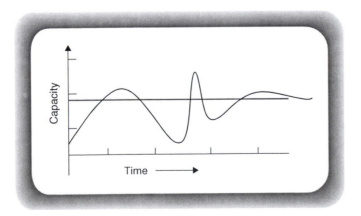

Figure 13.3 Level capacity

When the wavy line is below the straight line, some of the staff will be idle and the guests will have been served immediately. When the wavy line goes above the straight line, the guests will have had to queue for a short time until they were served.

Towards the end of this period it can be seen that the staffing resources and the demand for service from the guests are almost equally matched. It must be established for how long and how many times guests are prepared to wait. In some events they may go elsewhere, but at a wedding they are relatively 'captive' to that venue. However, it may be that they are sufficiently frustrated not to recommend that venue to others.

This approach can be used in many other situations. The time line can represent minutes or days or months. The event manager can use this analysis approach in a variety of different settings – for example, the number of mobile phone recharge points provided at an outdoor music festival. The time line could represent hours and the straight line represent the number of fixed mobile phone recharge points. In this example, the same figure (Figure 13.3) shows that at times the mobile phone recharge points are idle and at other times festival attendees will be queuing. The festival organizer will use this information and make decisions as to how many recharge points will be provided on future occasions.

Similarly, the time line could represent months at a conference venue, and the straight line the number of conference rooms available. In this instance the graph will show that at certain times of the year the venue is having to turn away business, and at other times it is under-booked.

A further issue to bear in mind when setting a fixed level of capacity, such as a set number of staff for the expected number of customers, is to ascertain whether the length of time each customer will need is the same for each customer. Planning is easier where the service provided is of the same duration each time – for example, at the registration of individual delegates at an international exhibition. It is more difficult when it is not known how long each service encounter will require, such as at one of the stands at the exhibition when delegates wish to discuss products and prices with the sales team. How many staff from the sales team should be seconded to the stand for the duration of the event?

When using a *chase demand management* approach, the opposite of a level capacity occurs. This is much more difficult to achieve, since an accurate forecast of demand has to be known. Wild (2002) discusses the uncertainty of demand and how the existence of a stable and known demand would simplify the problems of trying to match capacity to that demand. In Chapter 3, we discussed a factor in the typology of events as being the uncertainty in numbers attending, and how these numbers can change over a varying period of time. This uncertainty in numbers of, say, people attending or using our services gives rise to uncertainty about the number of resources required – i.e. the capacity we should provide at the event. It is useful to see this diagrammatically, as in Figure 13.4.

As in Figure 13.3, the time line on this figure represents hours. The vertical line represents the number of staff. The darker line again represents the staffing resources provided by the event manager to run a busy bar in a marquee at a large wedding reception. The lighter line represents the numbers of guests going to the bar to collect drinks.

It can be seen that the staffing resources and the demand for service from the guests are almost equally matched. This has been achieved by the event manager predicting the number of guests going to the bar to collect drinks over the period of time. Perhaps the speeches will have been taken into account, when drinks are not collected, and the fact that during the meal bar requirements would diminish. Later, using past experience, the event manager has realized that more drinks will be required. Another way of maximizing the use of the staff would be to use the staff elsewhere as the demand drops, but to keep them within calling distance or mobile phone range so they can

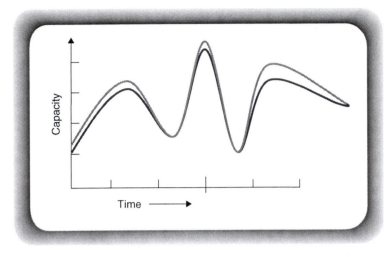

Figure 13.4 Capacity and resource provision chasing the fluctuating demand

return when necessary. Such staff would need to be multi-skilled and flexible. However, this flexibility of staff is only of use when there is another job to go to. For example, how many security personnel would you need at a busy outdoor venue, controlling entry points? Even as the number of attendees arriving drops, as they pass through the barriers, there is little else that the security personnel can do but stay at their assigned posts.

Using the example of mobile phone recharge points, this approach is not as practicable – the recharge points cannot be transported to another site and called back at short notice. Therefore this approach is only appropriate in those circumstances where the resources can be provided flexibly, or where prediction of the demand can be made accurately and the resources can be varied.

In most cases where demand levels are lower than expected there will be an under-utilization of capacity and a build-up of resources (Wild, 2002). In some cases where the demand exceeds expectations and more staff are required this can be offset against times when full capacity is not required but was expected, and less than a full staffing compliment was provided. Where it is difficult to accommodate short-term excess demand it may necessitate a provision of excess capacity, as we saw in Figure 13.3. At many events where demand is difficult to quantify this under-utilization of resources might be considered more profitable than the loss of customers.

The capacity of the staffing resources can be changed to some extent. Staff can work overtime, unskilled people can be employed in busy periods to free up skilled staff, and staff can be reallocated from their normal duties to help in situations where they are needed for short periods of time. However, as said before, they must be trained and willing to be flexible.

Where customers do have to wait, the event manager can make that wait more palatable – for instance, at some outdoor events there can be street entertainment. Customers can also be advised how long they will have to wait for. This second strategy does much to allay feelings of frustration, particularly if it is coupled with the fact that the wait is not quite as long as predicted.

The third approach is *demand management*. This approach represents an attempt by the event manager to manipulate the demand for services to match the capacity that is available. Common methods of manipulating demand include advertising, promotions, cheaper rates in the off season, cheaper meals for early diners, happy hours (half-price drinks) in bars and so on. Where demand exceeds capacity, prices can be raised to discourage customers coming at busy times. At events we can often see cheaper entrance costs for those who arrive early, and more expensive entrance costs if tickets are not booked in advance – for example, for runners in road races, where entry is made in advance or by the Internet. Some of these measures are now being criticized – for example, the cheaper prices of early drinks, since it has been reported that this can lead to excessive drinking. If this criticism is taken seriously, bar and club managers might have to reconsider how they can attract customers to their premises at times when their trade is low and their staffing costs static, but without using the lure of cheap drinks.

As in Figure 13.3, the time line on Figure 13.5 represents hours. The vertical line represents the number of staff. It is not appropriate to use the wedding guests/bar example here, since it would be inconceivable to try to manipulate the guests to come to collect their drinks during the speeches and whilst eating the wedding breakfast. However, smoothing can be seen at concerts where customers are asked to order their drinks in advance of the interval. This enables the bar staff to be working relatively constantly, receiving the orders and then delivering the drinks to a prearranged place for the interval. Identification of work that can be done in advance greatly relieves the affects of fluctuation of demand.

We could imagine that Figure 13.5 represents the attendance of 4000 people at a large agricultural show. Those attendees with families could be encouraged to come in the morning, when children's activities would be more prevalent, and other groups of people to come later in the day for different styles of entertainment.

By segmenting your market it is possible to delay and attract numbers so that your staff and the different facilities are used to a constant level through the event. The darker line again represents the staffing resources provided by the event manager, and the lighter line represents the numbers of attendees who have been encouraged to arrive at different times during the day.

It can be seen that the staffing resources and the demand for service from the guests are almost equally matched, and a steady, even flow is obviously easier to cope with than peaks and troughs.

The capacity can be managed at some events by asking customers to book in advance or to make reservations. If the capacity is then available to meet those prearranged needs, the customer is satisfied.

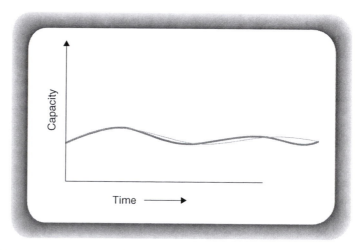

Figure 13.5 Demand being smoothed by encouraging a more consistent flow to and within the event

Another way of smoothing the demands of customers and increasing the match between the demand and the capacity is to ask the customers to participate in the service. For example, at a buffet bar customers can serve themselves, or they can book on line for an event, saving registration staff the need to complete forms.

Case study 13.3 provides an illustration of seasonal trends.

Case study 13.3

The Ice Cube, Millennium Square, Leeds, England, Winter 2001–2004

The 'Ice Cube' is a 1250 square metre real ice rink constructed each winter at Millennium Square, Leeds city centre, as a part of Leeds City Council's annual events programme.

Since the inaugural season in 2001, the Ice Cube has become one of Leeds' most popular events. During the 2004 season (16 January–29 February) the rink attracted approximately 71 000 skaters, and an estimated 250 000 non-skating visitors to the rink structure.

Having experienced four seasons of rink operations, it was clear from anecdotal operational evidence that there was a significant increase in demand at weekends (Friday evenings, Saturdays and Sundays) and during the school half-term holidays (period 6 in the 2001–2004 comparison).

By comparing total revenue from all years on scatter plots (see Figures 13.6–13.9), this trend is quite clearly shown.

(Please note that in Figures 13.6–13.9, seasons have been split into four periods to allow greater detail to be shown. Where seasons have started later (2001) or finished later (2002), this is accounted for within the table by the non-appearance of season data.)

When assessing data such as these, otherwise known as 'time series' data, results can be categorized into the 'decomposition model' as one of four components, trend, seasonal, cyclical or random factors. Clearly with emphasis on weekend and half-term trading peaks, the Ice Cube can be considered seasonal in nature. In addition there is an element of randomness – the weather – which explains the occasional sudden plunge in revenue figures.

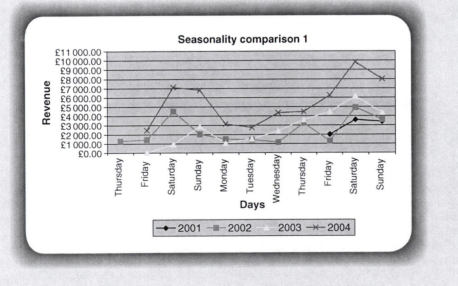

Figure 13.6 Seasonality comparison (periods 1 + 2)

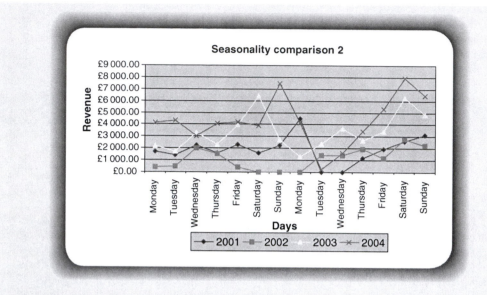

Figure 13.7 Seasonality comparison (periods 3 + 4)

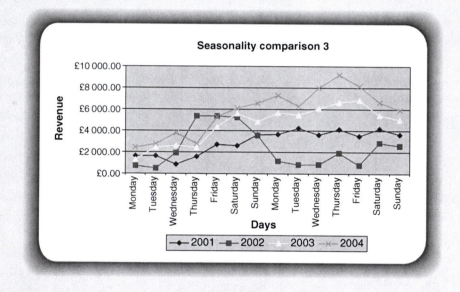

Figure 13.8 Seasonality comparison (periods 5 + 6): half-term holidays

Seasonal trends

The time series data above can also be used to assess trends throughout each individual operating period. With the rink only open for a 6-week season each year, does the rink get busier as word-of-mouth spreads, or does all the initial media coverage connected with the rink opening mean that the rink is less popular towards the end of the season?

This information would be particularly useful when planning the rink marketing campaign, so as to concentrate advertising spend to encourage visitors during quieter periods.

Presently the rink cannot accommodate all skaters during busy sessions (Saturday afternoons and during the half-term holidays). Due to the constraints of the site the rink cannot

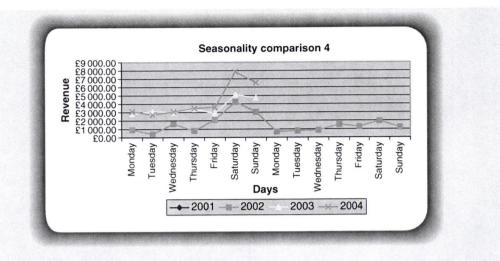

Figure 13.9 Seasonality comparison (periods 7 + 8)

realistically be extended beyond its current 1200 square metres, and therefore the challenge is to develop off-peak periods to further maximize income. It can be seen from Figures 13.6–13.9 that the trend in the 2004 season shows a positive increase over the 6 weeks.

(Patrick Loy, Senior Lecturer, Leeds Metropolitan University, England.)

Reflective practice 13.2

Regarding Case study 13.3:

1. How can the above information be used to smooth out variation in demand for the ice rink?
2. What strategies could be put into place to manage demand?

Queuing theory

Due to the random nature of customer arrivals (even when there is an arrival pattern) and the variability in time taken to satisfy each customer, no matter how good the planning of resources, queues will build up, disappear when there is a lull, and then reappear.

Reflective practice 13.3

During a coffee break-out session at a conference:

1. How long should a customer wait, what is 'reasonable', and how long on average do you think that customers will be prepared to wait for a drink?
2. How much idle time is acceptable for service staff?
3. What is the cost of having unused capacity?
4. What is the cost of not being able to provide a service?

Variability of arrivals

It is often not possible, unless an appointment book or reservation-type system is used, to control the actual moment of arrival of a customer. The number of arrivals and the length of time between subsequent arrivals is not constant. By recording the number of arrivals, a histogram can be used to show a frequency distribution.

The assumption in most queuing systems is that arrivals occur singly, and therefore the concern is with the probability of a customer arriving or no customer arriving at any point in time or period of time.

The simplest form for managing customers is a single facility through which all customers must enter if they are to be served or registered; more complicated systems will have several serving units which may not all be the same. At events this does not necessarily mean individual people; it may be groups of people arriving in cars or coaches. Multiple entry points can be arranged in parallel, so that customers might enter through a choice of points. On the other hand, a single queue may be encouraged to form and the next customer will go to the first point that becomes available. At large events, correct procedures are crucial to avoid crushing and prevent frustration.

Queue discipline

Customers might form orderly queues where newcomers go to the back of the queue and wait their turn (FIFO – first in first out), or the system might be that the last one to arrive is served first (LIFO – last in first out) – for example, in the processing of inward mail, the last letter received goes to the top of the pile and is processed first.

Other methods might be to have a priority system for serving certain customers first (for example, those customers with pre-booked seats at concerts), to have no system at all with customers being selected, or to have customers selecting themselves for service at random. Discipline or lack of discipline is not likely to affect the speed at which the service unit operates, but will affect the waiting time for customers and, consequently, their feeling of being equitably served.

Whichever methodology you employ when managing queues, Yeoman *et al.* (2004) advise the event manager to understand the psychology and feelings of people who do wait in queues. They recommend further reading, citing Maister (1985), and suggest how the event manager can reduce tension by recognizing that unoccupied time feels longer than occupied time and unexplained waits longer than explained waits. On the other hand, they cite that if the value of the service for which they are waiting is greater, the visitor will wait longer. This and other points are valuable phenomena that the event manager could utilize to reduce problems where the demand for a particular event outstrips the resources that have been provided at a particular point. Bear in mind that different countries might have different cultural approaches to queuing.

Service times

Some customers might take longer to serve than others, or all customers might need exactly the same amount of time to process. Nonetheless, as in the case of measuring the variability of arrivals, so too can the variability of service times be measured and averaged. It might be observed that as the queue lengthens the average throughput increases, with the serving staff allowing themselves less time per customer. If customers are being rushed through the system they might believe that the level of service is below standard, or if they are kept waiting they might become dissatisfied and leave the queue. There is the challenge for the event manager.

Queuing formulae

An important measure for a simple queue is customer intensity, where:

Customer intensity = Mean (average) rate of service / Mean rate of arrival

For example, if the inter-arrival time is on average 8 minutes and the service time is on average 6 minutes, then customer intensity will be $6/8 = 0.75$. Thus 0.75 is the probability (P) of a customer having to wait for service. When P is below 1 there will be idle time for the resource, but if P is more than 1 then the queue will get longer and longer (assuming that the service does not speed up but remains constant).

Developing this example, imagine that a client for a fortune-teller at a fête arrives at the beginning of the hour and another 'client' arrives every 8 minutes thereafter. The average 'service' time is 6 minutes. At the end of 60 minutes the fortune-teller could have seen ten customers, but as only seven have arrived with one due in 4 minutes, only seven have gone through the system. Therefore over a period of 10 hours the fortune-teller have will seen 75 people but would have been able to have seen 100.

If, however, the arrival time were to be every 6 minutes, starting at the beginning of the hour, and each interaction were to take 8 minutes, the customer intensity would be $8/6 = 1.33$. Thus at the end of the first hour seven people would have been seen, one would be half way through a consultation, one would have 4 minutes to wait, and the remaining one would have 12 minutes to wait. However, if at the end of the hour a new client walks in the door, that client is going to have to wait 20 minutes. At the end of 10 hours the fortune-teller will have seen 75 customers, and there will be a further 25 people waiting in the queue (that is, the last customer to arrive will have a wait of 3 hours and 12 minutes).

The question of queuing can thus be addressed from a customer service perspective i.e. how long do customers have to wait for service, or how long will they wait before they are lost to the system? OR from a resource use perspective – (how long are we prepared to have idle capacity in the system?)

There is a range of queuing models available; for their use within the event industry the reader is advised to refer to further work and details by Yeoman *et al.* (2004).

Reflective practice 13.4

You are the operations manager for a racecourse. You have a major 3-day event of races starting on Boxing Day, and need to plan all of your facilities to provide parking, catering, box office admissions, etc. for the 3 days.

1. Identify which forecasting procedures you would use.
2. Identify the advantages and disadvantages of each method.

Chapter summary and key points

This chapter has demonstrated that the knowledge of numbers of people attending and their different requirements is an important prerequisite for any event. Following on from having gained that information is the determination of the capacity and availability of resources to service those numbers and needs.

We began by explaining the need to forecast the number of people expected to attend an event. Capacity management is the matching of resources with demand.

Several techniques for forecasting demand have been introduced, and it was emphasized that whichever method was used that any forecast should be tested against past experience and take into account present circumstances and trends. When looking at forecasts the questions to ask include, are these figures sensible, what happened last time and what is likely to happen this time?

Once the forecast demand has been agreed, the next step is to determine what capacity management strategy will be adopted. The broad strategies are to have a fixed level of resources, to manipulate capacity to chase demand, or to try to manipulate demand. If the first strategy is adopted, a fixed level of resources, then it can be expected that at times resources will not be fully used but at other times customers will have to wait and queues will form. When queues form, there is the danger of losing customers.

Manipulation of demand requires flexibility of staff and customers and the ability to react quickly to changing numbers. Manipulation of demand might be through pricing or special promotions.

In conclusion it is worth repeating that the major resource in the events industry is people, thus training and motivation of people is important.

The chapter has ended with a section on queuing theory. This third stage of the event operations management model now moves on to researching different scheduling techniques that the event manager can use effectively in order for the event to run as planned.

Chapter 14

Scheduling and time management

Learning Objectives

After reading through this chapter you will be able to:

- Understand the importance of scheduling
- Apply the different techniques of scheduling and analyse the different stages
- Consider the importance of time management
- Apply techniques to your own use of personal time.

Introduction

In the last few chapters within the third stage of the event operations management model we have considered the importance of motivating one of our most important resources – our staff. We have also considered the essential nature of predicting how many people will attend our event and what they will want to do when they arrive. This then led on to the need to plan for those activities within the capacity of the venue and the resources provided.

Now we turn to scheduling all these activities so that they fall into place to give the desired event. Scheduling is a key issue for an event manager. As soon as a concept is thought of, as described in the life cycle of services in Chapter 7, then a decision should be made – can we deliver this in the time we have available? Further questions should identify all of the tasks that have to be completed, and how those elements will finally come together. Indeed, scheduling has to balance many different factors and many diverse needs in order to integrate them and deliver the production of the event at the required time.

Events are a series of unique projects. The finite nature of some of the critical resources, such as special skills, means that these have to be taken into account in the planning process, and the overriding priority is to complete the project within a given time, to a given date and hour (Slack *et al.*, 2004). Wild (2002) defines a project as an activity with a specific goal occupying a specific period of time. An event is a project, since it is a finite activity in terms of the time spent in its duration and in the use of resources. Therefore it is essential to plan the event thoroughly and to schedule all the activities so that as a whole they form the event. It is a different concept from planning repetitive activities, where problems can be resolved next time round.

At an event, all of the resources and skills have to be brought together in a planned fashion, and there is only the one opportunity to get it right and as per specification. Getz (1997) confirms that an event manager will require skills and experience in event or general project management. He cites that the manager's ability to organize, motivate and manage a team of experts and volunteers is a primary qualification.

The event manager faces uncertainty. The amount of time needed to complete all the different tasks is often uncertain, as are the amount of resources needed and the interdependence of all the activities. In some situations, the number of people who will attend is not certain. Scheduling therefore involves a certain amount of risk, and ideally allowances should be built in to enable revisions of the schedules. There is only one opportunity to start from scratch.

Waters (1996) points out that although there are many similarities between scheduling in manufacturing and in services, there are essential differences. First, in the service industry the customer is directly involved in the process – for example, sometimes customers serve themselves and form queues and wait. Secondly, services cannot be held in stock because, as discussed earlier, they are perishable and intangible. Thirdly, there are often wide variations in demand, as discussed in Chapter 12, and our schedules should be able to meet both high and low demand. All these points are particularly true in the event industry, and this chapter will explore these issues and offer solutions that the event manager can use.

Scheduling in the event industry

Scheduling is the art of:

- Event component breakdown
- Activity analysis
- Deciding the order of completing activities
- Arranging the necessary resources to complete each activity
- Arranging the timing of activities.

Different terms are used to cover these activities. Shone and Parry (2004) discuss logistics, and describe that function as being the discipline of planning and organizing the flow of goods, equipment and people to their point of use. This is essentially the same as scheduling, and an event is reliant on getting all elements to the right place in time for a range of deadlines.

At the start of planning for the event several activities can be started, but most subsequent activities will be dependent on others finishing. As more activities finish, even more can be started (Slack *et al.*, 2004). Some of these early activities may include getting special power and utility requirements to the event site (such as telecoms), and special licences may also need to be applied for. We can see in the example of organizing a simple craft fair that certain activities need to be completed before others. The date has to be set and the venue booked, and the admission prices and refreshments prices calculated before any advertising can be done. The exhibitors have to be sourced and invited before the layout and plan can be finalized. Only after a series of major decisions have been made can follow-on activities start. This pattern of a slow start followed by a faster pace and an eventual tail-off of activities holds true for many events.

For the majority of events, a *backwards scheduling activity* occurs – i.e. the finish date and hour is known, all the activities are listed, plus their expected completion times, and then the schedule is calculated backwards so that all activities can be sequenced appropriately and finished by the due date. Wild (2002) describes this technique as one where the time durations of particular activities are subtracted from the required completion date.

In practice, as discussed in Chapter 12, demand forecasts (i.e. the number of customers and their arrival times) are rarely exact. These provide a challenge to the event manager to have just the right resources available at the right time, but not in excess, since this would add on a cost to the project.

Case study 14.1 gives an overview of the scheduling required for the World Rally Championships.

Case study 14.1

World Rally Championships Production Cars, Tuesday 7 May 2002

The logistics of flyaways – a painstaking task

For European-based rounds, the Peugeot Sport road show is mainly freighted by truck.

However, the organization required for flyaway events such as the Rally of Argentina is a big challenge, as the French team's logistics wizard, Pietro Fornaris, explains:

Everything is transported by ship or by plane, which means lead times are very long. Scheduling has to be extremely tight to be sure that everything arrives at the correct destination, in the right order, on time and via the cheapest solution possible. The containers shipped by sea have to be ready very early. The crossing often takes a good month, and since there are generally only two ships a week, you always have to plan in a safety margin just in case. By plane, we send the test car and a stock of spares just prior to pre-rally testing. Other components and the rally cars themselves follow later. But here again, we build in a good margin for error.

The stress begins during the preparation phase at the workshop. For overseas rallies, we have seven 15-tonne, 12-metre containers. The specially dimensioned service trucks, the race cars, people carriers, electronic equipment and spares all need to be packed in the knowledge the containers shipped out to Argentina go straight from South America to Kenya, and then on to New Zealand and Australia. They only return to Paris at the end of the season.

That means that all the equipment sent onto the following destination has to be thoroughly checked after each rally. That can take up to 24 hours of practically non-stop work, and even twice that when the cars have to be squeaky clean: when going to rigorous countries like New Zealand or Australia, there's no way you'll get a car in if it still has traces of dirt from the previous event. Another headache is that certain used parts, or parts that need revising, are shipped back to Paris by plane, while replacement equipment, originally shipped out by plane, takes their place inside the containers. You can imagine how precise customs documents have to be.

Naturally, at the points of departure and arrival, and at certain ports of call along the way, we use agents in whom we have complete confidence to ensure that all goes well. In addition to the equipment, we also have to look after the transport of team staff, which means finding suitable air tickets for around 70 people. As a rule, each flyaway trip is prepared a good 6 months upstream of the event, except in cases of force majeur – for example, when the FIA decides to modify the World Championship calendar.

Schedule for Production cars for 2004

6–8 Feb	Uddehold Swedish Rally Production Car World Rally Championship (WRC)
12–14 Mar	Orona Rally Mexico Production Car WRC
16–18 Apr	Rally of New Zealand Production Car WRC
6–18 Jul	Rally Argentina Production Car WRC
20–22 Aug	Rallye Deutschland Production Car WRC
15–17 Oct	Rallye de France Tour de Corse Production Car WRC
12–14 Nov	Telstra Rally Australia Production Car WRC

(Printed by courtesy of Bryn Williams, MD of www.crash.net.)

In certain events the numbers of customers arriving is known, and in some cases at known specific times – for example, at a conference or for a dinner dance, or for some other pre-booked event. In these instances the event manager will make the availability of the resources coincide with the event starting; the manager can control the time of service delivery and the scheduling can be fairly exact. Efficiency is dependent on arrival of the customer at the prearranged time.

If, however, the customer is late, service will be delayed or not offered at all. In the case of a concert, the customer may miss the start of the programme. If the organizer agrees to the delay of the event, this may have an impact on other scheduled services and possibly on other customers. Nonetheless, if customers keep to the prearranged booked times, a high degree of accuracy, and efficiency in the scheduling of resources will be possible.

Customers who arrive early may have to wait, depending upon the policy of the event organizer. If the customer doesn't wait but is served, then there must have been some slack in the system and surplus capacity must have been held.

If the customer waits, then a queue starts to form. If the customer accepts that there may be a queue there will not be any conflict, but if the customer is expecting to access the event immediately there will be some dissatisfaction.

Where queuing is accepted to be part of the norm – for example at theme park rides, or whilst waiting for a mobile phone recharge at an outdoor festival – then customers will not be dissatisfied. The queues should be well managed so that there is no queue jumping and, provided that the queues are seen to be moving and there are no greater expectations, it is acceptable for the customer to be part of the resources available to the event manager. Theory of queues was covered in Chapter 12.

Case study 14.2 describes the scheduling required to provide St John Ambulance cover at a rock concert.

Case study 14.2

Robbie Williams Concert, 1–3 August 2003, Knebworth, England

St John Ambulance rocks at Knebworth, England

Brian Heron-Edmends, Assistant County Commissioner (Operations), describes three long days in August when fans flocked to see Robbie Williams play Knebworth and St John Ambulance volunteers flocked to minister first aid.

St John Ambulance Hertfordshire was asked to provide medical, first aid and ambulance cover at the Robbie Williams concerts at Knebworth Park over the weekend of the 1–3 August 2003, with 125 000 people attending each night.

The planning started back in February this year, when the basis of the concert was known, and the boundaries to which we would be working were being agreed. Over the following few months a number of people put in a great deal of work to ensure that there were sufficient numbers on duty each day.

The organizers had requested 80 first aiders per day, and four ambulances. This was to be supplemented by eight paramedics and two paramedic ambulances, which were to be supplied by the local ambulance service (Bedfordshire and Hertfordshire Ambulance and Paramedic Service NHS Trust).

It was agreed that there would be six first aid posts and a medical centre; four posts in the main arena and the remaining two backstage to treat people who were taken from the crowd via the pit. Each first aid post would have a 10 × 10 m marquee and a first aid unit; all the posts would have toilets (for members' use only) and running drinking water. The medical centre, a much larger marquee, was to be manned by St John first aiders, doctors and nurses.

Day 1, Friday 1 August

The day started wet and miserable – not good for an open-air concert. Members started to arrive and set about checking the equipment in their first aid posts in preparation for the gates to be opened. The afternoon saw a gradual increase of fans arriving, with most first aid posts relatively quiet to start with. As time went on, it became apparent that many fans were stuck in traffic jams on the A1(M) and surrounding roads. This included some of our members who were coming to the duty after work, as well as those coming from further afield.

The concert was divided into sections, with artists playing followed by a 45-minute break before the next artist took to the stage. Casualties who needed treatment made their way to the posts during these breaks, leading to a wave effect of patients requiring treatment and quiet periods when members could get themselves a drink and quick snack. As the evening went on the stream of casualties became more constant, even when the artists were playing.

Many members played the game of hunt the casualty after receiving a report of a collapsed fan in the crowd; most requests for help came via show security, various control rooms and finally to the members. The Chinese whisper effect on some occasions made tracking down the casualty a challenge.

The concert finished on time, even though people were still arriving from the motorway. Many St John personnel didn't leave the concert site until the early hours of Saturday morning.

Day 2, Saturday 2 August

Everything was reviewed for Saturday; problems that had been encountered on Friday evening were rectified, as far as possible. Some of the posts were rearranged by the members to free up more space for stretcher patients. This left less staff for the walking wounded. Again, members began to arrive during the morning ready for the 12 noon opening of the gates. The weather was totally different to Friday; the sun was shining and it was starting to get very hot. At the front of the stage where the noise was at its greatest Raynet personnel provided additional radio communications with the Control Room to speed the passing of non-medical messages. As the afternoon turned into early evening, the first aid posts and the medical centre became busier and busier.

Day 3, Sunday 3 August

Another hot day was forecast, and as the day progressed fans started to feel the full force of the sun and were even collapsing in the queues before entering the arena, so members were deployed to the gates with water and patient report forms.

Many people in the audience, having found themselves good vantage points, were reluctant to leave to get themselves fluids; this led to many people collapsing or coming to the first aid posts with severe sunburn. In an attempt to protect members as much as possible, they were all issued with sun cream and provided with bottled water.

The total number of casualties treated on Sunday was the highest of the three concerts.

Everyone who attended the duty had a great time and found they learnt a lot. The overall event was a great success for all involved; the planning that went on beforehand played a large part in this, but would have been pointless without the dedication and hard work of everyone who covered the duty. They made it possible for Hertfordshire to deliver the high standard of care and service that is always expected of St John Ambulance.

The official figures totalled 1387 patients over the 3 days.

Staff attendees: first aid units and medical centre staff

Doctors	5	Nurses	8
Paramedics	1 per shift	Pharmacist	1 (on-site pharmacy instigated by St JA)
First aiders	100 per shift	Radio operators	33 (Raynet)
StJA support staff	10 per shift		

These staff members were drawn from the following seven counties: Hertfordshire, Bedfordshire, Cornwall, Dorset, London District, Oxfordshire, Suffolk.

Resources on site

Front-line ambulances	6	Sitting car	1
4 × 4 ambulances	1	Minibuses	3
4 × 4 support vehicles	2	Command and/or first aid units	6

And what did we learn?

The pharmacy not only catered for people requiring painkillers for headaches but also with the many that were after plasters for blisters after the long walks from the car parks. The decision to have a pharmacy on site was by far the best decision taken during the planning stages, as it provided a much needed service to the public as well as helping reduce the need for people to attend the first aid posts with minor ailments. The pharmacy sold most products that you would expect to find in a high street pharmacy.

We would highly recommend anyone else who is providing medical cover at a concert of this size, or even smaller, to consider an on-site pharmacy, as we believe it reduced the members' work considerably, leaving them better prepared to deal with serious conditions which were referred to the first aid posts and medical centre.

Control rooms: At the event there were three control rooms, St John Ambulance, Beds and Hertfordshire Ambulance Service (BHAPS), and RAYNET. The control rooms were all separate, albeit within 10 metres of each other. However, it made the passing of information quickly between the different agencies very difficult.

Calls for medical assistance from the security and event organizers were directed via BHAPS, who then passed them on to St John; housekeeping calls came from the various first aid posts to the StJA Control Room via RAYNET.

After the first night it was agreed that at future events all three controls should be located in the same building, thus allowing for easier interagency communications.

First aid posts: The first aid posts were all large marquees, along with a conventional mobile StJA first aid unit, which was there to provide staff facilities along with additional space for the treatment of patients who needed additional privacy. Some of the posts had barriers around them; however, this was not the case for the posts towards the back of the arena, and it was only on the Saturday, as the sun shone brightly, that it became apparent that all posts needed to be 'fenced in', just leaving an entry/exit hole. As these large marquees provided some shelter from the sun, people did everything they could to get as close to them as possible. This meant that staff and patients inside were being knocked, albeit unintentionally, by those outside trying to avoid the sun.

The problem was further exacerbated when the only shelter from the sun was at the front of the marquee, and without careful management from the post manager it was not uncommon for the door area to become a sea of people avoiding the sun.

(Information supplied by courtesy of the Hertfordshire St John Ambulance Service; for more information see www.herts.sja.org.uk/.)

Reflective practice 14.2

Consider Case study 14.2.
From the information given, put together a schedule of activities for first aid cover for day 1 of the Robbie Williams concert, taking into account the lessons learned.

The stages of scheduling

The stages of scheduling are shown in Figure 14.1, and comprise event component breakdown, activity analysis and deciding the order of completion. We will now look at all the stages of scheduling, and apply some best practice techniques from the event industry.

Event component breakdown

A technique used within traditional project management is to create a product breakdown sheet (O'Toole and Mikolaitis, 2002). In the event industry the product is the event itself, which could be an exhibition with a supporting conference and seminars, followed by a conference dinner with entertainment. It is important to break down the whole event into its component parts, taking into account many of the intangible aspects of the event that have been described and considered necessary in its original objectives. This is called the *event component breakdown*.

The importance of having clear objectives was noted in Chapter 2, and it is essential that the event manager return to the objectives of the event so that those intangible aspects that have been cited as being most desirable and important are not missed. For

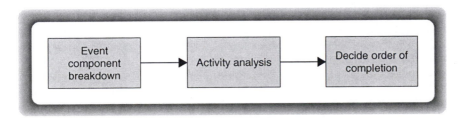

Figure 14.1 Stages of scheduling

example, the need to allow for networking opportunities may have been identified, or for a fun all-age embracing event, or to develop loyalty of a community towards their town within your objectives. It is important to refocus on all aspects of the previously stated hopes and wishes, so that the event breakdown reflects even the subtlest of objectives.

O'Toole and Mikolaitis (2002) say that this product breakdown is not merely effective as a means of identifying client objectives but it also provides a common language for the event. It is necessary for all groups of people who are responsible for different elements of the event to be aware of the final desired picture, and all unspoken assumptions should be clearly defined. If these assumptions can be aired, and ideally written down, they can be referred to as the event progresses. It may be that as the event arrangements proceed, some of the assumptions need rewriting and the documentation needs updating. If changes are made it is imperative that all parties are informed, to avoid some teams working to old versions and others to a different version.

A useful document is a contact sheet of all the relevant contacts, with mobile and email addresses, so that contact can be made swiftly and everyone is aware of those contact details should the need arise.

The event component breakdown information can be used to create the management structure for the event. It may be that several activities can be completed by certain groups of people and others should be outsourced to specialists, or that an additional team should be set up to concentrate on a particular aspect. The event component breakdown provides the client, the suppliers, major interested agencies (for example the Health and Safety Executive) and the different groups of teams working on the event a clear view of the overall event. Hence it can be seen that the event component breakdown has many important uses.

Activity analysis

Once the event components have been defined, the next stage is to analyse every element of work that needs to be completed during the planning, implementation and control of the event. This is a process of decomposition whereby a complex event can be broken up into smaller units of work that can be easily managed (O'Toole and Mikolaitis, 2002). The result of this is your activity analysis. There are several benefits to using this approach – these manageable units can be assigned to subcontractors or different event teams, or to different committees, dependent upon the set-up of the event and its managerial scope. These separate units of activities can also provide a basis for costing and a managerial structure, and they denote levels of responsibility.

Similarly, the costs for the entire event can be calculated by adding together the costs for each unit.

Subsequently each of these groupings can be broken down into more activities, so that eventually as each unit is expanded it will show all of the work that must be completed.

The *activity analysis* becomes the representation of the entire event project. As such, the event team, client, suppliers, sponsors and volunteers should easily understand it, and it gives a quick reference for all aspects of the event.

The aim is to ensure that nothing is forgotten or falls into a black hole with everyone thinking someone else is completing that particular task. Similarly, a comprehensive activity analysis ensures that nothing is forgotten or left undone.

Case study 14.3 shows the schedule for the event day of an actual University Awards Ceremony in 2003. The names of individuals and organizations have been changed.

Case study 14.3

A Business Awards Ceremony, a University Town, England, June 2003

Time	Activity	Area of responsibility	Company		Notes
09:00	Set-up of staging	Andy Close	Free Hotel	Completion 10:00	6 × 10′ × 5′ with red carpet and surround, central far wall kitchen side. Could we have Magpie divided into two?
	Stage set, sound and lighting	Iain Newman	Row Audio Visual, tel. 0123456738	Completion 13:00	Raven Suite, parking available at the front for off loading. Refreshments tea, coffee for Row × 3
09:30	Singing group arrives	Joanne, Jimmy	Event organizers, tel. 0777777711	Singing group contact number	Allocate rooms if possible, otherwise luggage etc. to changing room
10:00	Minibus for singing group	Joanne, Jimmy	Event organizers, tel. 0777777711		Pick up outside Free Hotel, go to Big Grammar School, followed by Little Grammar. Accompanied by Jimmy to give workshop
13:00	Lunch	Free Hotel			Sandwiches to be provided for Row × 3 people + 1
14:00	Audiovisual check	Joanne, Row			Run through lighting, graphics etc.
	Flowers arrive	Joanne			Delivery to front of hotel
15:00	National TV presenter arrives	Joanne	Event organizers, tel. 0777777711		Booked into suite, brief tour etc.
	Refreshments for crew				Tea/coffee/water
15:30	Singing group returns	Jimmy			Refreshments available, fresh tea, water, orange juice in changing room
15:45	Rehearsal singing group	Row	Row Audio Visual, tel. 0123456738		Sound check
16:15	Asian music group and brass ensemble, acoustic guitar and folk singer arrive	Joanne			Allocation of room for changing/ instrument cases

16:30	Awards Alive! Overture rehearsal	Singing group, Asian music group, brass ensemble			
17:00	Awards rehearsal	Sam, Sabi, Joanne, Jimmy	Awards clients, tel. 0123455673, 077777723		
18:00	Staff changing				
18:20	Staff to positions, folk singer to champagne reception, brass ensemble to front of foyer area of Free Hotel	Sam, Sabi, Joanne, Jimmy			Refreshments for artists in changing rooms; tea coffee, water, orange juice
18:30	Guests begin to arrive	Sam, Sabi, plus Awards client staff			
19:10	Raven suite to be lit, Asian music group to take their positions	Helen to call 19:08			
19:15	Guests invited to take their seats	Free Hotel manager		Local news presenter to be met at the door – Jimmy	Parking available outside the Free Hotel for dropping off
19:25	Call for Singing group and brass ensemble	Helen		Brass ensemble to move from foyer area to main suite	
19:28	Singers to mingle with guests in suite, brass ensemble to take their positions				
19:30	Awards Overture Awards Alive!	Asian music, brass ensemble, singing group			
19:36	Singing group exeunt				
19:36	Welcome speech	Sam			
19:45	Starters	Asian music group			Waiters to enter from two areas of the suite en masse to serve starters
20:03	Cue brass ensemble to main suite	Helen			
20:05	Asian music exeunt	Joanne to give cue			
20:05	Main course	Brass ensemble	Liaison between Free Hotel and Joanne re. change		Waiters to enter from two areas of the suite en masse to

				over from starter to main course		serve main course
20:43	Brass ensemble exeunt				
20:45	First three awards	Sam *et al.*	1. Presenter; 2. Presenter announces Awards; 3. Winner from seat – Award speech; 4. Repeat		
21:00	Cue folk singer	Helen			
21:05	Desert/coffee	Folk singer	Liaison between Free Hotel and Joanne re. change over from main course to dessert		Waiters to enter from two areas of the suite en masse to serve dessert; bar to open
21:30	Introduction to the singing group	Local news presenter			
	Cue singing group to reception	Helen			
21:33	Singing group Part 1				
21:44	Singing group exeunt				
21:45	Awards Part 2	Sam *et al.*	1. Presenter; 2. Presenter announces Award; 3. Winner from seat – Award speech; 4. Repeat		
21:55	Cue singing group	Helen			
22:00	Singing group Part 2				
22:15	Singing group exeunt	To reception area			
22:15	Keynote speaker; national TV presenter	Sam			
22:25	Singing group Part 3				
22:38	Cue folk singer to reception	Helen			
22:40	Singing group exeunt				
22:40	Music in reception area	Folk singer			
24:00	Close				

Deciding the order of completing activities

This can be referred to as critical path analysis. Critical path analysis is a planning and scheduling tool that can help to streamline all the processes to be undertaken (Getz, 1997). It examines the relationship between all the resources and the activities that need to be undertaken in order to 'deliver' the event – i.e. those listed in the activity analysis.

All these activities should now be arranged in chronological order, working back from the event date so that each prerequisite activity gets scheduled in proper sequence. The resultant schedule is a network of interconnected tasks, and the actual critical path in the network is the shortest possible sequence of activities needed to get the event operational (Getz, 1997).

When all the activities are linked and the dates by which those tasks should be finished by have been identified, a line can be drawn to establish how long the event preparation and lead up to delivery will take. There is a variety of computer software packages that are useful for analysing the enormous number of tasks and links that are essential to any event. However, it might be that the nature of events is too fluid for it to be put onto a software programme such as Microsoft Project.

Built into the software will be the ability to have a minimum of three estimates of time for each activity – the expected time (most likely), the most pessimistic, and the most optimistic. The software will also show the earliest start time, the latest start time, and the most probable start time. The program will calculate various critical paths and provide for printouts, on an exception basis, of a list of activities that are falling behind schedule, thus enabling the event manager to take action to correct the situation. Correction might include adding extra resources, or delaying one activity and transferring resources to another activity and so on.

However, research has been undertaken (Tum, 2004; unpublished) that shows that very few event managers in the UK use any computerized critical path analysis software.

The activity analysis has determined the critical dates when each task has to be finished by, and by whom. Some tasks can be done simultaneously, whereas others may have to wait until others have been completed. We identified examples of this in the introduction to this chapter. Other examples might include the promotion of a major sports event, which cannot start until the venue has been secured. Similarly, the delivery of expensive equipment cannot be accepted until it can be established that the level of security is adequate. However, in this scenario the event manager is then left with the challenge that it is often easier to accept delivery of large equipment onto a virgin outdoor site prior to the construction of the perimeter fencing. Many tasks at an outdoor venue cannot start until the generator has arrived. O'Toole and Mikolaitis (2002) suggest that planners of small events use sticky note slips. Each slip denotes one of the activities and can be placed on a large board, and the notes can then be easily rearranged to achieve the optimum sequence.

Network planning: the critical path method

Table 14.1 illustrates the critical path method of network planning, using the example of organizing an exhibition.

Table 14.1 Network planning: the critical path method

Activity		Duration	Preceding activity
Book venue	A–B	1 day	None
Decide on layout plan	B–C	5 days	A–B
Touch up paintwork and minor redecoration of venue	B–D	3 days	A–B
Order and delivery of display stands	C–D	7 days	B–C
Wire for stand lighting	C–E	3 days	B–C
Install display stands	D–F	2 days	B–D, C–D, C–E
Exhibitors set up	F–G	1 day	D–F

Table 14.1 depicts the order in which activities can occur. The convention of network diagrams is for the arrows to move from left to right across the page, with no backtracking. To maintain the logic, a dummy activity can be shown. In our example, E–D is a dummy activity. If E–D was not used there would be two activities designated C–D (wiring for stands and delivery of stands).

By adding the time required for each activity, it is possible to calculate the total time required to prepare for the opening of the event. If we follow along the path A–B, B–C, C–E, E–D, D–F, F–G, we can see these activities will take in total 12 days, whereas the path A–B, B–C, C–D, D–F, F–G totals 16 days and the path A–B, B–D, D–F, F–G takes 7 days. Thus the longest path is 16 days and the total time required to complete all the activities will be 16 days.

It follows that if any event on this path A–B, B–C, C–D, D–F, F–G takes longer than planned, the total amount of time required will be extended. For example, if B–C 'Decide on layout plan' takes 8 days instead of 5 days, the total time required will be 19 days. If time is critical, then no activity on the longest path, i.e. the *critical* path, can be allowed to extend beyond its allotted time. Activities not on the critical path can take longer, without affecting the total time. For example, activity B–D ('Touch up and redecoration') can take up to 12 days, and if all other activities are on schedule the total time required would still be 16 days. In the above example the only other activity that could be delayed is C–E, but then only by 2 days.

This example is very simple, designed to give the rudiments of network scheduling. A fuller example appears below.

Network planning and critical path analysis: organizing a conference

(The following explanation and work for critical path analysis has been provided by John Nightingale, BA (Hons), Events Management Course Leader, UK Centre for Events Management, Leeds Metropolitan University.)

The following network diagrams (Figures 14.2–14.6) work through the activity of setting up the basic requirements for a conference. It is important to know and understand the following terms:

- A *project* is any job – usually large. It can be split up into *activities* or *tasks*. A task is a part of a project that requires *time* and *resources* to complete.
- An *event* (in critical path jargon) marks the beginning or end of an activity or group of activities. Events take *no time*. We try to avoid the use of this term, as it can cause confusion for event organizers!
- A *milestone* is an important point during the progress of a project (often marked by a review meeting) – e.g. moving onto site, completion of set-up.

- A *predecessor* is an activity that must finish before a particular activity can start.
- The *EST* (earliest start time) of an activity is the earliest time it can start – after all its predecessors have finished. You work out ESTs by starting at the *left* of a network chart, and *add* the activity times to get the EST of the next activity. If there are two possible ESTs for an activity, use the *larger* one.
- The *LFT* (latest finish time) is the latest time at which an activity can finish, without delaying the whole project. You start working out LFTs at the *right* of the network diagram, and *subtract* the activity time to get the next LFT. If there are two possible LFTs for an activity, you take the *smaller* one.
- Activities on the *critical path* have the LFT and the EST the same at each event on the path.
- Activities off the critical path will have a *float time* bigger than zero. The float time is the maximum time that an activity can be lengthened or delayed. To find it, you work out LFT – EFT, or LST – EST.
- A *baseline* is the original version of the complete plan for the project. Progress of the project is compared against the baseline as the project progresses.

Figure 14.2 shows just one part of a network diagram.

EST		EFT
	G	
	2	
LST	Float	LFT

EST – the earliest time the activity could start

EFT – the earliest time the activity could finish

LFT – the latest time the activity could finish, without delaying the project

LST – the latest time the activity could start, without delaying the project

Float – spare time which could be used up by delays or lengthened activities, without delaying the project.

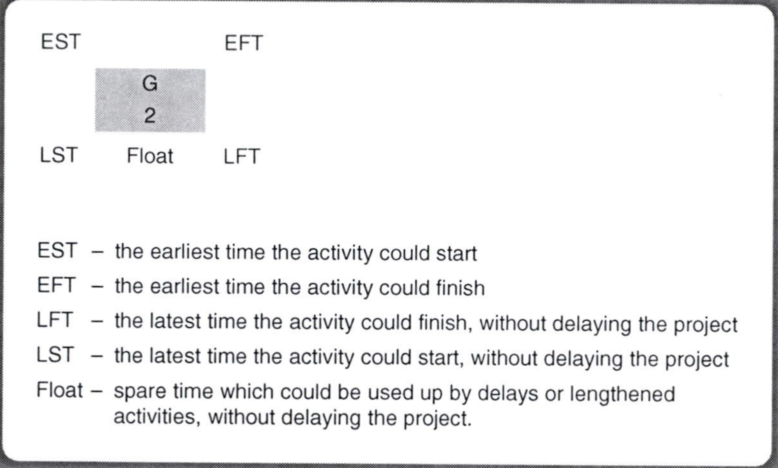

Figure 14.2 One part of a network diagram

Organizing the conference

1. Stage 1: break the project down into activities.

Activity	Duration	Preceding activities	
A	3	C	Arrange presentation systems
B	7	E	Arrange food
C	12	E	Arrange speakers
D	5	A	Set up room
E	8	G	Detailed planning
F	4	B, D, H	Stage conference
G	2	Start	Initial visit
H	9	A	Set up PA system

2. Stage 2: draw a network diagram, with precedents and times (Figure 14.3):

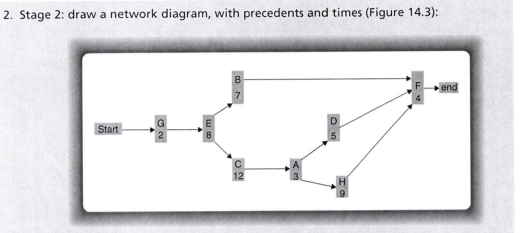

Figure 14.3 Stage 2: setting precedents and times

Key:

Activity	Duration	Preceding activities	
Start	0		
A	3	C	Arrange presentation systems
B	7	E	Arrange food
C	12	E	Arrange speakers
D	5	A	Set up room
E	8	G	Detailed planning
F	4	B, D, H	Stage conference
G	2	Start	Initial visit
H	9	A	Set up PA system
End	0	F	

3. Stage 3: add earliest start and earliest finish times (top left and top right) to each box (Figure 14.4). To get the earliest start time of the next activity, choose the *largest* EFT of jobs leading to it. To get the earliest finish time for an activity, *add* the duration to the EST.

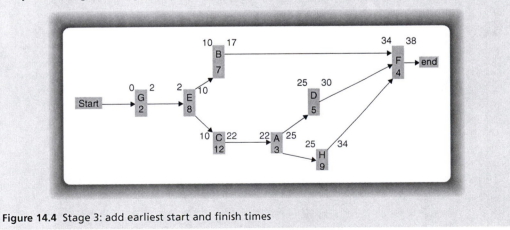

Figure 14.4 Stage 3: add earliest start and finish times

Key:

Activity	Duration	Preceding activities	
A	3	C	Arrange presentation speakers
B	7	E	Arrange food
C	12	E	Arrange speakers
D	5	A	Set up room
E	8	G	Detailed planning
F	4	B, D, H	Stage conference
G	2	Start	Initial visit
H	9	A	Set up PA system

This project takes 38 days.

4. Stage 4: put in latest finish time for each activity, starting at the right (Figure 14.5). To get the latest start time for an activity, subtract its duration from the latest finish time. When there is a 'disagreement' between two possible LFTs, take the smallest.

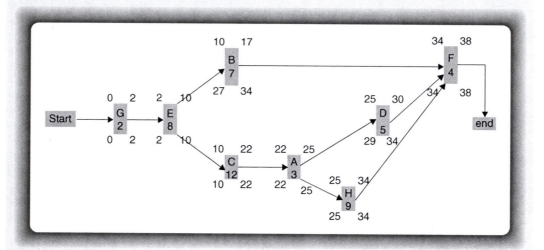

Figure 14.5 Stage 4: add latest finish time for each activity

Key:

Activity	Duration	Preceding activities	
A	3	C	Arrange presentation speakers
B	7	E	Arrange food
C	12	E	Arrange speakers
D	5	A	Set up room
E	8	G	Detailed planning
F	4	B, D, H	Stage conference
G	2	Start	Initial visit
H	9	A	Set up PA system

5. Stage 5: work out the float time (the difference between the bottom and top of each box; Figure 14.6). The critical path has zero float on every activity, therefore delays on the critical path are important. Could you speed up the critical path?

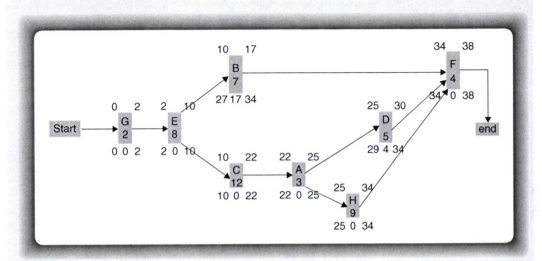

Figure 14.6 Stage 5: work out float time

Key:

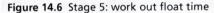

Activity	Duration	Preceding activities	
A	3	C	Arrange presentation speakers
B	7	E	Arrange food
C	12	E	Arrange speakers
D	5	A	Set up room
E	8	G	Detailed planning
F	4	B, D, H	Stage conference
G	2	Start	Initial visit
H	9	A	Set up PA system

Many standard computer packages exist for network planning. Generally software will enable three estimates to be made for each activity: expected time, best time, and worst time. The software will calculate the earliest start date and the latest start date, show the critical path, and provide for a printout on exception basis of a list of activities that are falling behind schedule, thus allowing the event operations manager to take corrective action. Corrective action might include adding extra resources, or delaying one activity and transferring resources to another activity. However, adding extra resource adds to the cost. A trade-off might be necessary where an acceptable delay occurs rather than adding the cost of an extra resource.

Gantt charts

Another technique that could be used is a Gantt chart. Henry Gantt first devised this chart in 1917. The bottom line of the chart represents time, and this time line can represent weeks, days or minutes. Each activity should be entered onto the vertical axis and plotted onto the graph to indicate the start and finish times. It is sometimes useful to have two Gantt charts: one with a weekly time line for the entire project starting at initial planning stages and leading through to breakdown and evaluation, and the other providing a running order of the event over the day/s when it is being delivered. This would then show the main components of the event.

These two Gantt charts have the beauty that most people who are involved with the event can easily understand them and they are extremely visual, and therefore effective. If kept simple, the Gantt chart will show the major tasks, i.e. the event component breakdown and the activity analysis.

The Gantt chart shows when each activity should start and finish, and enables everyone's responsibilities to be identified. It also shows their relationships to each other. As the activities are completed they can be coloured differently, and so the chart acts as a means of control to show which activities have been completed, which still have to be completed, and whether the timeframe is being kept to.

Tum (2004; unpublished) has found that a small percentage of event managers in the UK do use Gantt charts, and these are often created on word-processing packages or a spreadsheet.

Case study 14.4 illustrates the use of a Gantt chart in the scheduling of a Gala (see Figure 14.7).

The Gantt chart in Case study 14.4 shows the main activities required for the Gala Day. Accompanying this would be an activity schedule similar to the one for the Awards Ceremony, which would identify responsibilities and more minute-by-minute detail. Having the timescale on the top of the Gantt chart enables easier reading of the table.

Time management

This chapter has identified the importance of scheduling all the activities that must be completed for an event to occur. It has discussed the need to have resources available and at the right time.

The use of time is crucial. In the last pages of this chapter we are going to consider how you personally can manage your time better. As for all events, the first step is to know what the objectives are, and the steps or activities needed to achieve the objectives. It is also important to prioritize objectives and steps.

A five-step approach to personal time management is as follows:

1. List the problems/tasks facing you. Sort those that will advance the organization's interests and those that don't really add value to the business. Discard those that don't add value.
2. Prioritize – i.e. determine which objectives are the most important and the order in which they should be done. This includes deciding which cannot be delayed, and which are not important. Sometimes it is possible to get rid of several small tasks in a short space of time, but don't get bogged down with a trivial task.
3. Having decided the order of objectives, then in the same manner list the tasks required for each objective and assign priorities to them.
4. Make a schedule of jobs to be done and, in brackets, allot time to each.
5. Tick off items as they are completed (this is the best bit).

This approach can be done at the beginning of each week and then checked and reset each morning, but don't waste all morning reworking the schedule.

Most managers achieve 80 per cent of their important results in only 20 per cent of their time – in other words, 80 per cent of their time is spent on unimportant or

Case study 14.4

Gantt chart for Addingham Gala, 10 July 2004, West Yorkshire, England

Gantt Chart

Task	Saturday 3rd July	Sunday 4th July	Monday 5th July	Tuesday 6th July	Wednesday 7th July	Thursday 8th July	Friday 9th July	Saturday 10th July
One week to go								
Sell programmes	■	■	■	■	■	■	■	■
Put up bunting							■	
Put up balloons								
Cut grass on field			■				■	
Put up marquee							■	
Mark out field							■	
Build entrance gates							■	
Collect raffle prizes			■	■	■	■		
Saturday forms			■	■			■	
No parking cones								
Wrap prizes		■	■	■				
Make games		■	■	■				
Make signposts		■	■					
Print signage				■		■		
Progress meeting								

Figure 14.7 Gantt chart

Addingham
Schedule for
10th July 2004

Rope off ring 1 and 2

Close off car park
and site entrance
to general public

Put up officials
tent

Allocate space for
field stalls

Collect chairs and
put out in marquee

Collect tables and
put out in marquee

Mark out road for
procession

Check police cones

Put up tents for
gala committee
stalls

Bacon butties

Refreshments prep

Figure 14.7 (Contd)

Task	7 to 8	8 to 9	9 to10	10 to 11	11 to12	12 to 1	1 to 2	2 to 3	3 to 4	4 to 5	5 to 6	6 to 7
Receive competition entrants			▓									
Divide marquee in two sections		▓										
Arrival of stall holders and rides					▓	▓	▓					
Put up and decorate fairy dell				▓	▓	▓						
Put out committee stalls and games					▓							
Judging of competition entrants					▓							
Stewards from the Round Table arrive duties allocated						▓	▓	▓	▓	▓	▓	▓
Caravan for floats and cash counting						▓	▓	▓	▓	▓	▓	▓
Judging of best frontage competition, house and business						▓						
Signage on field					▓							
Programme selling and charity buckets						▓	▓	▓				
Floats and walking groups arrive at procession start						▓						

Figure 14.7 (Contd)

Task											
Judging of procession at 1:00					■	■	■	■	■		
Refreshments on gala site	■	■	■	■	■	■	■	■	■	■	■
Police road closure from 1:30 all roads					■						
Procession from 1:30					■						
Gala field open to public 1:45											
Gala opening on site, programme run re gala activity schedule						■	■	■	■	■	■
Health and Safety	■	■	■	■	■	■	■	■	■	■	■
Gala finishes 4:30								■	■		
Stall holders dismantle and leave								■	■	■	■
Litter pick								■	■	■	■
Remove ropes								■	■	■	■
Return chairs and tables								■	■	■	■
Dismantle marquee								■	■	■	■
Clear refreshments hall								■	■	■	■

Figure 14.7 (Contd)

Celebrate successful day												
	7 to 8	8 to 9	9 to 10	10 to 11	11 to 12	12 to 1	1 to 2	2 to 3	3 to 4	4 to 5	5 to 6	6 to 7

Figure 14.7   (Contd)

time-wasting tasks. It is easy to go home feeling that you have been busy all day, but in reality having achieved very little of value. Some writers suggest setting a regular amount of time aside each day for talking to staff, checking telephone messages, making phone calls, checking the email and sending emails. If you are working across time zones, 10 am in the UK will be 10 pm in New Zealand, thus messages don't have to be answered immediately.

By the same token, you should try and make it a rule that all messages, emails and faxes are replied to on the day received, if only to acknowledge receipt. Technology is wonderful, but don't get caught by the trap of thinking that just because you have sent a message it has arrived. Somewhere in the IT link a server can be down, and although you have not received 'message returned' advice this does not mean that your message has gone all the way down the so-called superhighway. If you don't get a reply in a reasonable amount of time, don't be shy about sending a message asking for confirmation.

Meetings don't have to be a waste of time

A poorly run meeting can run on for hours, waste everyone's time, and achieve absolutely nothing. Minutes of meetings should only cover actions to be taken by members. At the next meeting, the first task should be to check whether actions have been completed, followed by a discussion of what else has to be done, what should be done, and agreement on a fresh list of actions. Unless any action follows on from a meeting, why have it?

One suggestion for running a meeting is to have no chairs; if everyone has to stand for the duration of the meeting, it is surprising how quickly it will finish. If this is too revolutionary, at least try not serving coffee. A meeting is not a social occasion; if it is it should be billed as such, and we should not expect to achieve any worthwhile business.

Chapter summary and key points

In this chapter we have considered the key task of scheduling work. We have shown that scheduling includes arranging resources and setting timeframes so as to achieve objectives as efficiently as possible.

Techniques and methods of scheduling have been considered, along with the importance of managing our own time.

This chapter concludes with the thought that time is a precious commodity, and whether you are doing time, marking time or spending time, time is running out. Your only hope is to do it now; procrastination is the thief of time.

Event Operations Management Model: Tum, Norton and Wright 2005

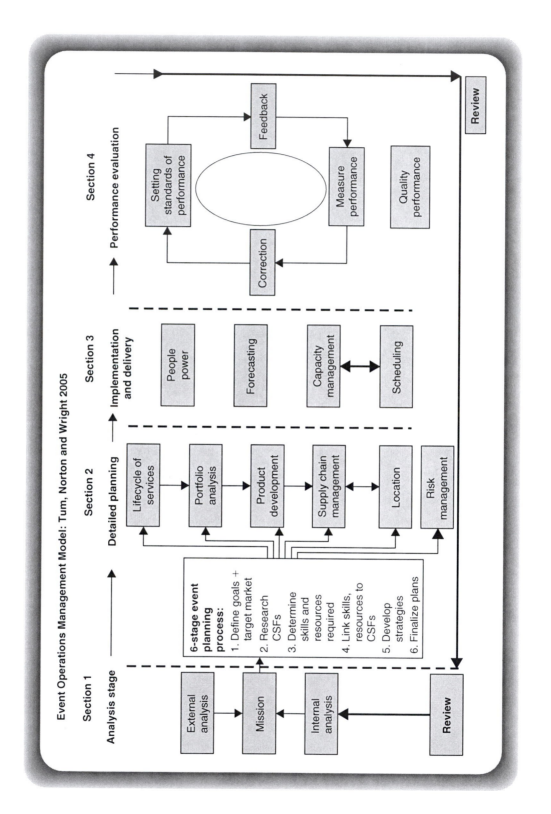

Section Four
Performance evaluation

Introduction

Section 4 covers the fourth stage of the event operations management model. This stage gives us an opportunity to look back on what has happened during the event, correct all that may not have gone as planned and build on what went right. It would be a mistake to think of evaluation merely occurring at the end of an event. The event manager looks on each event as a complete project, and it is not good enough to look at the event only after it has happened; there should be continuous evaluation throughout. The wedding celebrations cannot be repeated the following day, if all did not go as planned. The live concert performance cannot be restaged the next day, due to the event manager not having sufficient staff.

On the event operations management model it appears that evaluation is the last stage of the model, and yet evaluation, analysis and a myriad of decisions occur throughout the staging of an event. We can see evaluation within the analysis stage, the detailed planning stages, during the implementation and again at the review.

As Getz (1997) says, there are three types of evaluation:

1. Formative evaluation (i.e. part of the analysis stage)
2. Process evaluation (to improve effectiveness during the event)
3. Summative evaluation (after the event, to evaluate the impacts and overall value).

It is this last stage that most event managers are concerned with – did all go as planned, and are our clients and customers satisfied? These different distinctions are explored within Chapter 15.

Chapter 16 explores an equally difficult concept to plot on the event operations management model, that of quality. Quality, like evaluation, should be considered throughout the event operations management model, and quality procedures and awareness should be applied to the event from its conception to its completion.

Chapter 15 is concerned with two elements of evaluation – to establish whether the event has met its objectives, and also to assess whether the way that the event was planned was reasonable and was carried out in the best and most appropriate way. Event evaluation is critical to the event management process (Allen, 2000) and, if properly managed, is the key to continuous improvement. It provides a loop back to the start of the event operations management model, and can become a tool for analysis and development, and for feedback to stakeholders. Evaluation therefore provides a basis for improvement of both new and repeating events, and should occur throughout the event operations management model.

Chapter 16 is concerned with quality issues. The previous stages of the event operations management model have covered analysis, detailed planning, and implementation of the event. Despite quality being tackled as a separate subject in this stage of the event operations management model, it is argued that quality is not a separate discipline, such as accounting or marketing, but rather an integral part of all the event manager's activities. Chapter 15 identifies that unless there are standards and measurement of performance, control will be less than perfect, and without measurement it will not be possible to know if performance is improving or not. This chapter identifies that quality cannot be put into a separate compartment, to be picked up and put down when the occasion or management situation demands. The management situation in today's global economy will *always* require that quality be an integral part of all management actions. This is especially true in events where customers rightly expect high levels of service. The chapter explores the nature of quality and how it has evolved over the twentieth century to become part of every employee's remit, at every level within an organization.

Chapter 15

Performance evaluation

Learning Objectives

After reading through this chapter you will be able to:

- Understand the different methods of evaluation
- Identify, use and evaluate the control cycle and the control elements
- Apply profitability assessment measurements
- Understand the terms *balanced scorecard* and *benchmarking*, and evaluate their use in the event industry.

Introduction

We are now at the start of Section 4, which covers the last stage of the event operations management model. Evaluation requires us constantly to learn about how well we are delivering the event and whether it is appropriate within in its environment. Evaluation draws heavily upon all of the analysis and planning stages covered in the first two sections of this book.

Getz (1997) sums evaluation up as the need to learn about the environment surrounding the organization and the intended outcomes of the event, to be aware of the unintended outcomes of the event, and to consider ways that management can improve in the future. Since much of this has been covered in previous chapters, this chapter concentrates on evaluating whether the objectives of the event are being met and discusses how the event can be best controlled and delivered in the style originally intended. However, all of the aspects of evaluation covered earlier must still be considered.

Different forms of evaluation

The most common form of evaluation is post-event (or summative) evaluation (Watt, 1998). Here, success of an event is measured against the targets and objectives established in the first stage of the event operations management model. Data can be gathered from the event and analysed in relation to the objectives.

In order to do this successfully, *every* aspect of the event must be evaluated. The most obvious features to look at are customer satisfaction, profit made, and successful projection of the message or product of the event to the target audience. However, Wendroff (2004) points out that other factors, such as staff and volunteer training and performance, facilities, access, catering, atmosphere, timings, sound systems and acoustics, should all be appraised.

Shone and Parry (2001) and Wendroff (2004) agree that post-event evaluation should be undertaken soon after the event has taken place, whilst it is still fresh in the minds of all involved. However, evaluation after the event occurs too late to repair any problems that occurred during it. In many instances the event can be evaluated before it commences and also during its implementation. Torkildsen (1999) believes that evaluation should take place during the early stages of planning and when resources are being assigned, and likewise with the process and design and manner in which they are used.

Continual evaluation during the planning and implementation stages of the event operations management model ensures that the operation is up to schedule, as well as providing the event manager with the opportunity to hold feedback meetings with stakeholders to ensure they are satisfied with the development of the event (Bowdin *et al.*, 2001).

Keeping control of the event

Implementation of the event is an operational function. The event has been planned and based on clear SMART objectives set by the event manager and the customer. The location and the layout of the event have been carefully selected, the demand for the event forecast, and all relevant and reliable suppliers sourced for both tangible resources and intangible skills. As discussed in Chapter 14, critical path analysis is a useful technique for the event manager, alongside bar charts and Gantt charts. Gantt charts can be used to control and monitor the progress of the event.

Planning creates standards of action, and controls keep the plans and actions in line. Grundy and Brown (2002) state that implementation and control require continual cross-checking to the project's strategy and vision to ensure that the original purposes are being met. This is exactly the same with an event, where it is important to check continually whether the original aims can still be met as the planning continues and the event itself takes place.

This chapter will now discuss the different methods of control that can be used by an event manager.

The control cycle

The traditional approach for managers is to control subordinates, by supervision and measurement of performance, to make sure that what is being done is what is intended. Watt (1998) believes that control is the management function that checks to see if what is supposed to happen is happening or is going to happen. That is, it must not remain as a loose promise. Watt offers a four-stage control procedure:

1. Plan what you intend to do
2. Measure what has been done
3. Compare achievements with the blueprint
4. Take action to correct anything that is not as it should be.

The supervisory method of control relies on feedback of results, and consequently control tends to be in the past tense rather than in the present. This is obviously of little value to the event organizer, who has only one chance to get the event correct. A race cannot be re-run because the timing went wrong! When control occurs in the past tense, the manager checks after the event to see what occurred as being different to that which was intended.

A manager cannot control without a plan consisting of goals and targets. The more detailed the plan, the more control can be achieved.

The alternative method of control is to empower each member of the staff, or a team of staff, so that control is exercised directly by each person. The event manager should provide the staff with the right resources and full support. The control of the event is then within the immediate remit and authority of the staff responsible for it. This approach has obvious benefits to the event organizer.

Wright's model (Wright, 2001) allows for control to be exercised at the lowest level possible, if staff know what the standards are and have the ability and authority to take corrective action.

Wright's four-stage control cycle is as follows:

1. Set and agree standards of performance
2. Provide timely and relevant feedback
3. Compare actual performance to the agreed standards (staff need to know what to compare)
4. Empowered staff to take corrective action.

It would seem logical that the earlier a variance to a standard is detected, and thus a problem is noted, the less it will cost to put right and the fewer the consequences, provided it is put right as soon as possible.

Control elements

For any activity, whether control is top-down from the event manager or where control is exercised directly by the staff, the same four elements of control apply (Figure 15.1):

1. Setting standard specification
2. Feedback of actual performance
3. Measurement of performance against the specification
4. Correction of deviation from the specification.

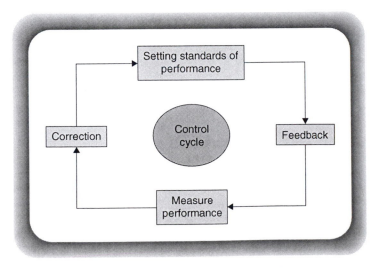

Figure 15.1 The control cycle element of the fourth section of the event operations management model

An appropriate and reliable approach to each event can exist when specifications are known and are communicated. The difficulties are first in setting the standards, and secondly in ensuring that deviations do not occur.

Setting standard specification

Standards are usually expressed in terms of the specification and objectives desired by the customer. They can be imposed by the company or the client, or can be set by the staff themselves, either as individuals or as a team. Standards were discussed in the detailed planning stage of the event operations management model. The standards of performance should be judged by its own set of SMART objectives.

It is envisaged that when the culture is right, 'empowered' staff will be able to work to the standards set, which are both explicitly and implicitly expressed. Implicitly expressed objectives are all the assumptions regarding the event that have not been written down but should be understood and shared by everyone.

In events it is often considered difficult to set quantifiable standards. How, for example, do you measure 'courteous service'? Nonetheless, if customers *perceive* that there is a lack of courtesy, then corrective action must be taken. In other areas of service, standards can be set quite readily – for example, how long do customers wait before being registered? Did the customer receive the information pack in time? Was the service effective?

Tangible criteria are measurements such as meeting deadlines, number of failures, wrong deliveries, time taken to attend to a customer, and time taken to reply to a letter or an email. Such measurements are quantifiable, easily understood, and cannot be disputed. However, even when the tangible criteria are met successfully by the event manager and the team, it is often the intangible criteria that influence a customer's decision whether or not to attend an event again, or to spread word-of-mouth recommendations or not.

Intangible criteria include the atmosphere of the event, cleanliness, well-groomed staff, attitude of the staff – are they friendly and is the advice given helpful; is there empathy, is the smile genuine, and do they really mean what they are saying? For instance, at a product launch other intangibles will become important – such as ethical conduct, sound and lighting appropriateness, appropriate theming carried throughout the event, and subtle opportunities for potential buyers to see the product in its best surroundings.

If the service includes food, then its smell, colour, taste and temperature when served all become important. When the culture of the organization is right and all the staff genuinely believe in the value of what they are doing, then enthusiasm and a desire to help will overcome the adverse effect of a late delivery or some other shortcoming. No manner of control imposed from above can substitute for people who want to get things right and who want to help the customer, providing that they are empowered to do so.

Feedback of actual performance

Figure 15.1 includes a means of feedback of actual performance. Feedback needs to be reasonably precise, recognizable and timely. For example, with budgetary control there is little point if actual results are notified 3 months after the event. The importance of key measures cannot be emphasized enough. What should be measured is what really matters. Too often the desire for total accuracy takes too long and the information provided is often so detailed as to be of little use to the recipient. Effective control for an event manager requires some key measurements that are sufficiently accurate to enable corrective action to be taken.

As discussed before, the key measures can be either tangible or intangible. They should be determined and agreed so that everyone knows the minimum level that is acceptable. These key measures are also known in the operational management literature as benchmarks.

In some organizations, especially those relying on the skill, expertise and creativity of staff, standards are often poorly defined, and variation from standards is a matter of perception rather than measure. Too much measurement and too many standards may stultify creativity, and so it is important to keep measurement to the areas where it will do the most good.

Care has to be taken not to impose detailed measurement on people who have been hired for their creative ability. One of the targets of an event manager should be to devise a performance measurement system that balances having only a few key measures, which may not reflect all of the event objectives, and having too many detailed measures, which then become overwhelming.

Some key measures that could be used include the statistics of attendees and financial returns. Others might include questionnaires and customer focus groups. Questionnaire design and meaningful surveys are essential skills that must be learned and developed. There is a range of authors who cover this aspect extraordinary well, and so questionnaire design is not covered in this text.

Case study 15.1 provides an illustration of event evaluation.

Case study 15.1

British Association for Counselling and Psychotherapy Research Conference, May 2004

10th Annual Counselling and Psychotherapy Research Conference, London, England

Evaluation Report by Nancy Rowland and Stephen Goss

The 10th annual conference was held in May 2004 with 180 delegates each day from around the world, including America, Australia, Canada, Germany, Ireland, Kenya, Malaysia, New Zealand, Portugal and Turkey.

The 2 days saw a total of 77 presentations, made up of 62 papers, 7 workshops, 8 posters and a plenum paper.

The conference had a wonderful atmosphere and gained enormously from a wide mix of cultures and nationalities. The exhibition hall was decorated with traditional cloths and items from some of the co-host organizations, making a fantastic display. A congenial social evening on Friday ensured old friends met whilst new friendships were formed over the international cuisine and dancing. Networking opportunities abounded, and once again the evaluation results emphasized the importance of this aspect of the conference, along with appreciation of the warmth and friendliness of the event.

An evaluation form was completed by 44 per cent of delegates, using scores of 1 = Poor and 10 = Excellent. Scores continued to display good levels of satisfaction, with administration of the event scoring a notable 9.2 and 73 per cent of respondents giving the highest score of 9 or 10. Programme structure and the venue scored 8.5 and 8.7 respectively, with an overall satisfaction rating of 8.9, with 68 per cent of respondents giving a 9 or 10 in this category. Friday's papers gained an average score of 7.5 (from a range of 6.0 to 9.3), with the average for Saturday's being 7.8 (from a range of 5.3 to 9.5). Workshop presentations registered an average of 8.1 (from a range of 6.0 to 9.0), and posters scored an average of 7.4 (from a range of 6.8 to 7.8). Appreciation of the general warmth and friendliness of the event came through strongly in the evaluations, which is an element of this event we are keen to foster.

The following table shows the comparison of average marks over the past six research conferences:

	2004	2003	2002	2001	2000	1999
Venue	London	Leicester	London	Bristol	Manchester	Leeds
Return rate for evaluation forms (%)	44	59	48	70	53	79
Overall satisfaction (average score)	8.9	8.3	8.6	8.7	8.4	7.7
Structure of conference programme (average score)	8.5	8.3	8.3	8.4	8.1	7.1
Quality of the venue (average score)	8.7	8.2	7.8	8.1	8.5	8.1
BACP administration (average score)	9.2	9.0	8.9	8.9	–	–
Satisfaction with papers (overall average score)	7.6	7.5	7.5	7.4	7.6	6.9
Satisfaction with workshops (overall average score)	6.9	7.3	7.9	7.4	7.6	6.7
Satisfaction with posters (overall average score)	7.4					

(Information supplied by the British Association for Counselling and Psychotherapy, BACP House, 35–37 Albert Street, Rubgy, Warwickshire CV21 2SG. More information about their research can be found at www.bacp.co.uk.)

Reflective practice 15.1

1. Using the information from the evaluation report in Case study 15.1, in which areas could improvements be made for the 2005 conference?
2. What would you suggest to improve these areas?
3. If you were organizing the conference, what other feedback would you like to receive and how would you gather this information?

Measurement of performance against the specification

As shown in Figure 15.1, the crucial issue at this stage of the control cycle is knowing what the feedback means, and how to measure performance and compare results so as to be able to recognize deviations. In many cases there are suppliers providing staff and other resources at an event, and they may have their own policies to determine whether success has been achieved or not. However, it is in the interest of the event manager to ensure that the event has gone ahead as planned and as expected by the customers. Typical questions could be:

- How can the service be judged against expectations?
- Can service be improved?
- Can the service be improved at no extra cost?
- How, and by whom?

Correction of deviation from the specification

Once the first three steps of the control cycle are in place, then irrespective of whether this is an outdoor festival, an annual dinner and fundraising event, a product launch or a teambuilding event, the outputs can be compared with the plan or standard and with the

SMART objectives. Where necessary, corrections should be made so as to eliminate divergences. Ideally, the level at which this is done should be as low as possible. If a corrective action has to be reported up through five levels of management and down again before action can be taken, time is lost and errors can often be compounded. If a customer is waiting for a decision to be made, customer satisfaction will diminish at a rapid rate.

If a member of staff is facing a customer, that staff member needs to know the limits within which decisions can be made. The ability and knowledge of the staff member has to be taken into account when limits of authority are given. Some staff will welcome flexibility of action, whereas others are afraid to make decisions.

Not everyone is comfortable with being empowered, and this also will need to be taken into account when limits of authority are being set. Each member of the organization has to have mutual trust and confidence in the others. Management needs to be confident that staff are well trained and competent, and that every person understands the goals. Staff have to be confident that they are empowered to take action and will be supported by management in difficult situations.

Where it is found that deviations to the required standard are consistently above or below the set level of performance, then the original conditions must be checked. If the level being achieved is *above* the set standard, it could be that conditions have changed – such as new suppliers, improved technology or an improved process – or the workers themselves have found better ways to provide the service. It should be investigated whether the customer welcomes this improved standard, or whether time or money is being spent on an unnecessary resource or activity. If the level of performance has fallen *below* the standard, it is important that action is taken to determine why this should be and what needs to be done.

In Case study 15.2, it is clear that the Sydney Festival organizers aim for continuous improvement, gaining feedback by both formal and informal means.

Case study 15.2

Sydney Festival, Art Gallery Road, The Domain, Sydney, Australia

Access for the disabled – improvements to existing facilities

The Sydney Festival is held over 3 weeks in January each year, and has a number of popular free outdoor events where the attendances can reach 150 000. Sydney Festival organizes Symphony in the Domain, Opera in the Domain and Jazz in the Domain. Around Christmas, the Domain also hosts Carols in the Domain.

The Domain is officially part of the Royal Botanic Gardens of Sydney, and Festival Domain Manager, Stephen Champion, cooperates with the Gardens to stage these events. Providing for crowd entertainment is his specialty.

'These annual events are really popular. It grows each year … As much as we can, we make sure people can get into the enclosures on the site, get around, see the stages and use the facilities,' says Champion.

An outdoor site presents particular challenges for organizers providing access including parking or areas for transport drop-off and pick-up. Champion's access strategy has been devised in conjunction with the Royal Botanic Gardens. Though 'it is not formal,' says Champion, 'we have a protocol which developed from consultations and from our experiences year after year'.

In relation to feedback, Champion says: 'We receive a lot of requests from individuals or groups wanting access to events, and it's in talking to them that we have tailored some of our solutions each year.' Feedback from spectators generally comes informally, via discussions with staff at events or approaches to Festival organizers. However, the Festival also consults with peak disability groups through regular meetings. This informal and formal information plays a vital role in Champion's planning.

'We respond to perceived as well as solicited needs. For example, one woman brings a group each year to hear the Symphony in the Park,' says Champion. She has become an important source of information and consultation on particular needs of the group – such as access, parking and toilet facilities.

They strive for continuous improvement, and management and operations are assessed each time an event is presented. As Champion says, 'There are things that could be done better. We need to look at the issue of signage, together with the Gardens, and come up with a better strategy.'

'Each year at the Festival outdoor concerts, we try to increase the amount of temporary lighting. Since the Olympics, there has been more acknowledgement of issues relating to risk assessment and occupational health and safety.' The next step will be a formal approach to government to consider solutions and to fund ongoing works.

The ongoing solutions also include more Sydney Festival staff training on the issues of access and disability awareness. 'We do have a handbook, which is given to staff each year so they remain aware of the issues and the organizations that the Festival works with are also chosen for their application to access issues.'

(Extracts from website; for more information see www.sydneyolympicpark.com.au.)

Reflective practice 15.2

The information in Case study 15.2 indicates the informal structures in place at the Sydney Festival for improving access for the disabled at the Domain.

1. During events, what formal structures could be introduced, and how would you do this?
2. What are the benefits of informal structures?

Profitability measurements

We all recognize that if any company is to stay in business it has to make sufficient profit to service its debts, make a return to the owners and invest in new resources for future growth.

For not-for-profit organizations, efficiency has to be demonstrated and management has to be accountable for the funds and assets that have been provided.

Most people would see that recording and reporting profitability and/or being accountable for the funds used is the responsibility of the accountants. However, event managers must know how the figures are compiled and be able to read standard accounting reports.

Accountants work on historical data of what has happened, and their reports cover arbitrarily set periods of time. They make little allowance for the fact that business activities do not stop on 30 June or 31 December, or whatever other date has been designated as the time to take a snapshot of the financial position of the business. From a conventional point of view, and from the point of view of stakeholders such as shareholders and bank managers, there has to be a way of measuring the financial performance of an organization, and currently there is no better method than accounting reports. It follows, therefore, that for accountants to do their job of reporting to meet the conventional and regulatory requirements, information will be required from the operating arm of the business. If information is being provided, then it is useful to try and use that information to improve the efficiency of the organization.

This text does not deal with financial control and accounting measures, but it is suggested that readers study these aspects further.

The balanced scorecard approach

This approach was first taken by Kaplan and Norton (2001). The balanced scorecard, according to Lashley and Lee-Ross (2003), recognizes that the evaluation of the performance of an organization needs to be viewed from the perspectives of different stakeholders. The stakeholders typically used are the customers, employees, shareholders and the community. Other approaches use the finance perspective, customer perspective, employee perspective, and an innovation and learning perspective (Johnson and Scholes, 2002). The scorecards combine both a quantitative approach and a qualitative approach whilst acknowledging the expectations of the different stakeholders. Without a scorecard, it is not possible to see if improvement is being made. As Slack and Lewis (2002) state, the advantage of the scorecard is that it brings together an overall picture of the organization's performance into one report. We would add that a further advantage is that it does not just measure activities and success from a financial perspective, but also allows the voices and considerations of our customers and staff, and opportunities for creativity, to be taken into account.

Slack and Lewis (2002) argue that a balanced range of measures enables managers to address the following questions:

- How do we look to our shareholders (i.e. a financial perspective)?
- What must we excel at (i.e. an internal business perspective)?
- How do our customers see us (i.e. a customer perspective)?
- How can we continue to improve and create value (i.e. an innovation and learning perspective)?

It is important to link the scorecards not just to a short-term approach but also to a long-term view since, for example, innovation and learning are critical to long-term success (Johnson and Scholes, 2002).

Eaglen *et al.* (1999) believe that the prime success of an organization from a shareholder's perspective is dependent on customer satisfaction and repeat custom, and this is in turn dependent on employee performance and customer satisfaction. Eaglen *et al.* (1999) reported increasing numbers of leisure organizations using the balanced scorecard to evaluate organizational performance.

This approach brings together many different parts of the organization, and could be useful within an event company or for a one-off event. It also has the benefit of reducing the number of measures and focusing only on those that are considered essential. It is beneficial if the entire organization is involved with creating and agreeing on the measures that are to become part of the scorecard. This way it ensures that everyone is fully committed, and agrees with the concepts to be measured and how.

Slack and Lewis (2002) believe that one of the advantages of the scorecard is that it presents an overall picture of the organization's performance on one report and encourages a company-wide approach rather than just the self-interests of separate departments.

To understand this concept as applied to the event industry, see Table 15.1. In this scorecard an event to celebrate the New Year in a capital city is illustrated. This event had been organized by the city, for its local community, and to attract tourists and economic wealth to the city. This example of the scorecard takes three headings – vision, strategy and objectives, and uses four different perspectives i.e. financial; customer; internal and innovation and learning in order to measure the success.

Table 15.1 Partially balanced scorecard for New Year's Eve celebrations in a capital city

Vision	Strategy	Objectives	Balanced scorecard
To attract visitors to the city	To provide services that exceed customer expectations and provide complete satisfaction	*Financial*: return on expenditure, satisfactory cash flow, reliability of performance and adequacy of suppliers	*Financial perspective*: cash flow, within budget, economic impact on city
		Customer: value for money, high level of satisfaction, creative and fun	*Customer perspective*: satisfaction surveys
		Internal: provide customer satisfaction, exceptional event project management; excellent use of resources and suppliers	*Internal business perspective*: conformance of design, keeping to time, numbers of attendees
		Internal growth: innovative; empowered workforce, and continuous improvement	*Innovation and learning perspective*: creativity and design, new ideas, use of employee specialisms, training
To raise the profile of the capital as an international venue	To engineer continuous improvement throughout the planning process from the concept formulation to the implementation		
To provide a high-quality event for the enjoyment of all participants, including the residents of the city	To ensure that all staff and suppliers involved with the event should match expectations		
	To ensure that during the event planning all the stakeholders be consulted and plans agreed with them as far as possible		

The vision is to attract visitors to the city, to raise the profile of the capital as an international venue and to provide a high-quality event for the enjoyment of all participants, including the residents of the city.

The strategy that needs to be taken to achieve this is to provide services that exceed customer expectations and give complete satisfaction. It was decided that there should be continuous improvement throughout the planning process from the concept formulation to the implementation. All the staff involved with the event should match expectations, and during the event planning all the stakeholders should be consulted and plans agreed with them as far as possible.

In order to achieve that strategy, a number of objectives have to be set that can be measured for their success and are achievable. Table 15.1 then also depicts the different perspectives that success can be measured by in the final column. This is deliberately not complete; further ideas can be added when considering the reflective practice below.

Reflective practice 15.3

You are the chief executive of an event management company who has been selected to organize the New Year festivities in a capital city.

1. Complete the scorecard shown in Table 15.1 to show all of the targets that each of the four perspectives could take.
2. Establish measures that should be set to identify how closely you are achieving your objectives and how you would assess individual performance.

Benchmarking

The purpose of benchmarking is to measure your performance against a similar operation. Slack *et al.* (2004) identify two types of benchmarking:

1. Internal, where there is a comparison between operations within the same organization
2. External, which is a comparison between an operation and other operations that are part of a different organization.

Benchmarking can take place against other event organizations, whether they compete in the same market or not. The benchmarking could consist of comparing your own performance against another event management company or their means of completing activities – i.e. what can be learned from looking at another event, and could different practices be adopted?

Griffin (1999) describes benchmarking as the process of learning how other firms do things in an exceptionally strong manner. The technique enables an organization to stay abreast of any improvements and changes their competitors are making.

The accountant's method of benchmarking is to compare published annual financial reports. It is fairly simple to obtain your competitors' audited accounts and compare them with yours by means of ratios and by looking at various key figures, such as stock turnover, return on investment, cost of sales and so on. It doesn't matter if company X has $50 million sales and companies Y and Z have $200 and $80 million sales respectively. If all three are in the same sector of the event industry, it could be expected that the percentage of costs to sales should be roughly the same – or that there should be some clearly defined reasons why not.

Internally, benchmarking can be achieved by comparing key measures of like departments, or even comparing over the organization as a whole. Absenteeism could be a benchmark (if considered to be a problem area). Similarly, the number of days taken off sick each year can be compared as a moving trend, and with other companies, or branches of the same company. The changes and trends that are identified can be extremely useful to highlight excellence and below-excellent performances.

Further benchmarks might be staff turnover, and growth of numbers of staff employed per £1000 sales. Clearly there are many instances where benchmarking can be used usefully to compare your own event management company against competitors, or against your own achievements and benchmarks from previous events.

Benchmarking is a form of measurement, and is useful in highlighting areas that can be improved. It is also concerned with searching out new ideas and practices that could be copied or adapted (Slack and Lewis, 2002). It stimulates creativity, and makes organizations consider how they could be serving their customers better. Thus it is ideal for event management companies who thrive on creativity and who are able to see competitors' events often at first hand.

Case study 15.3 discusses the practical use of benchmarking.

Case study 15.3

Edinburgh Festival, Edinburgh, Scotland
The Edinburgh Festival is held annually in August in Edinburgh

Edinburgh is one of the premier festival cities of the world. The unique combination of the International Festival and the Fringe makes for one of the biggest festivals in the world. The festivals help to fix Edinburgh's image in tourism terms, and on the back of them come hundreds of thousands of staying visitors every year, across all seasons.

As well as the International Festival and the Fringe, there are the other summer festivals – the Jazz & Blues, the Film and the Book, and of course the Tattoo. The packed programme of events in Edinburgh's Winter Festivals, Hogmanay and Capital Christmas, also attract large numbers of staying visitors to Edinburgh and the Lothians, bringing a short, sharp boost to business in what was a quiet time for tourism. The other three major festivals, the Easter, the Science and the Children's, are less hectic, taking place in the spring and bringing in welcome day and staying visitors.

Long-running art exhibitions of international stature, major outdoor concerts and international events like the Tall Ships, the Rugby Union World Cup and the Edinburgh Marathon have all given significant boosts to tourism. (**NB**: individual games of the RWC have been played at Murrayfield, but Edinburgh hasn't ever been host nation. The final of the Challenge Cup (Rugby League clubs) has been played there, however.) There is a host of other events, such as the Festival of Flight in East Lothian, as well as smaller, often community-based events, staged as one-offs or annually.

Edinburgh has on the whole held up well in terms of visitor numbers, even during a period when Scottish tourism has been experiencing a tough time. However, in this position it would be easy to become complacent about standards. This tendency has been noted in other cities with big cultural festivals and events, and some have taken action to address their problems. Quality is a key challenge – to make sure that visitors get the kind of overall experience they expect. As a recent review of Amsterdam as a city of culture asked:

> *Is it content, quality and development, rather than simply quantity, that we should be focussing on for the future?*

With such a volume and diversity of major events, the tourism partners have decided that a coordinated approach to development is called for. The Edinburgh Tourism Action Group, a partnership of the private sector, the City Council, SE Edinburgh and Lothian and the

Edinburgh and Lothians Tourist Board, is undertaking a wide-ranging review of festivals and events policy and practice, and investigating the establishment of a dedicated Events Unit.

Benchmarking is something of a buzzword, perhaps, but for very good reason. Because there is so much to be learned from other cities, benchmarking is underway to establish what 15 other European cities are doing, and how Edinburgh compares. This will help to set standards and guidelines against which the city can measure its future performance. If Salzburg or Barcelona can teach us something, that's great, and of course Edinburgh can share with them its own good practices, built up over decades of experience.

(Information supplied by the Lothian Exchange; for more information see www. lothianexchange.net.)

Reflective practice 15.4

Consider Case study 15.3.

1. What are the advantages for a city like Edinburgh in benchmarking its events with other European cities?
2. What areas could be benchmarked?

Evaluation of an event

As previously discussed, at the completion of an event there should be a meeting with all of the interested parties, or stakeholders, to evaluate its success or otherwise. A good evaluation should use all the sources of information available to it, and not just rely on the customers' points of view (Shone and Parry, 2004). Care should be taken, since it is an aid to future planning.

There may be activities within the event that went well and could be strengthened further, and there may be those that need improving upon, if they went badly. In all cases, the evaluation should be provided speedily – for example, to speakers at a conference before they leave, or even before they present again at the same conference. Adjustments can then be made quickly.

As the event evaluator, you should determine what is to be evaluated and why and how. Silver (2004) believes that research and evaluation will give the information required to devise effective practices and controls, which could lead to good results. This process is shown in Figure 15.2.

There are two key issues, according to Shone and Parry (2004):

1. Did the event meets its objectives?
2. What can be improved for the next event?

Sources of information for evaluation (adapted from Shone and Parry, 2004) include:

- Event attendees' comments derived from questionnaires and other observations
- Security and police views on crowds, traffic and other incidents
- Specialists comments, for example from lighting and sound specialists
- Council comments and community views
- Any mystery guests and other participants
- Staff comments, including volunteers
- Sponsors' views
- Financial statistics and reports.

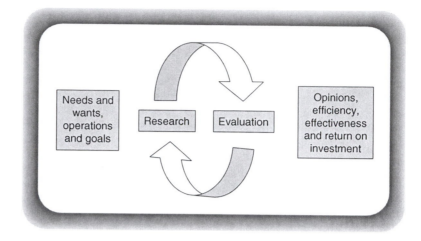

Figure 15.2 Silver's research-evaluation continuum model

All constructive criticism should be taken seriously, since the goal is to improve events in the future and to improve your organization and planning of the event.

The information is also invaluable to different groups of people. For instance, those groups that have financed the event or sponsored elements of it need to know that their money was well spent. The numbers of people attending the event and their geographical range and demographics are of interest to future sponsors of a similar event. At the end of each year, the budgeting process begins for the following year. Since many corporate events may have to compete for funds, the evaluation from previous events will become invaluable. The event manager must be able to demonstrate that an event can efficiently and effectively achieve corporate objectives (O'Toole and Mikolaitis, 2002).

The evaluation results provide facts that can be used to compare the cost of the event to the value generated.

A well-designed evaluation assists the manager, the sponsors and the client to determine whether the event met the desired outcomes, and hence whether it will be repeated next year. It also is useful for future clients as a record of past successes. As such, it can be communicated to potential clients and may increase future business and contacts. The evaluation data will also be useful when the event manager compares costs and return on investment to propose alternatives to potential clients.

O'Toole and Mikolaitis (2002) suggest that the evaluation covers two areas; first the content of the event, and secondly the destination and the facilities provided. The first focus relates to how the attendees feel about how the event was organized and designed, while the second focus relates to the appropriateness of the venue. This was covered in Chapter 10, where we discussed a series of criteria for choice of destination. The evaluation information should determine how well all the SMART objectives have been achieved as a whole, and how well the event managed to weave together all the elements required.

As O'Toole and Mikolaitis (2002) suggest, the evaluation can determine whether a particular part or element of an event is responsible for either its success or its failure. If a particular activity has increased the overall success of an event, the data could be used to include this element in future events. For instance, if there was sufficient return on investment for guests to attend an event due to a particular activity, then the client should be made aware of the added value. Not only does this information help your future events with a current client; it also demonstrates to potential clients that you have a policy of evaluation, which could help them in the future.

Quantitative and qualitative evaluation methods

Surveys of numbers of attendees, money taken, computer records, and telephone surveys all provide accurate quantitative data. On the other hand, face-to-face interviews and open-ended questions on a well-designed survey can provide detailed insight into the attitudes and feelings of the event attendees. Indeed it is useful to apply these to non-attendees to find out the reasons for their non-appearance. In either method there may be a pattern of response that can provide clues for the future or warrant further investigation.

Further literature sources should be consulted on the design of useful questionnaires, since it takes time and expertise to complete these in order to get the information that is required (see O'Toole and Mikolaitis, 2002, Chapter 12; and Silver, 2004, Chapter 14).

The information collected should not just be the outcomes of some of the problems, but also the underlying causes of the problem. For example, if there were long queues was this due to insufficient staff, or to a poor layout and design, or to insufficient resources, or to a higher demand than forecasted?

Shone and Parry (2004) recommend that an event manager identifies persistent problems and ranks them in order of seriousness. With this list of priorities it is possible to confront the issues, increase the success of your event and decrease its problems.

One method that can be used to solve problems arising from an event is an Ishikawa diagram, also known as a fishbone diagram due to its shape. The idea is to identify one problem at a time and then draw the fishbone diagram on one sheet of paper. See Figure 15.4. It provides a good opportunity for group discussion and brainstorming. Adapting a procedure from Slack *et al.* (2004) for events, the following steps could be used to construct a fishbone diagram:

1. State the problem in the effect box
2. Identify the main categories that may have caused or have the solution to the problem
3. Use systematic fact finding and the information from the evaluation process to generate possible causes and solutions
4. Record all the comments generated and add onto the diagram as extra fins to the main fishbones.

The most common causes of problems are people, the equipment used, the method of using the resources provided, the finance available, and lack of communication. However, the group discussion will establish the most relevant areas for the specific problem under discussion.

For instance, imagine a concert is being held in a church on an evening in November in the UK. All the equipment has arrived, and all the rehearsals, schedules etc. are going to plan. A final walkthrough reveals that the portable toilets for the use of the audience, which are based outside the church, do not have interior lights.

The Ishikawa diagram in Figure 15.3 (see next page) deals with this problem.

An interesting concept proposed by Grundy and Brown (2002) is that of the 'bonefish' diagram. Here the problem starts on the left of the fishbone and leads to multiple consequences on the right. This amplifies the point (Grundy and Brown, 2002) that the fishbone is a way of showing an ongoing cause and effect chain. The bonefish diagram identifies the problems of getting some aspect of your event wrong. Many of the activities within an event are interdependent, and as one thing goes wrong there may be many other consequences as a result.

As an example, this concept could be used for a major wine festival held during the summer tourist season in Italy. It could be envisaged that following unprecedented media focus on the event, there may be many thousands more people attending than

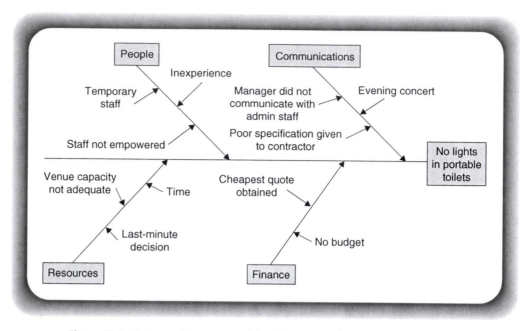

Figure 15.3 Ishikawa diagram examining the causes of no lighting in portable toilets

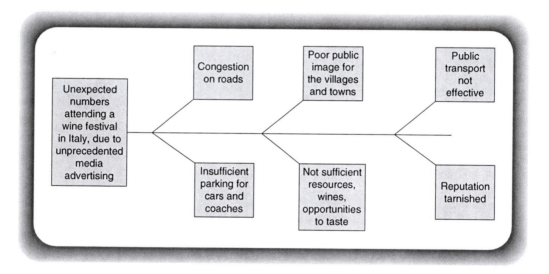

Figure 15.4 Fishbone diagram examining consequences of unexpected high attendance

in previous years. Using the bonefish diagram and following detailed discussions, the possible consequences of the problem and any extra costs incurred could be identified. Figure 15.4 is only hypothetical, but it can be seen that the fishbone diagrams and the bonefish diagrams show an ongoing cause and effect chain (Grundy and Brown, 2002), and would highlight the cost of failures and poor planning. This could be a useful tool to persuade the client to resource the event fully.

Reflective practice 15.5

1. From the information shown in Figure 15.3, what steps should be taken to ensure that the portable toilets all have lights in the future and that this does not happen again?
2. Draw a bonefish diagram. This is the reverse of the fishbone diagram, with the problem at the head end on the left. Your diagram should identify the effect of poor weather being the cause of cancellation of a horseracing meeting at Kempton Race Course, England, on Boxing Day, after 22 000 people had already arrived and some programmes had already been sold.

Reflective practice 15.6

You work for a company that has won the contract to manage the Annual Gala for your local town. This Gala has been running for 20 years, but has got a little tired in its format and the income it raises for local charities has not grown appreciably over the years. In the past it has had a very mixed format. It opens with a parade through the town, with floats from many of the local businesses and a Gala Queen. It culminates in the town's municipal park, where many different organizations are able to rent space to display their services and activities to all of the townspeople. Many uniformed organizations take part, and there is a large display area.

Standards of performance

1. List the tangible standards that could be used by the following four different groups of people to judge the success of the new Gala event:
   - Your own company
   - The Town Council
   - Local businesses
   - Gala attendees.
2. Consider what intangible criteria might be important to these four groups.
3. Now consider each of these standards, and put them together into a composite list and into an order of importance or priority.
4. Who could set the final standard or specification so that these standards could be met, fully or in part?
5. Is there any way that any of these standards could be improved without extra cost?
6. Identify for each of the standards included in your composite list the key measurements that would determine success (or otherwise) in meeting the standard of performance.

Chapter summary and key points

This chapter has introduced a four-step model for control. If the culture of the organization is positive, the events manager will be able to concentrate on the important higher-level issues if staff know what is expected, have agreed the standards of performance, get accurate and prompt feedback, know what to compare, and are empowered to take corrective action if required. For this to work, staff have to want to take responsibility, and management has to believe in and trust their staff.

Communication and prompt and accurate feedback of information are essential if control is to be exercised.

The event manager has the responsibility of deciding what should be measured and why. If no advantage can be gained from keeping a particular record, then the gathering of that information should cease. Record gathering in itself does not add value. There is some truth in the adage that if it can't be measured, it can't be managed. On the other hand, too much measurement will stultify, lead to extra expense, and inhibit creativity.

Measurement should be used in a positive manner to advance the aims of the organization, and not as a means of power play to rule and subjugate.

Chapter 16

Awareness of quality

Learning Objectives

After reading through this chapter you will be able to:

■ Define quality and understand its application in the event industry
■ Appreciate the development of total quality management
■ Calculate the costs of conforming to quality, and the costs of non-conformance
■ Apply the concepts of just-in-time management to an event organization and use the SERVQUAL method of measuring customer satisfaction.

Introduction

This is our last chapter, and it explores the subject of quality, which has featured implicitly throughout the book. It is discussed here as a separate, explicit topic, but the concept of total quality should be apparent throughout all the event management work that you, as manager, are involved with, from the very first conception of the event. It should also be evident throughout your organization's structure and culture.

Volumes of books and learned papers have been written on the subject of quality. In 2005, some universities offer Quality as a separate degree (University of Wales, University of Paisley, Queens University Belfast), the inference being that quality has become a 'discipline' or subject in its own right, which can be studied in isolation from other disciplines. There are many different definitions of quality and, as Getz (1997) points out, there are many different connotations of quality. To some it is a mark of excellence, to others it is simply the best, while to others it indicates reliability or exceeding expectations.

This chapter does not intend to repeat and apply much of the excellent material written on quality and how it can increase competitive advantage. The work presented here will focus on what quality is, the costs of conforming to quality standards and the costs of non-conformance to those standards. It will then consider two of the quality initiatives, just-in-time management (JIT) and SERVQUAL, and apply those in an event management context. We believe that although the study of quality can be taught separately, it is in fact inseparable from any management action. Quality cannot be put into a separate compartment, to be picked up and put down when the occasion or management situation demands. The management situation in today's global economy will *always* require that quality be an integral part of all management actions. This is especially true in events, where customers rightly expect high levels of service and there is no opportunity to repeat the event if it is not just as planned.

The underlying theme in all of these chapters has been customer satisfaction and efficient use of resources. Both of these objectives require quality considerations. An event manager cannot offer customer satisfaction without an understanding of what quality is; likewise, efficient use of resources requires a total quality management approach. This chapter will start by exploring some of the definitions of quality.

What is quality?

Quality has different meanings for different people. Griffin (2000) believes that, for managers, understanding the basic meaning of quality is a good first step to managing it more effectively. A manufacturing sector approach and a sector providing a service, as in the event industry, might consider a definition of quality as being one that provides a service that is free of error (Slack *et al.*, 2004). Although the product or service may not be the 'best' that is available, it could be described as a quality product if it conforms to its original specification.

On the other hand, our customers may be looking for a product or service that is fit for its purpose. This definition demonstrates Slack *et al.* (2004) concern not only that the service adheres to its specification but also that it is appropriate for the customer. For example, a conference designed to introduce delegates to new business opportunities in China may be well run and organized very professionally, but if it fails to create any networking opportunities between business colleagues in the host country or to share ideas of good trading opportunities, it has not served its purpose.

A further approach is one where the product or service has quality stated as a measurable set of characteristics that would satisfy the customer. In the event industry, this could be an exhibition that states in its marketing promotional material that there will be 200 stands over a period of 3 days, a 2-day seminar programme with four different keynote speakers on each day, full catering facilities, and a potential market of 3000 visitors from the relevant industry arriving on each day. It would be relatively simple for the attendees and the exhibitors to check whether the characteristics stated in the advertising literature were being achieved or not, and to what degree.

Finally, Slack *et al.* (2004) cite the value-based approach, where the customer may be willing to accept a slightly lower specification of quality if the price is less. Within the event industry, an illustration would be the acceptance of a less convenient location for a special event provided this is reflected in the price.

Slack *et al.* (2004) define quality as having consistent conformance to customers' expectations. You can see that this definition brings together the concept of having a well-planned, designed and controlled event, which keeps to the original specification and matches the expectations of the customer. Slack *et al.* (2004) prefer the word 'expectations' to 'needs' or 'wants'. 'Needs' implies a basic requirement, and 'wants' could be anything that the customer desires. As Slack *et al.* (2004) point out, though, there is a problem with trying to match customers' expectations in that individual expectations may be different and may change.

The various authors within the quality management and operations management literature all offer different views on the interpretation of what is quality. Waters (1996) says that in its broadest sense, quality is the ability of a product to meet and preferably exceed customer expectations. Appropriately, Swarbrooke and Horner (2001) remind us that we have both customers and consumers in our industry. This distinction was discussed in Chapter 2. To remind you, customers could, for example, be those organizations that employ the delegates who attend our events, or the council that pays for a range of entertaining events and community-orientated events that are provided for the local communities. The consumers are those who actually attend our events and use the service. It can be seen immediately that the customer in this context will expect an event at the right price, and the consumer will expect a different range of other attributes, including entertainment value, fun and an informative experience.

Drummond and Anderson (2004) cite three of the quality gurus' definitions of quality:

1. Deming (1982) defines quality as being aimed at the needs of the consumer, present and future
2. Crosby (1979) defines quality as conformance to requirements
3. Feigenbaum (1993) say that quality is in its essence a way of managing the organization.

We can see in the first two definitions similarities with the work of Slack *et al.* (2004), but the third approach, from Feigenbaum (1993), refers to the way the organization is managed. This requires a focus on satisfying the customer and changing the organization to achieve that objective (Drummond and Anderson, 2004). For further reading, the Drummond and Anderson's chapter in *Festivals and Event Management* is recommended (see the bibliography for full details). The chapter focuses on service quality at events, and the management of people.

Wild (2002) defines quality as the degree to which a product or service satisfies customers' requirements. He discusses the degree to which the design specification would satisfy the customer, and how closely it conforms to specifications. Similarly, Campbell *et al.* (2003) believe that quality is meeting customers' needs or expectations.

It can be seen that the myriad of different definitions of quality all consider that the service, or in our case the event, should match customer expectations, and that the specification should be clearly set and achievable through good organization.

Total quality management

If we now consider the concept of total quality management (TQM), Campbell *et al.* (2003) state that TQM is a holistic approach that provides awareness of the customer–supplier relationship, and that there should be continuous improvement and effort made throughout the organization.

TQM includes setting standards and the means of measuring conformance to standards, but an organization that truly has embraced TQM does not need the ISO stamp of approval. ISO Standards are discussed later in this chapter.

Bowdin *et al.* (2001) believe that the integration of all the practical aspects of controlling quality with the overall strategy of an event is TQM. Any organization aspiring to TQM should have a vision of quality that goes far beyond mere conformance to a standard. TQM requires a culture whereby every member of the organization believes that not one day should go by without the organization in some way improving the quality of its goods and services. The vision of TQM must begin with the event manager, or the chief executive of the organization. It is this person who should have a passion for quality and continuous improvement, and this passion should be transmitted down through the organization. TQM seeks to create an event company that continually improves the quality of its services (Bowdin *et al.*, 2001).

It is generally those staff members such as security staff, stewards, receptionists, guides, drivers and car park attendants who are the contact point with the customer and the wider public. They have a huge part to play in how the customer perceives an organization. It is on these staff that an organization must rely for the continuing daily level of quality. Often outsourced companies may employ these staff, and so the challenge for the event manager will become greater. Once the culture of quality has become ingrained, it is hoped that it will be driven from bottom up rather than achieved by direction or control from the top. Management will naturally have to continue to be responsible for planning, and for providing the resources to enable the workers to do the job. However, unless the telephone operators, the cleaning staff, the driver and the cloakroom attendant are fully committed to quality, TQM will never happen.

The event manager and all of the personnel working towards the successful staging and completion of an event should be totally customer orientated. Everyone should be encouraged to look for ways continually to improve all their activities, and rather than having control measures (discussed in Chapter 15) to monitor performance, they should have a quality focus to prevent errors occurring in the first place.

Case study 16.1 describes a re-enactment of the Battle of Tewkesbury.

Case study 16.1

Re-enactment of the Battle of Tewkesbury, 9–10 July 2005, Lincoln Green Lane, Tewkesbury, England

A free Medieval Festival that takes place on some of the fields where the battle was actually fought in May 1471, the battle is recreated by more than a thousand soldiers from Britain and Europe, many in full plate armour, others wielding the famous English longbow. Early cannon are also used.

Historically victory was gained by the House of York, which put King Edward IV firmly on the throne of England and defeated the House of Lancaster. Edward Prince of Wales was dead, and his mother, Queen Margaret of Anjou, was forced to flee for her life.

Other activities that take place at the re-enactments include creating weapons and armour for fighters, and demonstrations of other fifteenth century crafts such as pottery, spinning and blacksmithing. There are Victorian fairground sideshows and a wide variety of stalls, art exhibitions, and a tavern that sells ales and mead.

Along side this are strolling players with tales of monsters, fabulous beasts and great adventures, whilst fire-eaters, jugglers and acrobats offer displays of courage and skill.

Regular guided tours of the battlefield are conducted during the festival, with a full description of the events leading up to the Battle of Tewkesbury, the conduct of the battle, and the aftermath. The walks are leisurely, and last about 2 hours.

Tewkesbury Medieval Festival is a not-for-profit company that organizes and runs Tewkesbury Medieval Festival, with a considerable amount of help and support from the re-enactment community and from organizations in Tewkesbury. One of Europe's premier medieval events, the Festival attracts tens of thousands of visitors and involves well in excess of 2000 performers.

(Printed by courtesy of Tewkesbury Medieval Festival; for further information see www.tewkesbury-medieval-fayre.org.uk/.)

Reflective practice 16.1

Look at Case study 16.1.

1. From an organizational point of view, how can TQM be applied to the Tewkesbury Medieval Festival?
2. Consider the different types of organizations involved in this Festival. How can the organizers of the event ensure that consistent quality of customer service is given?

As seen in Chapter 2, customers have basic requirements regarding aspects of a service that will make them choose that service – i.e. their critical success factors. The example used in Chapter 2 was the courtesy bus service. First, unless the bus is travelling to where it is intended as per the detailed specification, it is of no value. The second requirement is timing; if it is intended to be part of a timed tour and is due to take passengers to another site by a specific time, it is of no value if it doesn't keep to its timetable. The third consideration is cost. The route, the time and the cost are therefore classified as basic requirements, and probably, depending on circumstances, they would be ranked in that order.

The courtesy bus service may meet all the above requirements but still not be a quality service. If the service is unreliable, i.e. sometimes late, sometimes early, sometimes not keeping to the route, then we would not consider it to be a reliable quality service. To be a quality service, the bus service needs to meet the customers' basic requirements and be reliable.

These requirements conform to a simple definition of quality – i.e. the right thing, in the right place, and at the right time. However, supposing the bus does all these things, arrives at each destination on time and at a reasonable cost, BUT is dirty, the driver is surly, the seats are hard and the bus leaks exhaust fumes. Then, although it is meeting the criteria of right thing, right time and right place, there is no way the service could be described as a quality one.

Thus apart from the basic needs there are certain higher order needs that must be met. In this case, we would look for polite service, a clean bus, reasonably comfortable seating, and certainly no exhaust fumes. A truly high-quality bus service might be spotlessly clean, have carpet on the floor and piped music as well as all the other attributes. However, no matter how comfortable the ride, how polite the service and how cheap the fare, unless the bus is going 'our way' we won't be interested in catching it. In other words, the specification must be reasonably satisfied.

Quality service at an event occurs when the consumers' expectations of the event match their perceptions of the service received. According to Bowdin *et al.* (2001), because this is based on perceptions rather than something tangible, not every customer will be satisfied all of the time.

Another typical definition of quality is to 'get it right first time'. This is often more of a slogan aimed at encouraging a sense of responsibility amongst staff to be accurate in their work. For anyone to be expected to do something right first time, they first have to know exactly what they are meant to be doing and then to have all the available and appropriate resources.

Case study 16.2 illustrates the difficulty of getting it right first time.

Case study 16.2

The Baftas (British Academy of Film and Television Arts), 24 February 2002, London, England

The Baftas move to February last year was widely seen as a master stroke, placing the event smack in the middle of the awards season, between the Golden Globes and the Oscars (the awards had previously been held in April, after the Oscars).

However, February in London brings its own problems, and on Sunday evening the film industry's great and good had to negotiate a red carpet that became so wet with rain it started foaming with detergent from its last clean. The offending substance turned out to be a flame-retardant chemical that was used in the manufacturing process, which was reacting with the rain.

The red carpet foamed and squelched as celebrities including Nicole Kidman, Kevin Spacey, Dustin Hoffman, Baz Luhrmann, Halle Berry and Renée Zellweger tiptoed their way into the Odeon, Leicester Square.

(Information supplied by BBC News at bbcnews.co.uk.)

Reflective practice 16.2

Regarding Case study 16.2:

1. 'Getting it right first time' – could it be feasibly expected that the organizers would know the effect of rain on the red carpet? What could they have done? What are the cost implications?
2. Bearing in mind that these events are for the press and public to see as many and as much of the stars as possible, and that designers use these types of awards ceremonies to show off their latest creations, what could be done to prevent a repeat of the wet carpet in the future? Or do the stars have to put up with the inconvenience for the sake of publicity?

'Fitness for purpose', 'getting it right first time', or 'right thing, right place, right time', may all fit the basic requirements of people attending events. However, in their eyes these are the minimum requirements expected. Without satisfying the basics, you won't be able to give an acceptable level of service. To have your event described as a quality event, the customer will expect higher-level benefits such as courtesy, attention to detail, pleasant surroundings etc. These higher-level benefits are what give an event and the event company a competitive edge, and often the difference may cost very little to achieve.

However, there is no point in an event company concentrating on being friendly and having efficient service in the hope that this will make the difference if the event does not meet the basic specifications, costs too much, or is not available when the customer wants it. For example, a conference may be held in a good location with very good rooms and conference facilities, and tasteful décor; the menus may offer a good variety of dishes and styles at the right price for a range of differently priced functions, and the waiting staff are well-groomed and helpful. However, if the food is poorly cooked and the gateaux are still frozen in the centre you won't go back, and you will tell many people of your experience. Of course, these people will pass the bad news on, often with embellishments.

No-one ever knows how many potential customers are lost as the result of sub-quality products or inferior service. Such a figure cannot be quantified; it is unknown and unknowable.

The cost of quality

Quality does not come cheap. It is not free. To instill a quality culture into an organization will take time, require total commitment, and have associated costs. Oakland (2000) says that the costs of achieving a high degree of customer satisfaction must be carefully managed so that the long-term effect on the organization is a desirable one. The costs should be budgeted for and measured just like other resource costs. The payback for the investment in quality may be long term, and the event manager will at some point be able to reap the benefits of higher quality in the reduction of costs, higher profits, growth and, ultimately, survival.

Costs of conformance

The costs of conformance (i.e. preventing poor-quality events) include the costs of:

- Quality inspection and quality control
- Quality assurance and ISO 9001/2000
- Training
- Appraisal.

Quality inspection and quality control

Quality inspection and control rely on supervision to make sure that no mistakes are made. The most basic approach to quality is inspection and correction of errors, and the next stage, quality control, is to inspect, correct, investigate and find the causes of problems and to take actions to prevent errors recurring. Both methods rely on supervision and inspection, and hence a cost is incurred.

In some cases, a modicum of common sense might help. However, generally, second-rate organizations (i.e. those that have not embraced the philosophy of getting things right first time, or of giving all levels of staff responsibility for their actions) will resort to inspections, tests, close supervision and audits. This approach challenges the event industry, since testing of some of the various components of an event (e.g. the adequacy of the sound amplification when the venue is full), can only be carried out properly when the event itself is in full swing. Another example would be the simultaneity of the plasma screen vision at an outdoor concert with the sounds emanating from the stage – this can only be balanced as the event is occurring.

Hence although control and inspection may be considered essential in many instances, this is not always possible.

Quality assurance and ISO

Quality assurance includes the setting of standards, with documentation, and also includes documentation of the *method* of checking against the specified standards. Oakland (2000) sees quality assurance as the creation and maintenance of the quality system. Quality assurance generally also includes third party approval from a recognized authority, such as ISO. With quality assurance, inspection and control is still the basic approach, but in addition there would be the expectation of a comprehensive quality manual, recording of quality costs, perhaps the use of statistical process control, and also the use of sampling techniques for random checking and the overall auditing of quality systems.

Quality inspection and control and quality assurance aim at achieving an agreed, consistent level of quality, first by testing and inspection, then by rigid conformance to standards and procedures, and finally by efforts to eliminate the causes of errors so that the defined accepted level will be achieved. *This is a cold and often sterile approach to quality.* It implies that once a sufficient level of quality has been achieved, then, apart from maintaining that level (which in itself might be hard work), little more needs to be done. This does not mean that the event manager is not taking into account what the customer wants, or is ignoring what the competition is doing. It just means that the managers believe that they know what is best and how this can be achieved. To this end, supervision and inspection become an important method of achieving the aim, with little input expected from staff members.

This approach could be used successfully in elements of organizing an event – such as those aspects that are repeated many times over. An example might be the registration at a conference and the taking of details of delegates prior to entering the main conference room. A further example might be the service of meals at a large silver service dinner, where certain aspects of the service could be perfected and repeated with the assurance that a full quality of service is being delivered.

Training

Further costs are those associated with preventing errors occurring. These include training for both staff and managers, and also training of suppliers to an event to make sure that they understand exactly what is expected of them, and how they can contribute to a well-planned quality event and environment.

Appraisal

Appraisal costs result in your staff and the event team checking that their work is right and that all is to plan. This might include sound checks at a major function, or telephoning a supplier to ensure that the deliveries will be on time and the product as specified. It can also include appraisals with staff to see how they are managing and developing within the organization, and whether they require any assistance to continually perform as expected.

The costs of non-conformance

Non-conformance is when work or service is not performed to the standard set by the organization, and therefore has to be corrected or repeated, or the customer has to be recompensed. Such costs should be captured and recorded. In the event industry this is slightly different, as this is not always possible. The event has occurred, and it may be that it was not delivered at the standard required. It cannot be repeated.

If it is possible to calculate how much extra expense is incurred owing to mistakes, then errors can be analysed and procedures changed to make sure that such mistakes are not repeated.

Flow-on effects resulting from mistakes include forgetting to include items when loading up containers taking event materials to an outdoor event and overtime worked as a result of errors. These costs may not readily be apparent, but can sometimes be calculated after a lot of soul searching and recriminations.

Costs of lost opportunities and loss of enthusiasm by workers cannot be measured. Some of the workers may not always be on your own payroll; they may be regular staff that work for you and are paid by a supplier, such as outdoor security staff or stewards.

Eventually, if errors and second-rate performance become the norm, morale will be such that there will be a general unwillingness to accept responsibility, and an attitude of fatalism will pervade with the feeling that second best can be tolerated. If a staff member is bold enough to raise a concern but their fears are proved groundless, and the supervisor is sarcastic or disparaging, it will make the employee reluctant to speak up or make suggestions next time.

Kaizen

The Japanese have a word for continuous improvement: *kaizen*. The word is derived from a philosophy of gradual day-by-day betterment of life and spiritual enlightenment towards a long-term goal. Kaizen has been adopted by Japanese businesses to denote gradual and unending improvement, but with a firm goal in mind. The philosophy is the doing of little things better to achieve a long-term objective.

Wild (2002) says that there are two prerequisites for the effective use of kaizen:

1. Setting demanding but achievable objectives
2. Feedback of achievements against these objectives.

Kaizen is 'the single most important concept in Japanese management – the key to Japanese competitive success' (Masaaki Imai, 1986).

Kaizen moves the organization's focus away from the bottom line, and the fitful starts and stops that come from major changes, towards a continuous improvement of service. Japanese firms have for many years taken quality for granted. Kaizen is now so deeply ingrained that people do not even realize that they are thinking kaizen. The philosophy is that during every day there should be some kind of improvement being made somewhere in the company. The far-reaching nature of kaizen can now be seen in Japanese government and social programs. It is a philosophy, and has much in common with total quality management (Wild, 2002).

Zero defects

The core belief of TQM is that it is possible to get things right the first time, and therefore there should be zero defects. However, to make this happen an organization has to know at every level exactly what the goals are and how to achieve them. There has to be a prompt and accurate method of feedback and a philosophy of continuous improvement, and everyone at every level should be looking for ways to make improvements.

This approach is exactly what is needed in the event industry, since there are no second opportunities. It is a positive statement if we hear the event manager say at the end of an event 'if we were to do this again we could do it much better'. This would not be inferring that major incidents had happened but that, in accordance with the philosophy of kaizen, there is always room for improvement.

Quality circles

In the 1960s, Juran said:

> *The quality-circle movement is a tremendous one which no other country seems to be able to imitate. Through the development of this movement, Japan will be swept to world leadership in quality.*
>
> (Juran, 1988)

Certainly Japan did make a rapid advance in quality standards from the 1960s onwards, and quality circles were part of this advance. However, quality circles were only one part of the Japanese quality revolution.

Quality circles involve representatives of employees meeting with the managers to discuss quality management improvement (Lashley and Lee-Ross, 2003). The overall philosophy of quality circles should be of trust and empowerment. The management of the organization has to be seen to be willing to trust the members of the circle to act responsibly, and they must be active in supporting the circle. Although initially within an event management company the circle may not appear to be addressing hard quality issues, as the confidence of the members increases very real benefits can be expected and seen within the organization and implementation of events.

Side benefits of quality circles, but nonetheless important ones, are the fostering of a supportive environment which encourages workers to become involved in increasing quality and improving productivity, and the development of the problem-solving and reporting skills of all staff.

Just-in-time-management (JIT)

We have decided to discuss this topic here, but it could easily have sat within Chapter 14 and featured within the scheduling issues. However, it is our contention that JIT can only be effective if you have a quality organization and a quality approach to the event – hence its place towards the end of the chapter and discussion on quality. As Wild (2002) stated, JIT philosophy has been used within manufacturing for 50 years.

The emphasis of JIT is on achieving customer service, with a focus on cost and timing. Some of the benefits, according to Wild (2002), include reduced inventories; reduced space requirements; greater employee involvement, participation and motivation;

improved service quality; and improved customer service. In order to achieve these most desirable benefits the event manager must have a reasonably stable and known demand for the services offered, reliable suppliers, and defect-free resources. There should be good communications, total management commitment, and employee involvement and flexibility.

All of the outsourced products and resources should arrive at an event just in time to be assembled and used. For example, the sound and lighting systems should arrive at the venue at the latest possible opportunity, to remove the need for security and the costs of extra hire time. In order to be assured that the equipment is without fault and can be set up quickly and efficiently, it should be sourced from a reputable supplier. The same philosophy can be used for staffing levels. Only the staff required for a particular part of the event should be on duty at the particular time. There is therefore a reliance on quality, accurate forecasting of demand and accurate translation of the needs into how many staff are needed.

If this philosophy of accurate forecasting and accurate estimations of how many staff are required is met, then there should be an excellent supply of reliable and error-free resources. Therefore, the costs for the event company could be reduced. This is because there is a lower inventory of goods and no time-consuming checking-in of goods because they are sourced from a reputable supplier.

JIT also requires increased flexibility from the staff (Slack *et al.*, 2004). In certain circumstances, staff may be required to work in different areas and functions within the event as required. The implication of such job flexibility is that a greater emphasis must be placed on training, learning and knowledge management (Slack *et al.*, 2004). This will result in staff who are adept at multi-skilling. This may have an effect on salary scales, where remuneration is not based on the number of hours worked or the productivity of a particular group, but on the range of skills possessed by each individual.

It should now be immediately obvious why this concept of JIT is placed within the chapter related to quality. JIT can only be successful if the organization is working efficiently and effectively. Consider the arguments that would arise if we were to rely on the latest point of delivery of supplies and minimal staff levels:

- What if our staff are late or are ill prior to the event, and therefore the low numbers of staff are not sufficient?
- What if the equipment does not arrive at the right time?
- What if the wrong equipment arrives?
- What if the equipment does not work?
- What if the staff need extra training prior to the event?
- What if our forecasts are inaccurate and we need more staff?

The traditional approach to these questions is to provide extra, well-trained staff just in case; to provide extra resources just in case the other item fails; to order just a little more since we are not quite sure about the accuracy of our forecasts. All of these solutions increase the costs to the event management company.

A useful way of describing this is to imagine a boat out at sea (Figure 16.1). The boat is sailing along and is protected from knocking into problems, which we can imagine as rocks below the surface. In fact, by increasing the costs the boat can be well protected from the rocks – more staff than ever needed can be hired and more equipment purchased or leased, just in case. A truly deep sea.

However, if we were to lower the costs and hence the water line, the boat would hit the first and topmost rock. To avoid this collision, something should be done about the problem. To solve the problem, remove the rock. Improve the forecasting, hire and employ only reliable staff, and use only reputable suppliers. For your company you

Figure 16.1 Just in time management

can imagine your own rocks, which prevent you operating just in time and increase your costs.

This approach leads to a different viewpoint about the operation. Waters (1996) believes that there are at least five areas that can now be reappraised:

1. Stock management: at an event this can include stationery supplies, catering products, back-up generators.
2. Reliability: this refers to the reliability of equipment and how it should be operational at all times when needed. This may therefore mean that it should be maintained more regularly or efficiently.
3. Quality: if we can use resources that have zero defects, then we would not have to have a buffer to act as a stand by – just in case.
4. Suppliers: the JIT system has total reliance on the suppliers, and therefore it is essential to build up a partnership and create common objectives in order to work together and with equal respect.
5. Staff: the success of the event depends on all staff working well together, so all staff should be treated with equal respect and appropriately trained.

SERVQUAL

The best-known approach to service quality is described by Parasuraman *et al.* (1991). They argued that quality in services can only be defined by first considering the customers' expectations, experiences and ultimate satisfaction. It is often the case that we concentrate on the tangible aspects of service, since they are easier to measure and put right. However, research has shown that it is more often the intangible aspects of service that lead to customer dissatisfaction (Gilmore, 2003).

Parasuraman *et al.* (1991) research identified that all the aspects of quality demanded by customers could be grouped together into five different dimensions. They argued that these dimensions are used by customers to compare their expectations of a service with their ultimate perceptions and satisfaction. The dimensions are:

1. Reliability: at an event, this would include whether the event ran to time, and whether it was consistent with what had been agreed with the client in advance
2. Assurance: at an event, this would include courtesy, ability to communicate effectively and aspects of security

3. Tangibles: at an event, these would include the venue, the appropriateness of the theming, the setting of the venue, and waiting and queuing times
4. Empathy: this refers to the caring nature of the staff at the event and individualized attention
5. Responsiveness to customers: this includes promptness and accessibility.

An event manager could expand on these points and consider a much fuller range for any particular event.

We would recommend that the event manager survey the customers prior to the event to see what aspects are important, and to what degree, to ensure their enjoyment of a particular event. Armed with this information, the event manager can then organize the event to ensure maximum satisfaction. Parasuraman *et al.* (1991) recommend that after the event the customers should again be surveyed to establish, using the same weighted criteria, how closely their expectations were matched. This may be a cumbersome piece of research, but it produces a result that shows how closely the event came to satisfying the customers' expectations.

When an event is staged there are always going to be gaps between expectations and satisfaction. However, if these can be reduced or understood, the event manager will be closer to satisfying the customer. The gap model provides the basis of the SERVQUAL instrument, which aims to increase customer satisfaction by improving the quality of a service.

Parasuraman *et al.* (1991) site five gaps that open up between expectations and ultimate customer satisfaction:

- Gap 1: we do not fully understand what our customers want at the event. This may be due to poor communication, misunderstanding, or customers not being clear about this themselves. Previous research may have generated lots of new ideas, and it is difficult to translate these into a clear understanding.
- Gap 2: we cannot clearly translate those needs into an unambiguous specification, and some experimentation is needed.
- Gap 3: something goes wrong on the day, and what we had expected to happen does not. This could be due to poor deliveries, or poor training or neglect.
- Gap 4: everything is going well, but we failed to market the event properly and our guests either did not arrive in sufficient numbers or they expected something slightly different.
- Gap 5: our customers do not get what they expect and they are dissatisfied. The event manager must undertake the research outlined at the start of this section and establish those aspects which the customers value, and to what degree.

The work covered by Getz (1997) covers this subject very fully. Similarly, you are encouraged to read Gilmore (2003), which again covers this concept exceptionally well.

Reflective practice 16.3

You are organizing a dog show, which includes dog agility events, fly ball and obedience trials. You are expecting 4000 spectators, 200 owners and 200 dogs.

1. How many supervisors do you need?
2. What is the cost of supervision?
3. What type and style of supervision would you need if every member of the company knew what they were meant to be doing, did it right first time, and were confident enough to take action or to seek advice if they thought things were not going the way they should be?

Reflective practice 16.4

Make a list of costs of non-conformance to quality standards for the first day of a major sales promotion at a large retail store.

Chapter summary and key points

This chapter has covered the question of quality. Our approach is that quality is not a new or separate discipline, and that quality pervades all management actions. Our philosophy is that quality is too important to be left to the managers; it is everybody's concern – not only members of the organization, but also suppliers and other stakeholders.

The chapter has defined the key words in use within the literature about quality. It has also examined the cost of making certain that a quality culture and performance is put into practice within the organization. It investigated the cost of not having a quality culture, and saw that these costs are manifest in loss of business and reputation, as well as in the cost of recompensing the client.

Two concepts have been introduced and applied to events management: just in time management (JIT) and SERVQUAL.

References

Ackoff, R. L. (1986). *Management in Small Doses*. John Wiley and Sons.

Allen, J. (2000). *Event Planning*. John Wiley and Sons.

Ansoff, H. I. (1987). *Corporate Strategy*. Penguin.

Bennet, J. and Jayes, S. (1998). *The Seven Pillars of Partnering: A Guide to Second Generation Partnering*. Thomas Telford.

Berry, L. L., Parasuraman, A. and Zeithaml, V. A. (1988). The service quality puzzle. *Business Horizons*, **Jul–Aug**, 35–43.

Bowdin, G. A. J., McDonnell, I., Allen, J. and O'Toole, W. (2001). *Events Management*. Butterworth-Heinemann.

Bubshait, A. and Farooq, G. (1999) Team building and project success. *Cost Engineering*, **41(7)**, 34–38.

Campbell, D., Stonehouse, G. and Houston, B. (2003). *Business Strategy*. Butterworth-Heinemann.

Carlzon, J. (1989). *Moments of Truth*. Harper Row.

Catherwood, D. W. and Van Kirk, R. L. (1992). *The Complete Guide to Special Event Management: Business Insights, Financial Advice, and Successful Strategies from Ernst & Young, Advisors to the Olympics, the Emmy Awards and the PGA Tour*. John Wiley and Sons.

Christopher, M. (1992). *Logistics and Supply Chain Management*. Pitman Publishing.

Cicmil, S. (2000). Quality in project environments: a non-conventional agenda. *International Journal of Quality and Reliability Management*, **17(4/5)**, 554–570.

Cooke-Davies, T. J. (1990) Return of the project managers. *Management Today*, 119.

Crosby, P. B. (1979). *Quality is Free*. McGraw-Hill.

Czuchry, A. J. and Yasin, M. M. (2003). Managing the project management process. *Industrial Management and Data Systems*, **103(1)**, 39–46.

Deming, W. E. (1982). *Out of Crisis*. Cambridge University Press.

De Wit, B. and Meyer, R. (2004). *Strategy: Process, Content, Context: An International Perspective*. Thompson.

Drummond, S. and Anderson, H. (2004). Service quality and managing your people. In: I. Yeoman, M. Robertson, J. Ali-Knight *et al.* (eds), *Festivals and Event Management*, pp. 80–97. Elsevier Butterworth-Heinemann.

Dulewicz, V., MacMillan, K. and Herbert, P. (1995). Appraising and developing the effectiveness of boards and their directors. *Journal of General Management*, **20(3)**, 1–19.

Eaglen, A., Lashley, C. and Thomas, R. (2000). Modelling the benefits of training to business performance in leisure retailing. *Strategic Change*, **9**, 311–325.

Evans, N., Campbell, D. and Stonehouse, G. (2003). *Strategic Management for Travel and Tourism*. Butterworth-Heinemann.

Feigenbaum, A. V. (1993). *Total Quality Control*. McGraw-Hill.

Freeman, R. E. (1984). *Strategic Management: A Stakeholder Approach*. Pitman.

Getz, D. (1997). *Event Management and Event Tourism*. Cognizant Communication Corporation.

Gilmore, A. (2003). *Services Marketing and Management*. Sage Publications.

Goldblatt, J. J. (1997). *Special Events: Best Practices in Modern Event Management*. Van Nostrand Reinhold.

Gray, C. and Larson, E. (2000). Project Management. McGraw-Hill.

Griffin, R. W. (1999). *Fundamentals of Management*. Houghton Mifflin.

Griffin, R. W. (2000). *Management*. Houghton Mifflin.

Grundy, T. and Brown, L. (2002). *Strategic Project Management*. Thomson Learning.

Hall, C.M. and Rusher, K. (2004). Politics, public policy and the destination. In: I. Yeoman, M. Robertson, J. Ali-Knight *et al.* (eds), *Festivals and Event Management*, pp. 217–231. Elsevier Butterworth-Heinemann.

Harrison, L. and McDonald, F. (2004). Event management for the arts: a New Zealand perspective. In: I. Yeoman, M. Robertson, J. Ali-Knight *et al.* (eds), *Festivals and Event Management*, pp. 232–245. Elsevier Butterworth-Heinemann.

Herzberg, F. (1966). Work and the nature of man. Cleveland: World Publishing. Herzberg, F. (1968). One more time, how do you motivate employees. *Harvard Business Review*. Jan–Feb pp. 58–62.

Ibbs, C. W. and Kwak, Y. H. (2000). Assessing project management maturity. *Project Management Journal*, **31(1)**, 32–43.

Johnson, G. and Scholes, K. (2002). *Exploring Corporate Strategy*, 6th edn. Pearson Education.

Juran, J. M. (1988). *Juran on Planning for Quality*. Free Press.

Kandampully, J. (2002) *Services Management*. Pearson Education.

Kaplan, R. S. and Norton, D. P. (1993). Putting the balanced scorecard to work. *Harvard Business Review*, **71**, 134–147.

Kaplan, R. S. and Norton, D. P. (2001). *The Strategy-focused Organization: How Balanced Scorecard Companies Thrive in the New Business Environment*. Harvard Business School.

Kerzner, K. (1994). The growth of modern project management. *Project Management*, **25(2)**, 6–8.

Kotler, P. (1991). *Marketing Management*. Prentice Hall International.

Lashley, C. and Lee-Ross, D. (2003). Organization behaviour for leisure services. Butterworth-Heinemann.

Laybourn, P. (2004). Risk and decision-making in events management. In: I. Yeoman, M. Robertson, J. Ali-Knight *et al.* (eds), Festivals and Event Management, pp. 286–307. Elsevier Butterworth-Heinemann.

Lee-Kelley, L. (2002). Situational leadership. *Journal of Management Development*, **21(6)**, 461–476.

Lewis, B. R. (1994). In: B. G. Dale (ed.), *Managing Quality*. Prentice Hall.

Magee, S. (2002). *Ascot: The History*. Methuen Publishing Ltd.

Maister, D. H. (1985). The psychology of waiting times. In: J. A. Czepiel, M. R. Solomon and C. F. Surprenant (eds), *The Service Encounter*. Heath and Co.

Masaaki Imai (1986). *Kaizen: The Key to Japan's Competitive Success*. Random House.

Maslow, A. H. (1943). A Theory of human motivation. *Psychological Review*, **50**, 370–396.

McDonnell, I., Allen, J. and O'Toole, W. (1999). *Festival and Special Event Management*. Jacaranda Wiley.

Mullins, L. J. (2002). *Management and Organisational Behaviour*. Financial Times Prentice Hall.

Oakland, J. S. (2000). *TQM Text with Cases*. Butterworth-Heinemann.

O'Toole, W. and Mikolaitis, P. (2002). *Corporate Event Project Management*. Wiley.

Parasuraman, A., Zeithaml, V. A. and Berry, L. L. (1985). A conceptual model of service quality and its implications for future research. *Journal of Marketing*, **49**, 41–50.

Parasuraman, A., Zeithaml, V. A. and Berry, L. L. (1991). Understanding customer expectations of service. *Sloan Management Review*, **32(3)**, 39–48.

Robbins, S. P. and Coulter, M. (1998). *Management*. Prentice Hall.

Shone, A. and Parry, B. (2004). *Successful Event Management: A Practical Handbook*. Thomson.

Silver, J. R. (2004). *Professional Event Co-ordination*. Wiley.

Skinner, B. F. (1971). Contingencies of re-inforcement. Norwalk: Appleton-Century-Crofts.

Slack, N., Chambers, S., Harland, C., Harrison, A. and Johnson, R. (1998). *Operations Management*. Pitman Publishing.

Slack, N. and Lewis, M. (2002). *Operations Strategy*. Financial Times Prentice Hall.

Slack, N., Chambers, S. and Johnson, R. (2004). *Operations Management*. Harlow, Pearson Education.

Sonder, M. (2004). *Event Entertainment and Production*. Wiley.

Swarbrooke, J. and Horner, S. (2001). *Business Travel and Tourism*. Butterworth-Heinemann.

Thompson, J. L. (2001). *Strategic Management*. Thompson Learning.

Torkildsen, G. (1999). *Leisure and Recreation Management*, 4th edn. E & FN Spon.

Tukel, O. I. and Rom, W. O. (2001). An empirical investigation of project evaluation criteria. *International Journal of Operations Management*, **21(3)**, 400–416.

Turner, J. R. (1999). *The Handbook of Project Based Management*, 2nd edn. McGraw-Hill.

Vroom, V. H. and Yetton, P. W. (1973). *Leadership and decision making*. Pittsburg, University of Pittsburg.

Vroom, V. H. and Jago, A. G. (1988). The new leadership, managing participation in organisations. Englewood Cliffs, NJ, Prentice Hall.

Waters, D. (1996). *Operations Management*. Addison-Wesley.

Watt, D. (1998). *Event Management in Leisure and Tourism*. Longman.

Wendroff, A. L. (2004). *Special Events: Proven Strategies for Nonprofit Fundraising*. John Wiley and Sons.

Wild, R. (1995). *Production and Operations Management*, 5th edn. Cassell.

Wild, R. (2002). *Operations Management*. Continuum.

Wood, E. H. (2002). Events, civic pride and attitude change in a post-industrial town: Evaluating the effect of local authority events on residents' attitudes to the Blackburn region. Presented at the Events & Place Making Conference, Sydney, July 2002.

Wood, E. H. (2004). Marketing information for impact analysis and evaluation. In: I. Yeoman, M. Robertson, J. Ali-Knight *et al.* (eds), *Festival and Events Management: An International Arts and Cultural Perspective*. Butterworth-Heinemann.

Wood, H. (1982). *Festivity and Social Change*. London, Leisure in the Eighties Research Unit, Polytechnic of the South Bank.

Wright, J. N. (2001). *The Management of Service Operations*. Continuum.

Yeoman, I., Robertson, M. and McMahon-Beattie, U. (2004). In: I. Yeoman, M. Robertson, J. Ali-Knight *et al.* (eds), *Festivals and Event Management*, pp. 65–79. Elsevier Butterworth-Heinemann.

Zeithaml, V. A., Parasuraman, A. and Berry, L. L. (1990). *Delivering Quality Service: Balancing Customer Perceptions and Expectations*. The Free Press.

Index

Breinigsville, PA USA
28 October 2010
248092BV00002B/1/P